D.G. Hogg

WORKING SMART WITH ELECTRONIC SPREADSHEETS

MODELS FOR MANAGERS

TIMOTHY BERRY

HAYDEN BOOK COMPANY
a division of Hayden Publishing Company, Inc.
Hasbrouck Heights, New Jersey

Acquisitions Editor: DOUGLAS K. McCORMICK
Production Editor: DENNIS MENDYK
Cover Design: JIM BERNARD
Text Design: JOHN M-RÖBLIN
Compositor: MAPLE-VAIL BOOK MANUFACTURING GROUP
Printer and Binder: FAIRFIELD GRAPHICS

Library of Congress Cataloging in Publication Data

Berry, Timothy J.
Working smart with electronic spreadsheets.

Includes index.
1. Electronic spreadsheets. 2. Business—Data processing.
I. Title.
HF4458.2.B424 1984 658'.05425 84-6643
ISBN 0-8104-6203-6

Printed in the United States of America

1 2 3 4 5 6 7 8 9 PRINTING

84 85 86 87 88 89 90 91 92 YEAR

To Vange, with thanks

CONTENTS

PREFACE

Remember the story of Alexander the Great and the Gordian knot? The people of Gordium believed that whoever untied the knot would rule all of Asia. When Alexander came to the knot, he raised his sword and cut through it with a single stroke. He went on to rule all of Asia.

We live now in a world full of a new kind of Gordian knot, the tangled messes of jargon and buzzwords that surround so many of our modern, specialized professions. The doctors, lawyers, butchers, bakers, and candlestick makers all have their own private words and phrases. Each little professional dialect is another Gordian knot.

This book is dedicated to the idea of cutting through two of those knots: microcomputers and business analysis. Computer hackers and the MBA-types treasure their insiders' words and magic phrases, which they sometimes use like passwords in a cult group. By locking this knowledge up in this verbal knot, they keep it to themselves.

I'll confess to being both a computer hacker and an MBA. But I was a journalist first, a writer, and I like nothing better than cutting through those knots to shake the mysticism out of the insider groups. I believe that the microcomputer is not some magic and mysterious cult object, but a very powerful new tool for writing, numerical analysis, list management, graphics, and education. And I believe that basic spreadsheet business analysis can be a simple and very effective tool for solving some business problems. These tools are for everybody, not just the insiders. So is this book. I want to tell the hacker about business, the business analysts about spreadsheets, and the normal reader about both.

Timothy Berry

ONE

About This Book

Introduction

One of the best studies of style comes from Strunk and White's *The Elements of Style*, a little book about writing and the English language. It says that beautiful, elegant writing is simple, clear, and functional. Spreadsheets are a new kind of language, one that can also be beautiful and elegant when it is simple, clear, and functional. The best spreadsheet models are the ones that look obvious as soon as you've examined them. If this book works, you won't be referring back to it to copy models; you'll be creating your own.

This book is a "what-to" instead of a "how-to." The "how-to" books give you pre-built models for solving pre-cooked problems on specific spreadsheet programs; this book wants you to build your own models, using the pre-built ones as first cuts, examples, or starting points—it's about creative spreadsheet planning and analysis.

The best way to learn this is by doing it. Thus, the book takes you through a series of basic examples. Then you go on to sales forecasts, budgets, investment analyses, and pro forma statements. Finally, in the last chapter, you learn about writing a business plan. We'll show you models we've used and suggest how you might vary yours. The business plan in the last chapter draws most of these models together into a single document that summarizes a new business idea. We provide a sample business plan outline, some examples, and thoughts about your own business plan and what you might want to include in it.

What is a spreadsheet? At one time, it was a piece of paper that accountants and business planners used for putting a lot of numbers into rows and columns. The numbers could then be added and subtracted and compared, one to another. Now, the spreadsheet is a computer software package that's running on almost every small business computer. This program puts rows and columns into a computer's memory and manipulates them according to formulas.

Figure 1
An Old-Fashioned Spreadsheet

	MONTH1	MONTH2	MONTH3	MONTH4	MONTH5
REVENUE	10,000	12,000	14,000	16,000	18,000
EXPENDITURES					
RENT	3,000	3,000	3,000	3,000	3,000
SALARIES	5,000	5,000	5,500	6,000	6,000
SUPPLIES	500	750	750	1,000	1,000
MISCELLANEOUS	1,000	1,250	1,500	1,750	2,000
EQUIPMENT	12,000	500	250	2,000	1,000
TOTAL EXPEND.	21,500	10,500	11,000	13,750	13,000
NET CASH	(11,500)	1,500	3,000	2,250	5,000

Why are spreadsheets useful? Consider a new business plan. In Figure 1, for example, a manual (pre-computer) spreadsheet is used to prepare an estimate for start-up costs of a new business. The hypothetical business is a computer software company. Its products, which are programs, are still being developed: Easy-to-use menus and help facilities have to be designed, manuals have to be written, and the programs have to be made to run on Apple II and IBM-PC computers, as well as on an original CP/M system. This work is estimated to take three programmers about six months to complete. The best way to figure how much the product will cost to go from the present state to marketability is to make a spreadsheet. Take a big sheet of paper and mark months one through six on top, leaving rows along the left side. (See Figure 1 for an example.) Mark one row for your rent, one for your own salary, one for additional programmer wages, one for required computer equipment, one for supplies, and one for miscellaneous items. Each expenditure takes up a row. Now, fill in the numbers, month by month, row by row. Add it all up, and you'll have a first, solid look at how much money it's going to cost to get the new business going—a basic spreadsheet analysis.

Computers take this idea and supercharge it. Rows and columns are easy for a computer to understand. They offer a way to organize numbers and a way to follow comparisons and relationships among those numbers. Also, they look a lot neater when they're entered via keyboard and printed automatically than when they're written in pencil on green sheets of paper. Some people find keyboards a simpler tool for entering the basic numbers. But the spreadsheet program goes far beyond easily entered numbers and nicely formatted tables. The magic begins when you take that first cash-flow spreadsheet and change your monthly computer cost. All the other numbers change with it. Add $50 to monthly computer costs, and you end up adding $50 to all monthly grand-totals. The additional computer costs, however, reduce the programming effort, so the labor cost goes down by $60 per month. Miscellaneous goes up by $10 per month to pay for extra paper and electricity consumption with the additional computer. Try all that in pencil and paper, and it gets complicated very quickly. An electronic spreadsheet is ideal.

So, the spreadsheet is a powerful tool. "One keystroke," the ads say, "and the results change immediately." It's made to sound like magic—"what-if" analysis without really trying.

But no powerful tool is all that simple. It won't do a single thing you don't tell it to do. And you have to tell it right, or it won't understand. There is a lot more to it than just one stroke. You have to tell it what to do with the rows and columns, where to subtract, where to add, and where to multiply. You have to tell it what is going into which place. You have to build a "model."

This book is about how to use that tool, not which keys to push or how to load the disk. It's about how to think with spreadsheets, not which commands will insert or delete. It's about business analysis and number use. It's about sales forecasts, business plans, budgets, and financial statements, all implemented on spreadsheets. It's not about VisiCalc, SuperCalc, Multiplan, MicroPlan, CalcStar, PerfectCalc, or any other single calc program—it's about all of them. Everything we're talking about will also work on

Lotus 1-2-3, Lisa, VisiOn, Context MBA, and the newer integrated spreadsheet programs. It's about models. It's about thinking in models, planning in models, and making them work as simply and as smoothly as possible to do what they are supposed to do.

How to Use This Book

We will build sample models. There are models of sales forecasts, budgets, financial plans, investment analyses, and business plans. Some of these models will be close to what you need to do with your own model. Use them as examples or as approximations of what you want to do. Understand how and why they work. Your own special models will almost certainly be different in one way or another from ours, but they may also be similar in many ways. Notice how the models are built; you'll learn by doing.

We'll make sample business analyses and illustrate the techniques involved (for example, forecasting, budgeting, using balance sheets, and studying cash-flow-based investment, relationships between income statements, and pro forma cash flow). These are basic business tools made that much more useful by the power of the spreadsheet on the computer. Apply them to your own situation. We'll also go over some of the general rules of business analysis taken from business-school classrooms and corporate boardrooms. Use the models here as basic designs; modify and customize them to suit your needs.

We'll provide detail, in some cases, about actual commands involved in different spreadsheet techniques. The commands will usually be for VisiCalc, SuperCalc, and MicroPlan, and sometimes for CalcStar. These programs seem like fair representatives of the rest; more than half the spreadsheet products now on the market base their command logic on the original VisiCalc. Even the new generation, including Lotus 1-2-3, Context MBA, Multiplan, VisiCalc Advanced Version, and SuperCalc 3, are still following the same basic logic, changing things here and there to improve on it and adding more features.

This book is not, however, meant to replace any user's manuals. You will need to refer to your user's manual for many of the functions and commands involved in your spreadsheet and in model management. If you use a program other than one specifically mentioned, you can just as well apply our general theory of models, business analysis, and creative spreadsheet thinking. Some features may differ, and some manipulations may be more difficult (or easier) in one program or another.

The Spread of Spreadsheets

VisiCalc started it. The story goes that Daniel Bricklin thought it up while watching a Harvard Business School finance professor go back and forth on the blackboard to change numbers to change scenarios. "If sales came to half that projected, finance needs would be—'' and the class waited for five minutes of hand calculations across the rows and columns on the board. That was some time in 1978. Before the end of 1979, Bricklin and partner Robert Frankston wrote VisiCalc to work on the Apple II.

One year later, VisiCalc was changing the world of microcomputers. First, the spreadsheet program turned the rest of the world's idea of a small computer from a hobbyist's tinkertoy into a useful tool. Many thousands of Apple IIs were sold only because they were able to run VisiCalc. By the end of 1982, Bricklin's and Franklin's company was pulling in $7 million per year and was growing at a rate of about 100 percent per year. VisiCorp, which marketed VisiCalc almost from the beginning, had grown to a $35-million-per-year company with an expanding line of computer software products. VisiCalc was running on more than half a million computers, including those made by Apple, IBM, Radio Shack, Atari, and Hewlett Packard.

Meanwhile, the rest of the small computer world followed. There was a race to put VisiCalc look-alikes on other machines. Sorcim's SuperCalc raced into the market for the several hundred thousand computers that used Digital Research's CP/M operating system; using commands and logic similar to VisiCalc, SuperCalc became an industry leader. Dashung Chang, who went to school with the VisiCalc people, came up with MicroPlan. MicroPro, whose WordStar program was the leader in CP/M word processing, released CalcStar. Spreadsheet programs became as common as disk drives and help keys in a growing market of millions of microcomputers. Few systems could be found without one. They called them ''VisiClones'' or ''Calc-alikes.'' By the end of 1982, 80 or 90 percent of the computers costing more than $1,000 had spreadsheet programs—that meant about two million units.

Not all of them are that much like VisiCalc anymore. In early 1983, Lotus Development Corporation began selling the Lotus 1-2-3 spreadsheet, which includes graphics and some database capabilities as part of the spreadsheet package. It was an enormous success, knocking VisiCalc out of the top spot in a number of software sales polls. Ironically, the Context MBA package offered the three functions available on Lotus 1-2-3 plus a basic word processor and was on the market several months before 1-2-3, but was not as popular. Multiplan is part of MicroSoft's multi tools line, which allows the spreadsheet to be linked to other MicroSoft applications packages. Even VisiCorp has a new, advanced version of VisiCalc. Competition has been better at handling such row-and-column cosmetics as putting numbers in fixed formats (how many decimals, for example) and positioning titles across columns. Some of the better spreadsheets let you easily combine and consolidate whole models from parts of models, a useful feature for something like adding departmental budgets. Some have graphics modules that make bar charts or pie charts from the spreadsheet data. Some do fancy financial calculations, such as internal rates of return, net present values, depreciation, and tax calculations. Some run on new operating systems, integrated in packages that let you move quickly from spreadsheet to word processing to database management to graphics without having to save your work off the system as you call up each new program.

Figure 2
Lotus 1-2-3 Spreadsheet Includes Graphics

```
A2Ø:                                                                          MENU
Worksheet  Range  Copy  Move  File  Print  Graph  Data  Quit
Global, Insert, Delete, Column-Width, Erase, Titles, Window, Status
        A          B          C          D          E          F
 1 Hotel Analysis Model
 2                Category         1
 3                  Region         B
 4                          '8Ø Act     '81 Act     '82 Pro     '83 Pro
 5                     ------------------------------------------------
 6 Avg night rental          $72.ØØ      $74.ØØ      $77.7Ø      $87.Ø2
 7 Occupancy rate            66.4Ø%      59.76%      58.27%      56.81%
 8 Revenues             $16,612,324 $15,366,4ØØ $15,731,352 $17,178,636
 9
10 Expenses
11           Salaries    $3,752,242  $3,47Ø,824  $3,592,511  $3,971,282
12           Maintenance $5,814,313  $5,378,34Ø  $5,5Ø5,973  $6,Ø12,523
13           Supplies    $2,245,986  $2,Ø77,537  $2,126,879  $2,322,552
14           Utilities     $869,655    $8Ø4,431    $823,536    $899,3Ø2
15           Other       $2,844,Ø3Ø  $2,63Ø,728  $1,Ø22,538  $2,679,867
16 Profit (Loss)         $1,Ø86,Ø97  $1,ØØ4,64Ø  $2,659,915  $1,293,111
17
18                1982        1983        1984        1985
19 Inflation        5%         12%          9%          5%
20
```

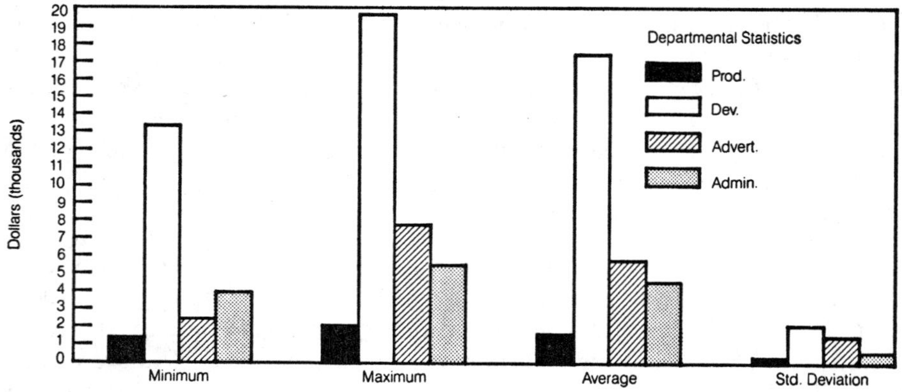

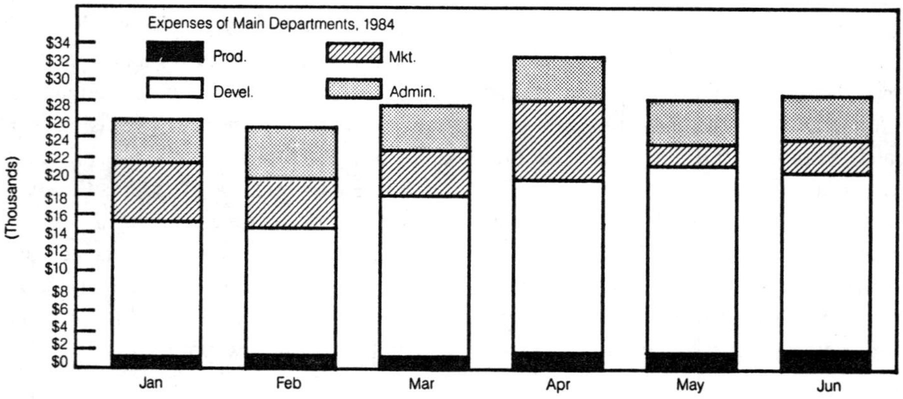

Some computer people say the spreadsheet program is a new and different kind of software. It isn't a program, because it doesn't really do anything by itself. A computer program takes some input and gives you some output, just as an accounting program or a Fahrenheit-to-Celsius temperature conversion program does. A spreadsheet program doesn't do anything unless you build a model for it; so the latest theory is to call the spreadsheet program an applications language. That would put it somewhere between an applications program and a programming language. It's an interesting thought, and it points the way to what a spreadsheet should be doing for you.

Using the Tool Well

A computer can be a fancy and expensive waste of time. What good is word processing, for example, to someone who writes drafts by hand, corrects by hand, and then types the final version on a keyboard, without making changes? The computer helps the writer only when the writer uses its capabilities to make changes, and rewrite, and shuffle blocks of text from place to place. The same is true with accounting and spreadsheets—more than one computer has been used to duplicate work done my hand without reducing the hand work.

Use the spreadsheet for what it does well. It's famous for "what-if" facilities, so use it for that. Write your models to show you the results of changes and plan on experimenting with those changes. Look for the model parts that might change. What happens when you get some extra money, and what if you spend more than planned? What if utilities double, or social security taxes increase? In a business model, what if insurance goes up, salaries rise, prices go down, and distributors ask for better margins? How do the salesforce commissions look if sales double? What if they fall by half? You have to plan for changes and use your spreadsheet well to consider those changes. That's a lot of what this book is about.

Consider the difference between forecasts and scenario analyses. Forecasts in their simplest form take the past and spread it out into the future. In 1972, oil price forecasts of a few dollars per barrel were thought to last forever; they had been at a few dollars per barrel for a long time. In 1980, oil prices were forecast to be $40 and $50 per barrel by 1983. In 1983, oil prices were forecast to hold steady or decline through 1987. But what if another war in the Middle East were to begin, or if a destabilizing crisis were to arise in Mexico? If you use your computer right, and your model is affected by oil prices, you build it so you can see what the business looks like at $15 per barrel, at $25 per barrel, and at $50 or more per barrel. Look at inflation at 6 percent and inflation at 16 percent, and see what the differences are in costs, selling prices, and profits. What about interest rates?

Spreadsheets are powerful tools for scenario analysis, which is little more than an MBA buzzword for "what-if" games. The world turns so fast nowadays that scenario analysis is a better way to look at the future than simple straight-line, or even curved-line, extrapolation of the past. Maybe that was always so, maybe not; maybe the electronic spreadsheet, properly used, makes scenario analysis practical in many places in which it wasn't once. Either way, it makes for much better planning, planning that considers what ought to be, what might go wrong, and what things will look like if something does go wrong. The best kind of planning looks at several different kinds of extrapolations, a few extra models here and there, and some relevant alternate scenarios; it then takes a well-considered stab at what to do when and what to do when things change.

We'll get more into these issues as the book goes on. There is a lot to be said for planning your "what-if" in advance so that, when the time comes, your computer can help you decide what to do. Maybe that's "what-if" squared.

Computers and Thinking

Computers don't think, they just do the numbers. Computers are very dumb contraptions that can be downright dangerous when you expect them to think for you. They are absurdly literal, and, worse still, literal in their own very narrowly defined languages. Tell a computer to tell you that 2+2=5, and it will swear that 2+2=5, over and over again if you want.

Use your models, but don't believe them—especially when dealing with spreadsheets. Because there is something magical about neatly ordered rows and columns of numbers shining at you through a computer screen or marching from the printer, you may forget how meaningless they really are. Most of us can think of at least one occasion in which we were lost in the luxury of reading a beautiful printout—"Aha! This shows we can make 30 percent return in the second year!"—without realizing that some important row had been added instead of subtracted. Two hours later, it hit you. Or, even worse, just as you were dazzling an important client, banker, or venture capitalist with your beautiful plan, you were drily told that taxes are added instead of subtracted.

So use the dumb thing for what it does well. You do the thinking, let the computer do the numbers, and the division of labor will work wonders. Remember the origins of the spreadsheet, back with the pencils and green lined paper, and think in those terms; you're still in that realm, but now you've got a team of tireless workers to change your numbers instantly. Now that's power!

The best analyst uses human judgment to guide the number-crunching. If you accept the great split between rational, analytic thinking and intuitive, creative thinking, then you probably realize the best work requires a little of both. Use your head to guide the analysis.

How do you get the right combination? The simplest way is by doing the numbers—running the spreadsheet models. Run them well and in volume. Change factors repeatedly. Each new version is another go at understanding a problem, each is another possibility to be considered. The world is far too complex for simple answers. Solving problems is akin to recording stereo albums: the artist sings multiple tracks onto a single tape and magnifies and multiplies the voice and voice effects. The more angles considered, the better the understanding of the final product and its alternatives. Look at your business plan at many different volumes, at many different prices, at many different kinds and levels of expense, and the set of numbers you finally accept will be a better representation of the full range of possibility.

There is an irony here. The best market forecasters use a lot of computer models, but they don't believe them. Output from different models stimulates thinking about alternatives, causes and effects, and different outcomes. But output is not to be believed, just considered.

Comparing Spreadsheet Products

Which one should you buy? That depends partly on which system you're using, partly on whether you have special uses that fit one spreadsheet's advantages, partly on how much money you can afford to spend, and a lot on subjective preference.

You can start from the assumption that most of the spreadsheets are almost the same product and do almost the same thing. These are the "VisiClones." Some have more formatting features, and some have more built-in functions, such as trigonometric or financial functions. Of these, if you buy whichever seems to be the leader in sales for the computer you're using, you'll do fairly well. If a spreadsheet comes with your system, it's probably about as good as most others.

If you've got a newer system like the IBM-PC, which runs the MS-DOS operating system, you have a lot of leaders from which to choose. You can assume that the new generation of spreadsheets generally includes features that were left off the earlier ones. Lotus 1-2-3 has been extremely successful, has a good tutorial, and runs reasonably fast on the PC. It seems relatively hard to learn, but that is because it can do a lot of different things. Context MBA is about the same, but it runs a bit more slowly (although it looks great and runs very fast on Hewlett Packard micros). The new Multiplan, VisiCalc Advanced, and SuperCalc 3 all added features that VisiCalc lacked.

You can have these products demonstrated. You can also get any number of printed comparisons, since magazines seem to publish many different tables that list all the features of all the market leaders. Your dealer should have this kind of information on hand.

If you have a specialized use, look for the features that match. MicroPlan, for example, is very convenient for many budgeting, accounting, and financial planning applications. It's not as versatile as some others, but it includes some very convenient financial functions, programming capabilities, and consolidation routines.

For the record, the models in this book were written on four different spreadsheet programs that include VisiCalc on the Apple II and SuperCalc, MicroPlan, and CalcStar on an 8-bit CP/M system. The models will also work on most other calc programs, including Lotus 1-2-3, Context MBA, Lisa, and Multiplan, with little or no modification.

TWO

Business Analysis

Business by the Numbers

This is the business age of numbers. You can't get a new company financed without a business plan full of believable, beautiful numbers. You can't get through your company's capital budgeting process (that is, you can't get your company to invest in your idea) without a business plan, usually with discounted cash-flow analysis. Correlations, regressions, and confidence levels, all jargon from statistics, have turned into business buzzwords. There was a time when a high school degree was enough, and a time when a college degree was enough (depending on where you were going). Now, in some fields (fancy management consulting and certain corporate staff areas, for example), you can't get anywhere without a masters degree in business administration, the MBA, which is in most cases training in quantitative business analysis.

Spreadsheets generate more numbers: more models, more forecasts, more budgets, and more plans. The ability to do this gradually becomes the need to do it. Managers have a powerful tool for keeping track of numbers, so there will be more numbers to keep track of. This has something to do with Darwin's theory of evolution, or the Peter Principle of incompetence, or some such law. Pierce's *The Crack in the Cosmic Egg* implies that the need is generated by the possibility, rather than vice versa; we wouldn't need all these number tools if it weren't possible to work with them on computers. Call it Berry's rule of index finger: The spread of number-crunching capabilities brings on an increased demand for crunched numbers; or, put more simply, more microcomputers means more budgets.

Figure 3

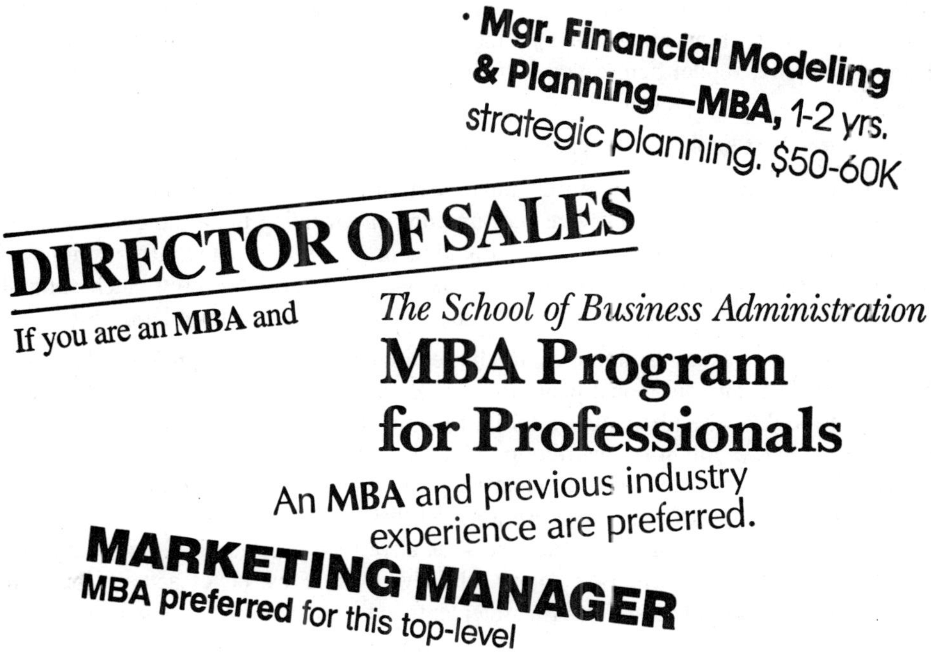

Basics of Business Analysis

Business analysis is supposed to make good business sense. It does, when it is done right. But business numbers can be frighteningly fictional, whether they are used for creative accounting (''Where did all the profits go?'') or for forecasting. The key is to recognize the use of business numerical analysis, which provides frameworks for decision making. The numbers help us understand what is going on; they are not of any real use in and of themselves. Even the accounting statements are really an enormous semi-fictional pageant, revolving around how much money is in the bank, how much we owe, how much they owe us, and how much we've spent. Business analysis, by its very definition, has to have some practical use. Time is money, and it has to be worth the effort.

The key phrase here is ''framework for thinking.'' Business is not in the numbers, it's in the decisions and their implementation. But the numbers provide the key framework for understanding the alternatives, the background, the cause and effect, and the decision itself.

Almost all of business analysis has the three main components of the framework for thinking: the statement of the problem, the definition of problem parameters, and, in the age of the electronic spreadsheet, contingency analysis.

Stating the Problem

Often, the main value of modeling is stating the problem. You can't model a business situation without understanding what makes numbers go up and what makes them go down, and by how much. Many times, you'll have taken 90 percent of the value from a computer model before you actually run it. You learned so much in building it that you don't need to run it.

This is best explained by example.

In the previous chapter, an example suggested that adding computer equipment might cut labor costs for a software start-up company. Stating this problem is more important than solving it. Already, we're thinking in a new and potentially profitable direction: Before we figure out how much costs will be reduced, or how much computer equipment should be taken on, we've already realized an important relationship.

Take a forecasting problem as another example. We want to project sales for our software product, an educational play program. Before we get to the details of the model, we have to look at the forces we're trying to simulate. We must consider which factors affect sales. These might be distribution channels, commissions and margins, seasonal factors (for Christmas sales), and advertising and promotion expenditures. Depending on how we state the problem, we'll use a model that runs a straight growth rate or makes sales depend on some other variables, such as advertising, promotion, and margins offered to links in the distribution chain. Already, even if we never actually build this model, we've absorbed some important elements in our overall business strategy. We've been thinking about the proper level of promotion and commissions and about the need to plan for seasonal variations in sales and income.

Sales might go into a model as a straight estimate, as in the 10 percent growth rate suggested here:

	1983	1984	1985	1986
Sales	100	121	133	146

But they might also be influenced by promotion, adding a new element to the formula:

$$\text{sales}(1984) = 121 + [X]$$

where X is additional sales determined by the level of advertising and promotion. Then we can add a Y for the influence of distribution channel decisions and a Z for a seasonal effect. We'll be using some formulas like this in the sales forecasting chapter. The point to be made here is that even before we decide what values to assign for our new X, Y, and Z—

$$\text{sales} = 121 + X + Y + Z$$

we must recognize their importance. There is great value in stating the problem.

Looking at a common foundation of investment analysis, you find the same thing. What is a stock worth? There are many different answers, depending on whom you ask. If you decide it's worth its estimated future cash flows, discounted to present value, you've merely stated a problem: What can we expect in dividends and future sales value of this stock? In so doing, you've added a lot to your effort of valuing the stock. Now you know you will estimate dividends plus final selling price and discount them according to some assumed future inflation rate.

Notice what happens: You learn by stating the problem. The definition of the model may be a more valuable exercise than actually designing it.

Building the Model

Designing a model may be more valuable than running it. To design the model, you must define the relationships in detail and set up formulas to simulate cause and effect. One variable is the sum of several others, another is a fraction of the first, a third depends on several different ones in several different ways. Set your formulas and define your limits.

We've said that sales of a software product may vary according to distribution channels, promotion, and seasons. That's the problem as defined. In the second phase of the process, we come up with formulas to represent the way things actually move. We define our vague X, Y, and Z. That makes sales a function of several different, definable variables. We add up the expenses and arrive at a figure for total money needed to start the company. We subtract funds that are available from the bank and add the interest expenditure they'll cause.

Running the Model

Running the model should provide good food for further thought. With a properly built model, and an electronic spreadsheet system, you can play with many different assumptions, thus giving you a good feeling for how many different ways things can go.

Running the model leads to contingency planning. The impact of good business analysis is an awareness of the business's sensitivity to, say, interest rates, product prices, or labor costs. What if new competition opens up and brings on a price war, or what if the price of components doubles? How does the business look if it sells only half the projected units? What if it sells mainly through high-volume distribution channels in which revenue per unit is lower?

Remember, business analysis leads toward a very well-defined goal: the right decision. It may also be fun, and the right model can be elegant, beautiful, and truthful; but it ought to help you make the right decision. That is what it is all for.

Care and Feeding of Models: Rules to Remember

Rule One: Truth, Beauty, and Elegance

These are good goals for models. As representations of life, they ought to be valid and accurate first, but they can also be beautiful and elegant. Of course, a model that works is pretty close to beautiful.

Rule Two: A Model Is Just a Tool

Remember that a model is a tool for problem analysis. It is meant to help you, the human being, to make a business decision. It depends on your input and assumptions and is only as accurate as they are.

Rule Three: Never Believe a Model

Every so often, one business magazine or another examines the results of the better-known econometric models used to forecast the U.S. economy. Using these models and obtaining results are enormous intellectual efforts, normally incorporating thousands of equations run on multimillion-dollar computer machinery. They are seldom more accurate than the hands-on forecasts produced by the best economists in the business. That is because these models are used incorrectly. They are used to give answers when they should be used merely to point the way to answers.

They aren't a crystal ball, a magical answer box, or an Ouija board. Deal with them as you would deal with model airplanes: Build them but don't get on and try to fly them.

Corollary: You *can* believe your assumptions and the logical implications of your assumptions. You can believe that the formulas provide an accurate representation of what is going to happen. If the model seems right, then you believe your assumptions, your research, and the logical outcome. That's okay. But don't ever believe just because the computer says so.

Rule Four: Divide and Conquer

Break down your variables. Always start at the bottom, so you can build with the basic bricks. The line you put in as labor cost, for example, might have been direct labor hours times direct labor price per hour plus indirect labor hours times indirect labor price per hour. Then when you raise hourly wages, you don't have to change the model, just a single line. Don't hand-calculate the new labor cost; let the computer compute it. Make unit cost the sum of several components times each component's respective price, plus some direct labor times its price, plus a prorated overhead number.

Rule Five: Models Illustrate Relationships

Use models to illustrate relationships between different factors, such as between sales and advertising or between cost per unit and volume of units. Use them to show cause and effect and the more complicated implications of changes that affect several different business items at once. Use them to carry simple assumptions into complex limits, following their implications when the calculations would otherwise make things far too complicated for normal business use.

Some Practical Tips, Hints, etc.

Save Your Work Often

You can work with computers a lot better if you protect yourself from foul-ups. Save your work often, and when you have important models, keep back-up copies on another disk and in another place. What you have on a disk is a lot safer than anything in the computer's live, random-access memory.

If there is any real artificial intelligence in the world, it's that innate sense that tells computers to break down when you need them the most. Maybe it's something embedded in the silicon circuits. You should assume that as soon as you depend on a computer, it's going to foul up.

This theory is not as negative as it sounds. It was first voiced by a dedicated computer user who always saves his work and always keeps back-up copies of important models. So, the computers know that he doesn't depend on them that much, and they continue to work.

After you've written labels for the rows and columns, save the model on a disk. After you've done the first few lines of formulas and calculations, save it again. Many people save the file name under two closely related names, first one, then the other: If it's a forecast model, for example, you might name it FRCST; the first time you save it, use the name FRCST01, the second time FRCST02, the third time FRCST01 again. The original file is rewritten, because the computer will write over the first one when you give the third one the same name. You'll always have the latest saved version, plus the previous one. This way you won't accumulate a flock of similar files on the disk, and you won't get confused about which is which. When you're finished with a work session, save the model twice: once as its 01 version and once as its 02 version. If it's a very important model, back it up on another disk.

Tables as Building Blocks

Many people use tables and blocks within spreadsheet models as bricks for building other models. This saves a lot of retyping and allows you to multiply one table by another, as long as the spreadsheet is big enough to include both.

Here's an example that was used a lot to build the whole-market forecast in Chapter Four. First there's a table of computer brands and projected shipments for each in thousands of units in each of several years. Save this as one table. Then you read the same thing back into the spreadsheet *at a different place* but replace the shipment numbers with percentage numbers. Now you have two tables or blocks in the same spread-

Figure 4
Tables and Blocks in Tables

sheet. Save this on the disk. Then go to another empty place on the spreadsheet and read the first table back in. Write over those shipment numbers, this time with a formula that applies the percentage numbers in the second table to the shipment numbers in the first table. Now you have a third table in which the rows identify the computer brands, and the numbers associated with each brand are the product of the original shipments times the percentage. Save that off again.

Don't retype numbers. If you want to make an income statement from a cash-flow model, save the cash-flow model first, then put it back in the workspace, and convert it to an income statement. If you can, use the worksheet's rows and columns that weren't used by the cash flow so that you can have both of them on the same file. If you still have room, put the balance sheet there too; then you won't have to keep referring back to different models. Put them all in one file and save the subtables as separate blocks. You can even print the output of each of the subtables by itself, as a cash flow, income statement, or balance sheet, just by telling the computer which parts of the spreadsheet to print.

Spreadsheets and Word Processing

Most spreadsheets allow you to print your output to a file on a disk. Then you can call that output file into a word processing program for further work. Most of the tables in this book, for example, were done with SuperCalc, VisiCalc, CalcStar, or MicroPlan, with output printed to a disk file and then incorporated in WordStar text.

Bringing the output into the word processing program allows you to improve your presentation. You can polish the format, insert comments between key lines, and so forth.

Switches, Variables, and the IF Function

Most spreadsheets give you some kind of "IF" function. Most of them copy the VisiCalc original, which goes:

```
@IF(equation,formula,formula)
```

If the equation is true, then VisiCalc uses the first formula; if it isn't, it uses the second. Check your manual for how this works on your system.

Use these functions to build switches based on simple variables. In the mortgage payment table in Chapter Six, for example, the model uses an IF function to check whether we've got an interest-only or an amortized loan in a real estate deal. If the loan is interest-only, the model uses one formula; otherwise, the model uses another. Put a variable on top of the model used as a switch above, inputting 1 for interest-only or 0 for amortized. If the variable is in cell B10, for example, then the equation is B10=1.

Some of these calc programs have some sophisticated logic functions: and, or, if, etc. These functions can simplify some real modeling situations. Try them.

Loops and Circular Problems

Spreadsheet logic is going to catch you on occasion with a circular loop. It's very hard to avoid them in all cases, but watch for them.

A circular loop occurs when a formula refers to a row, column, or cell appearing somewhere else on the spreadsheet, and the first cell is updated before the reference cell. If this happens, recalculate, perhaps several times, to make sure you have the right values.

Some examples of this are in the pro forma section. Several different accounts are the product of last month's balance plus this month's transaction, which produces this month's balance. Take a look at the pro forma balance sheet in Chapter Seven for details.

The solution is always the same. Just keep recalculating until the numbers stop changing. Then you're safe.

Write Check Lines

It's a lot easier to make simple mistakes than to catch them once they're made. The output looks perfect, everything seems fine, and you can present the numbers to your boss before you realize you forgot to add in such-and-such, which is on the model but not in the totals line. You just skipped it when you wrote the formula.

You can prevent this with check lines. Find a different way to add the totals up, subtract from the total back to the largest single item (or something similar). Especially when the models get complicated, throw a check line into them. It can help a whole lot, and it doesn't have to show on the printout.

Use Cursor Functions

Most of these spreadsheets have a way of entering cell identification in formulas by moving the cursor. When you enter a formula in SuperCalc, press the ESCAPE key, and suddenly your cursor location is written into the formula. Then move the cursor, and the cell identification in the formula changes. In VisiCalc, as the cursor keys move while you're entering a formula, this happens automatically. CalcStar uses the @ key. Almost all systems have this feature, which is very convenient as you work on a complex model. Instead of going to your reference cell, committing it to memory, and then going back to where you want to write the formula, you can call the cursor into action. Go to the reference cell, press RETURN; the cell is in the formula, and your cursor is back where it started. Try it.

THREE

Getting Started—Some Simple Spreadsheet Models

Let's look at the fundamentals. First we'll talk a bit about the matrix organization of spreadsheets, and then we'll put a couple of simple models into rows and columns. This might also be a good place to go back to your spreadsheet user's manual to compare what we are giving as commands with those used in your own spreadsheet.

The Matrix and the Calculator Function

Spreadsheets are based on a matrix, the mathematical name for a layout that has rows and columns. There is a fair body of mathematical literature, plus some tricks in probability and statistics, that are based on a matrix layout.

Rows are always horizontal, columns vertical. In formal uses, you can refer to any single cell in the matrix by listing its row number first, its column number second, and by then enclosing both in parentheses. Thus, (4,1) stands for row 4, column 1 of the matrix; (23,17) is the entry in row 23, column 17.

For years, programmers have used matrix organization to simplify number-handling. Many programming languages allow the programmer to set up a matrix and use it to identify variables. For example, the results of a calculation might include 24 numbers:

the program might assign these to the matrix by row and column numbers and name the matrix by some simple variable. For example, X(3,4) identifies one number in a matrix named X. The computer programmer can easily manipulate these numbers by referring to that number: Y, for example, might be equal to X(3,4) multiplied by some other constant. Or X(3,4) might be equal to the sum of X(3,1) + X(3,2) + X(3,3).

VisiCalc, SuperCalc, CalcStar, Multiplan, and most other calc programs use similar logic but simplify it by using letters instead of numbers to identify columns.

1. VISICALC

In VisiCalc, you would do the sample addition problem by making cell D3 equal to the sum of A3 + B3 + C3. Move the cursor into cell D3 and type in the formula

A3 + B3 + C3

You could also type in

@SUM(A3...C3)

and get the same answer.

2. SUPERCALC

In SuperCalc, you would do the sample by making cell D3 equal to the sum of A3 + B3 + C3. Move the cursor into cell D3 and type in the formula

A3 + B3 + C3

You could also type in

SUM(A3:C3)

and get the same answer.

3. MULTIPLAN

In Multiplan, you would do the sample by making cell D3 equal to the sum of R3C1 + R3C2 + R3C3. Move the cursor into cell R3C4 first, give the value command, move the cursor back one cell, type +, go back another cell, type plus, then back another cell. Multiplan doesn't let you type the formula in and asks you to move the cursor to identify the cell.

4. MICROPLAN

MicroPlan uses different logic, based on rows rather than on cells. The calculation used here would be done by moving to column 4 and using the sum command to add columns 1 through 3. MicroPlan doesn't include the title columns and title rows as part of the data matrix, so the numbering will change. In the calc programs, titles on the left will occupy column A, and the column titles will occupy row 1. In MicroPlan, titles don't count as rows or columns.

Now we see where the "calc" part of the name comes from. Logically we use the matrix organization to keep track of the different entries, and then the mathematics of most spreadsheet models is as simple as what you could do easily with a calculator. You take this entry, which is the sum of those entries above, and multiply by that entry over there. It would be slower, but still quite possible, even in the larger models and even in those requiring some of the IF-THEN logic allowed in some of the better programs.

Some Simple Examples

Most of your spreadsheet manuals have some simple examples that show you how to get started. The best way to learn any new computer program is to use it. Now we'll set up the job cost estimate and a simple office budget.

Job Cost Estimate

In our fictional software business, we meet with a potential customer who wants a customized general ledger accounting package to use in her business. She says she also wants us to recommend and help her buy a small computer and some packaged software for word processing and budgeting. She wants a single price for the job, because she wants to know how much it will really cost before she gets into it. She also wants a fixed schedule, with penalties taken out of payments if we fall behind. After she walks out of the store, we sit down at the computer.

Step One: Call Up the Calc Program

This procedure varies by computer, but in most cases you must turn the machine on first and "boot up" the operating system. In the more traditional Apple computer with VisiCalc, you put in the VisiCalc disk, turn on the computer, and you are ready for Step Two.

The operating system, for you newcomers, is a collection of computer programs that handle the business of the system, such as putting letters and numbers on the screen, running an applications program, providing a directory of files on the disk, and so forth. Apple's operating system is usually Apple-DOS, Radio Shack's is TRS-DOS, and the IBM-PC's is PC-DOS or others. (DOS is a common term that stands for Disk Operating System.) CP/M, which has several different versions, is used on many different computers and at one time came closest to being the standardized operating system. MS-DOS, which is almost identical to PC-DOS, is becoming a standardized operating system among those microcomputers that have the same processor chip as the IBM-PC.

To "boot up" the operating system is to take the computer from its "catatonic," or resting, state into its operative state. Your hardware manual tells you how to do this.

Figure 5
VisiCalc Screen

F8/A MP: V1F:
ATTRIBUTE:E H M T L V D

	A	B	C	D	E	F	G	H	I	J	K
1				MARKETING DEPARTMENT							
2				2ND HALF REVISED BUDGET ($ØØØ)							
3											
4		F				3RD				4TH	2ND
5		A	JUL	AUG	SEP	QTR	OCT	NOV	DEC	QTR	HALF
6		-	----	----	----	-----	----	----	----	-----	-----
7											
8	SALARIES	F	26.6	3Ø.5	35.Ø	92.1	35.Ø	37.5	37.5	11Ø.Ø	2Ø2.1
9		A	26.5			26.5				Ø.Ø	26.5
10											
11	TEMPS	F	Ø.4	Ø.4	Ø.4	1.2	Ø.5	Ø.5	Ø.5	1.5	2.7
12		A				Ø.Ø				Ø.Ø	Ø.Ø
13											
14	BENEFITS (17%)	F	4.5	5.2	6.Ø	15.7	6.Ø	6.4	6.4	18.7	34.4
15		A	4.5	Ø.Ø	Ø.Ø	4.5	Ø.Ø	Ø.Ø	Ø.Ø	Ø.Ø	4.5
16											
17	SUB-TOTAL	F	31.5	36.1	41.4	1Ø9.Ø	41.5	44.4	44.4	13Ø.2	239.2
18		A	31.Ø	Ø.Ø	Ø.Ø	31.Ø	Ø.Ø	Ø.Ø	Ø.Ø	Ø.Ø	31.Ø
19											
20				F=FORECAST		A=ACTUAL					

When the operating system is booted up, you'll get a signal that it is waiting for a command. In CP/M or MS-DOS the signal looks like this:

A>

with the A standing for the disk drive that is logged in to be searched first for the applications program you ask the computer to run.

If you are one of those privileged microcomputer owners who has a Winchester disk system, you may be able to go already. If you use the floppy disk drives that most of us use, put one into the drive to boot up the operating system, and that may or may not be the same one that has your calc program on it. If not, get a calc program disk into one of your drives, and tell the operating system to run your calc. Either way, it might look like the following in a CP/M system or IBM-PC running SuperCalc:

A>SC<RETURN>

Figure 6
MicroPlan Screen

```
CASH FLO                         MODE=NORMAL   ORDER=R/C  ROW=1-28  COL=1-4
     ROW 1 (DATA FROM TABLE 1) <--
ENTER COMMAND:
                                        DEC        JAN        FEB  1 format:
ROW                                    1982       1983       1983  2 data:
------------------------------- ----1----- ----2----- ----3-----  3 math:
 1 DATA FROM TABLE 1                                               4 finance:
2 ACCOUNTS PAYABLE-MATERIALS      20,000.00                        5 print:
3 NET OPERATING EXPENSES               0.13                        6 status:
4 SALES PROJECTION                30,000.00  33,000.00  36,300.00  7 HELP
5 INCOME TAXES PAYABLE            25,000.00                        8
6 CASH                            15,000.00                        9 STOP
7 CREDIT SALES                    22,500.00  24,750.00  27,225.00  10 utility:
8                                                                  11 program:
9 CASH RECEIPTS                                                    12 stats:
10    CASH SALES                              8,250.00   9,075.00  13 tables:
11    COLLECT'S OF CREDIT SALES              22,500.00  24,750.00  14
12       TOTAL CASH RECEIPTS                 30,750.00  33,825.00  15
13                                                                 16 format:
14 CASH DISBURSEMENTS                                              17 INSERT
15    MATERIALS                              20,000.00  22,000.00  18 DELETE
16    OPERATING EXPENSES                      4,125.00   4,537.50  19   rows:
17    TAXES                                                        20 ROW TITLE
```

The <RETURN> means to press the RETURN key after you type SC. The command might also look like these:

B>CS<RETURN> (CalcStar on drive B:)
A>PLAN<RETURN> (MicroPlan)

Specifics will of course depend on which spreadsheet you're using, which computer you own, and how your system's storage memory is set up.

Now you are into the spreadsheet program. Your disk drives will buzz a bit, some logos and serial numbers will show up on the screen, and you will end up with an empty spreadsheet, ready for you to enter numbers.

The spreadsheets vary, of course. But, you are likely to see on the screen numbers running down the left side, letters running across the top, and a lot of empty space. A prompt signal for commands and basic information about memory usage are at the bottom. That's the VisiCalc look, which most of the others copied. MicroPlan gives you commands on the right (a menu), numbered rows and columns with zeroes in them, and some information at the top, with a command prompt at the left a few rows down from the top. Now you are ready to go.

Step Two: Label Some Rows and Columns

Now, you want to label some of your cost headings to begin to build that matrix. In most cases, you must look at your user's manual to figure out how your spreadsheet program wants you to fill in the text labels. SuperCalc, for example, gives you an error message if you write text into a cell without first telling the program—by inserting an apostrophe—that you want text instead of numbers. You have to move the cursor from row to row, according to whichever technique your hardware and software specify. You might use arrow keys such as those on the Apple computers: The space bar turns the arrows from horizontal to vertical. Many versions of SuperCalc and CalcStar use the CONTROL or CTRL keys along with some letters—C-E moves the cursor up, C-X moves it down, C-S moves it to the left, and C-D moves it to the right. In MicroPlan, you give the 20 command, called "change desc", and then write labels in the rows on the left. Write one, press RETURN, and you'll be dropped down automatically to the next one.

Try it on your computer. Many people are slow as they begin, and they are afraid that they don't know enough. And they don't. But they won't break the thing by typing into the keyboard. At the very worst, they'll have to reboot the system, which is no big deal. Try it.

Label some of your costs. In Table 3-1, we started with hardware costs. Then we went through the time involved in evaluation. Refer to your user's manual and enter the figures.

Early on, we distinguished between hardware costs, which are measured in dollars, and consultant/programmer time, which is measured in days. It could be hours, weeks, months, or minutes, depending on the job at hand. We chose dollars and days and then wrote the column titles in the job estimate (Table 3-1).

Consider the Model Relationships

This starts the thinking process. You have to define your cost items and how you want to keep track of them. As we said in an earlier chapter, stating the problem is taking a major step toward solving it. Look at Table 3-1, the job cost estimate we're building. It is the product of a trial-and-error thought process: We considered how we might best keep track of costs and present job estimates. We made several false starts and some corrections and refinements along the way.

Don't spend forever trying to figure out the problem in your head. You are much better off getting it onto the spreadsheet, then changing it. Doing Table 3-1, for example, we first estimated hardware costs at $3,500. Then we remembered a printer and changed the costs to $5,500. Then we decided our customer would probably be better off buying a Winchester disk drive and a floppy disk drive, instead of two floppies. At that point, we opted to itemize the hardware components and used the spreadsheet facility to insert some new rows. The result is better, because our customer would also want more detail in the hardware cost estimate. To be able to change factors as we proceeded was one of the main reasons we got onto a spreadsheet program in the first place. So use the power your tools offer; get going, refine later.

Table 3-1: Job Cost Estimate

(Columns: A	B	C	D)
(Rows:)			
1 Job Cost Estimate	Materials	Time	Duration
2	(dollars)	(days)	(days)
3 Specifications		1.00	5.00
4 Hardware evaluation		2.00	10.00
5 Software evaluation		1.00	0.00
6 Hardware Cost			
7 CPU	1700.00		
8 Monitor	350.00		
9 Drive A	450.00		
10 Winchester	2500.00		
11 Printer	2500.00		
12 Miscellaneous	100.00		
13	----------		
14 Total hardware	7600.00		
15 Installation and test		2.00	20.00
16 Packaged Software			
17 Operating System	250.00		
18 Word Processing	300.00		
19 Spreadsheet	250.00		
20 DBMS	900.00		
21	----------		
22 Total packaged software	1700.00		
23 Custom Software			
24 Detailed Specs.		1.00	
25 GL basic module		4.00	
26 A/R basic module		2.00	
27 A/P basic module		1.00	
28 Payroll module		2.00	
29 Menus		2.00	
30 Test, de-bug		5.00	34.00
31 Totals:			
32 Materials	9300.00		
33 Days worked		23.00	
34 Duration (days)			69.00
35 Estimated Invoice Amount			
36 Materials	10230.00		
37 Consultant days	5750.00		
38	----------		
39 Total Invoice Amount	15980.00		

Itemizing the hardware costs also goes back to Rule Two in the preceding chapter. That's the one about breaking things down into parts. By breaking down hardware costs, we'll be in a better position to modify costs if the need arises. If our customer already has a monitor, or wants a cheaper printer, we can revise instantly. We've already got a variable set up.

Step Three: Fill and Refine

Once we have a basic model going, we can begin to fill and refine. Follow whatever order comes naturally, filling in variables, adding new items, completing the numbers.

Note that some numbers are simple entries, and some are formulas of one kind or another. In Table 3-1, the hardware total is the sum of all the hardware parts. This is written as a sum function in cell B14:

@SUM(B7... B12)	(VisiCalc)
SUM(B7:B12)	(SuperCalc)
SUM(B7>B12)	(CalcStar)

In these spreadsheets, when the cursor is on the right place, you simply enter the above formulas to get a sum function. Note the use of the parentheses, which are taken from conventional computer programming styles. A few paragraphs from now we'll take that SUM function and enclose it entirely in parentheses to make something else happen to it. You might also write in:

B7+B8+B9+B10+B11+B12

This works out to the same thing. In MicroPlan, you would get your data pointer on row 14 and give the command 55 to sum rows. The system would ask you from which row to which row.

The formula and function facilities lead to many different ways to introduce truth, beauty, and functional elegance. This is part of the magic of electronic spreadsheets. Just as you can tell the computer to sum a part of a column, you can tell it to follow complicated decision rules in a complex model or to perform much more complicated calculations. Many of the spreadsheet software products now offer financial functions, such as present value calculations or internal rates of return. We will be using these as we go on through additional material in later chapters.

In Table 3-1, the column called "Duration" (column D) is another refinement. We are used to estimating costs in terms of materials and programming/consultant days. But often there are blocks of time that interfere, and we can't do our work straight through from start to finish. Hardware evaluation, for instance, may require appointments with several different vendors or visits to several retail outlets. Hardware delivery may take weeks. So the duration column attempts to absorb these doubts in order to give our client a better idea of how long, in real time, this whole process might take.

In most cases, duration is simply a given number entered directly as an estimate. For custom software, however, duration was clumsy to estimate, so we used a formula. The D30 formula is (in SuperCalc language) as follows:

(SUM(C24:C30))*2

It is the sum of C24 through C30, multiplied by two. VisiCalc users would write this formula like this:

(@SUM(C24...C30))*2

Note once again the use of the conventional computer formula notation with parentheses. The asterisk signals multiplication, the parentheses determine what is done first and how the math functions are bundled. We mentioned earlier that we would enclose a SUM function in parentheses, and here it is. The above formula tells the computer to take first the sum of C24 through C30 and then multiply it by two. If you wanted to divide two entries, A1 and A2, and then add 10 to the product, you would write

(A1/A2) + 10

To divide all that by 3, you would write

((A1/A2) + 10)/3

And to multiply that by another entry, A3, you would write

(((A1/A2) + 10)/3)*A3

Obviously, there will be some differences in the handling of details by each separate spreadsheet program. CalcStar is quite similar to the above VisiCalc and SuperCalc formulas, but it uses a ⟩ instead of a colon, making SUM(C24⟩C30) the CalcStar version of SUM(C24:C30). MicroPlan uses a different logic entirely, as we mentioned earlier; the SUM is a command instead of part of a formula. Multiplan uses about the same logic, but it identifies cells by R1C1 notation. As we go through the rest of the book, you should become familiar with the differences, if any, between the more standard products and the one you use. Up until we get to some of the more complicated elements, such as manipulation of tables and financial functions, all these products do about the same thing, even if they use different details in the language.

Notice that duration doesn't appear in the final tally of job costs. It is a convenience figure used to help estimate the total time lapse from start to finish. It is not part of the formal estimate.

The model tallies hardware costs and adds a 10 percent surcharge for the value added by evaluation and installation. Since subtotals appear already in column B, we can't do a straight SUM function. Instead, we add B14 and B22 and then multiply the sum by 1.1. This is written in cell B36 as

(B14 + B22)*1.1

The services cost is total days of work times our standard $250 per day. That comes out as

(SUM(C3:C30))*250

Or, since we already have SUM(C3:C30) in another entry, C33, we may just as well make the total labor formula (that's B37, called "consultant days") simpler, as in

C33*250

We should also follow our own Rule Three on models to break the formula down further, putting the daily consultant rate in a separate entry, which we could change if needed. If we used, say, E35 for that entry, we could then make C37

C33*D35

This is trivial at this point but could come back to haunt us later. In fact, we wrote the model correctly, with D35 reserved for the price, and then we simply left the E column off the printout.

When we're done, we get a job cost estimate. We might easily re-use the same form to do the next job cost estimate for the next customer. We have a model to use if our customer wants to substitute hardware and software materials from the original list. We have fair justification for charges for added value. We can save the justification (as well as the model!) on the disk and then compare the estimate with the actual costs when we've finished the job. Repetition makes estimation better, but only when you take the trouble to compare estimated with actual.

Simple Office Budget

Now we're going to write a simple office budget for this software company. We'll use the situation we discussed in Chapter One: A software product is six months and three programmers away from being finished. To calculate how much that six months is going to cost, we estimate the monthly expenditures on a spreadsheet program. Table 3-2 gives us some initial results:

Table 3-2: A Simple Office Budget

	month 1	month 2	month 3	month 4	month 5	month 6
Office rent	1200.00	1200.00	1200.00	1200.00	1200.00	1200.00
Utilities	220.00	221.10	222.20	223.31	224.43	225.55
Programmer salary	3000.00	3000.00	3000.00	3000.00	3000.00	3000.00
Programmer salary	2500.00	2500.00	2500.00	2500.00	2500.00	2500.00
Programmer salary	2500.00	2500.00	2500.00	2500.00	2500.00	2500.00
Payroll taxes	800.00	800.00	800.00	800.00	800.00	800.00
Computer rental	200.00	200.00	200.00	200.00	200.00	200.00
Stationery	150.00	150.00	150.00	150.00	150.00	150.00
Postage	20.00	20.00	20.00	20.00	20.00	20.00
Incidentals	50.00	50.00	50.00	50.00	50.00	50.00
Total monthly	10640.00	10641.10	10642.20	10643.31	10644.43	10645.55
Total expenditure						63856.61

The procedure is similar to the step process we used to estimate costs in Table 3-1. First, we must get ourselves into the calc program, following the same systems procedure we went through. Then we set an initial definition for our rows and columns.

This is a matter of entering them. Use the commands your calc program requires. Remember, in SuperCalc you request text by typing a quotation mark or an apostrophe as you enter data; in MicroPlan you use a 20 or 25 command, and in CalcStar or VisiCalc you just type the text.

The model starts simply enough. We did a similar one with pencil and paper in Chapter One. Column headings are obvious, and row headings are defined by actual expense items. Already, of course, we begin to think about the problem, but we may have forgotten payroll taxes or utilities.

Then we get to Step Three, in which we fill in the bones of the model. Rent is a straight-line estimate. Utilities are expected to cost a certain amount, with an average half percent increase per month (our own way of paying respects to inflation). To do this in the calc programs, type a number under month 1 (which would be row 3, column 2, or entry B3). We choose to estimate utilities at $220 per month. Then we enter a formula for month 2 as follows:

month 2 utilities = (month 1 utilities) * 1.005

Or, translated into calc language, entry C3 is equal to the following:

B3*1.005

To enter that formula, you move your system cursor—that's the pointer, or whatever the system uses to tell you in which cell you are entering information—to C3 and write the formula. In many calc programs, this formula works better:

+B3*1.005

The *plus* sign at the beginning tells the system that you are entering a formula, not text. In most programs, this formula will work either way.

Now you want to continue this formula through month 6—quite simple with a REPLICATE command (in VisiCalc and SuperCalc; copy in CalcStar). Using a / (; in CalcStar) to get the system's attention, you then give it an R (C in CalcStar). It will ask you what cell you want to replicate, and you tell it C3. Then it will ask you what cells you want to spread that over, and you tell it D3 through G3, written D3:G3 in many calc programs, D3〉G3 in others.

People are sometimes put off in the beginning by the computer's way of asking you for information. But your system's "prompt" is something that you will learn to like. When you give the replicate or copy command, do not try to put all the information you need into the command. Wait, and the computer will come up with a message asking for the additional information required.

1. MOST CALCS

In most calc programs, the replicate facility will let you choose whether you want "relative" or static values. This is a very useful option. Relative values will adjust each entry to preserve the formula as you move across the screen. F3, for example, will be

E3*1.005

It won't be

B3*1.005

The calc programs also have a marvelous feature that will let you use more than one variable in a formula, making one relative and one static. In this case, one will change and adjust itself across the matrix, and the other will preserve a single value. You could put inflation at the top of a model, for example, and many formulas would key off that one value. One change in the inflation rate would then adjust all the related formulas in the model. We'll use that capability in a couple of models we'll see later in this book.

The salary estimates in the model run straight across the six months. We entered them in the month 1 column, then replicated the number across the other columns. That means getting the replicate (or copy) command and telling the system to copy, say, B4, into C4:G4.

2. MICROPLAN

MicroPlan works in a different manner. It is a row or column-oriented calc system, rather than a single-entry system. In MicroPlan, the utilities row would be entered by taking the data pointer to row 3 and by then giving a 31 command to enter data. The computer then prompts for options:

0 to key in values for all the entries in the row
1 to get a constant number across the row
2 to increase the row by a constant growth rate
3 to increase the row by a constant increment

For row 3, you would answer 2 to get a constant growth rate. The system then asks for a number for the starting point, and you would enter 220. Then it asks for a rate, and you would enter .5. The results would be the same row 3 shown in Table 3-2. The whole affair would look like:

```
ENTER COMMAND: 31 〈RETURN〉        (to enter data on row 3)
CHOOSE (VALUES=0, CONSTANT=1, GROW=2, INCR=3):2 〈RETURN〉
BASE VALUE: 220
RATE: .5
```

The salary estimates in the model run straight across the six months. In MicroPlan, we gave the 31 command to enter across rows, then gave the 1 prompt to get a constant, then entered the number. The results are exactly the same. The procedure for row 4, for example, will look like this (you have to be in row 4 when all this happens):

```
ENTER COMMAND: 31 ⟨RETURN⟩
CHOOSE (VALUES=0, CONSTANT=1, GROW=2, INCR=3):1 ⟨RETURN⟩
BASE VALUE: 3000 ⟨RETURN⟩
```

Payroll taxes require another formula. For the sake of illustration, we estimated payroll taxes as

payroll tax=(total payroll)*.1

The assumption is that this estimates only the incremental cost of payroll taxes paid by the company in addition to the gross salary. In the real world, part of that gross salary is paid to the employee and part is paid to the government. Since the payout on a $3,000-per-month gross is still exactly $3,000 from the company, we left that figure and added the additional taxes that the company itself pays over and above what it takes from the employees' checks. This affects row 7.

1. SUPERCALC AND VISICALC

Starting in cell B7, we enter the following:

```
+SUM(B4:B6)*.1        (in SuperCalc)
@SUM(B4...B6)*.1      (in VisiCalc)
```

Then we give a REPLICATE command, telling the computer to copy B7's formula into entries C7 through G7. It asks, we tell it we want relative values, and the row is completed.

2. CALCSTAR

In CalcStar, we use (B4)B6) to indicate the entries to be summed and use a COPY command instead of REPLICATE. Otherwise, the procedure is exactly the same.

3. MICROPLAN

MicroPlan uses the FORMULA command, which is number 35. Then you would enter the formula using L4, L5, and L6 to represent rows 4 through 6. This goes as follows (with the data pointer at row 7):

```
ENTER COMMAND: 35 ⟨RETURN⟩
FORMULA: (L4+L5+L6)*.1
```

You can get tripped up with row-and-column formulas. If you are entering in rows, L5 stands for row 5. If you are entering in columns, L5 means column 5. Be careful with this.

Most of the rest of the budget involves simple rows running straight across the columns. These are for computer costs, postage, supplies, and incidentals. They are entered as the above salaries are, using the simple entry plus REPLICATE or COPY or the MicroPlan CONSTANT option on data entry.

1. CALCS

The total monthly expenditure row takes a SUM command. In the standard calc formats, you move to cell B13 and enter the following:

```
SUM(B3:B11)          (SuperCalc)
@SUM(B3...B11)       (VisiCalc)
+SUM(B3>B11)         (CalcStar)
```

Finally, we get the last—and probably most important—number: How much did this additional work cost? The total cost is simple to produce on the calc programs, because it is a sum entry:

```
@SUM(B14...G14)      (VisiCalc)
+SUM(B14>G14)        (CalcStar)
SUM(B14:G14)         (SuperCalc)
```

2. MICROPLAN

In MicroPlan, the total monthly expenditure needs a TOTALS command, number 55. When you enter this command, the computer prompts you for what to sum. This command looks like the following:

```
ENTER COMMAND: 55 <RETURN>      (the TOTALS command)
BEGIN ROW (1–50): 3 ⟨RETURN⟩
END ROW (3–50): 11 ⟨RETURN⟩
```

You may notice that the MicroPlan row numbers are sometimes different from all the other calcs. This is because most calcs take a row to do underlining, while MicroPlan sends a message to the printer to underline.

Finally, we get the last—and probably most important—number: How much did this additional work cost?

MicroPlan is not quite as agile on this sum, because of its row/column orientation. But we could get it in row 14 under month 6 by using the MicroPlan CUMULATE command, as follows:

```
ENTER COMMAND: 49 ⟨RETURN⟩
```

VALUE: 0 ⟨RETURN⟩
ROW (1–50): 13 ⟨RETURN⟩

The CUMULATE command puts a cumulative total across the row. If we want to start at a number other than 0 (if, say, we already have a balance of expenditures and want to add to that balance), then we can enter that number when the system asks for a value.

We could also get the cumulative total in MicroPlan by getting the data pointer to column 7, the one that follows month 6, and then by summing all the entries in columns 1 through 6, as follows:

ENTER COMMAND: 34 <RETURN> (selecting a column)
COLUMN: (1–20):7 <RETURN>

ENTER COMMAND: 55 <RETURN> (the *sum* command)
BEGIN COLUMN (1–20): 1 <RETURN>
END COLUMN (1–20): 6 <RETURN>

Either of these MicroPlan options would put the numbers in a format slightly different from the one presented in Table 3-2. With cumulative handling, you would have a full row 14 with cumulative expenditure numbers in each of the six months. With the summing of columns, you would have a seventh data column, which would sum each of the expenditure items for the whole six-month period.

At some point you start to ask yourself whether all these commands are worth the effort. After all, these aren't very complex numbers. Why not just get pencil and paper and figure them out?

Table 3-3: Simple Office Budget

(Modified)

	month 1	month 2	month 3	month 4	month 5	month 6
Office rent	900.00	900.00	900.00	900.00	900.00	900.00
Utilities	180.00	180.90	181.80	182.71	183.62	184.54
Programmer salary	3000.00	3000.00	3000.00	3000.00	3000.00	3000.00
Programmer salary	4000.00	4000.00	2000.00	0.00	0.00	0.00
Programmer salary	0.00	0.00	0.00	0.00	0.00	0.00
Payroll taxes	700.00	700.00	500.00	300.00	300.00	300.00
Computer rental	300.00	300.00	300.00	100.00	100.00	100.00
Stationery	150.00	150.00	150.00	150.00	150.00	150.00
Postage	20.00	20.00	20.00	20.00	20.00	20.00
Incidentals	50.00	50.00	50.00	50.00	50.00	50.00
Total monthly	9300.00	9300.90	7101.80	4702.71	4703.62	4704.54
Total expenditure						39813.59

The answer is simple: Once you've set up the spreadsheet model, you can change it easily. In Table 3-3, for example, we experiment with the costs associated with a new, more expensive programmer who is also unusually productive. She would have to earn $4,000 per month, according to this assumption, but would speed the programming completion.

If you are using your tools right, that idea brings you back to the keyboard. A change here and there, a row gets zeroed out, and you save yourself about a third of the development cost. Rent is lower and utilities are lower because less space is needed to accommodate fewer people. Computer costs are lower. And salary expenditures are much lower, because we have one more expensive person doing the creative work that two competent people were doing.

On the spreadsheet, these recalculations would probably take you about 30 seconds to do. With pencil and paper, you would have to practically start at zero. The spreadsheet is most valuable when you have factors to change.

FOUR

Forecasting

The Art and Science of Guessing

Forecasting is more art than science. There are no magic methods that always work, let alone a computer program that will forecast by itself. The heart of forecasting is good guessing, and the best guess is an educated guess. So use your common sense and judgment and as much information as possible. Look at as many angles as you can and consider past trends, new developments, cycles, and anything else that can give you a hint.

Consider the weather forecast. It's one of the best forecasts available anywhere. The meteorologists study wind patterns, satellite pictures, air pressure, and years of past trends. Each forecast is based on careful analysis of what's going on, why it's going on, and why it might lead to something else tomorrow. If a storm is over the ocean and is headed toward the coast, then probably there will be rain tomorrow, the meteorologists say, because in similar conditions on hundreds of past occasions the results were the same. The probability of rain or sunshine is a very professional guess, based on a wealth of knowledge, some good judgment, and common sense. Computers, satellites, and other tools increase the store of knowledge, but they can't do it all alone.

The same general idea applies to many other good forecasts. The best forecast combines fancy information management with good common sense. The market researchers, the stock brokers, and even the political analysts base their guesses on huge volumes of carefully analyzed information. They might use computerized econometric or simulation models or complicated trends analysis. But even the most sophisticated computerized forecasting models do very little more than pull equations out of the past and spread them into the future. This is certainly a very good way of considering alternatives and a valuable check on the thinking process. These models make the forecast better. But there is still no substitute for common-sense consideration of trends and alternatives: the famous "what-if" we hear so much about lately.

Spreadsheet sales forecasting at its best is a good combination of computer power and common-sense judgment. The best spreadsheet session is a supercharged version of scenario analysis. Make some assumptions and then test them for logic and reasonableness. Try different assumptions. Try them again and again until you feel comfortable with your forecast and the assumptions on which it's built.

Home computer markets recently showed the world how much a forecast depends on art as well as science. Forecasters had a tough time projecting those markets into the future. From 1979 through 1981, home computer sales were disappointing—just a few thousand a year, a few hundred thousand in 1981. Then suddenly the prices went down and the volume shot up to more than two million in 1982. So how do you forecast 1983 through 1985? Not easily, and not by any blind formula methods.

This home computer market shows how wrong you can go by just assuming the past predicts the future. Many forecasters simply determine past growth rates and then project those rates into the future. Unfortunately, if you assume home computer sales will continue to increase by more than 100 percent per year, you probably will come up with an unrealistic number very quickly. By 1985, you would then have to say, people will buy almost 20 million of the things. That's more computers per year than even color television sets.

This kind of error ignores the size of potential markets and the importance of product life cycles. The home computer forecast needs to consider how many households will own computers. On your spreadsheet, indicate the total number of households and how many you think will own computers in each year: 10 percent, 20 percent, etc. Then have the spreadsheet multiply. Maybe you should divide your households by education and income levels and then assume different percentages for different levels. Have the spreadsheet multiply each and then add up the totals.

The best forecasting takes many different possibilities into account and considers many different assumptions. Good forecasters put them on the spreadsheet screen and think about them. Eventually, they might go with one analysis or another, or they might absorb all the numbers and estimate some in between.

The point here is to use the spreadsheet program to play with your guesses. Put a guess on the screen and look at it. Try another angle, a different growth rate, and think about it. The computer can help by speeding up the process. Scenario analysis, as we discussed in earlier chapters, is one of the best ways to consider future alternatives and their implications; use it in your forecast.

This chapter is about ways to educate those guesses, to make a good forecast. There are some tricks of the trade, some of which are ideally suited for your spreadsheet models. We'll run through a series of forecasts and discuss some of the methodology involved. Then you should be able to make your own forecasting models to suit the conditions you confront.

Before we start, remember what we've been saying about computers in business analysis. You do the thinking, let the computer do the numbers—nothing else.

Forecasting from the Ground Up

In Chapter Two, we said you should try to "divide and conquer" when you can. You want to break your problem down into smaller pieces, work on the pieces, and then add them up again to get the whole picture. This is especially true when you're forecasting sales. It is often easier to forecast in detail and then to add up the details to produce a whole forecast.

One of the easiest sales forecasts to make is based on an actual poll of customers. This is sometimes possible in an industrial context in which sales are composed of large volumes of material or high-priced items sold to only a few very important customers.

In this case, ask your customers what they'll need next year and add it all up. The spreadsheet model is quite simple: Label your rows for customers; label your columns for years, months, or quarters; fill in the blanks; and then add the numbers up. Table 4-1 is an example. Salesman Smith had asked his customers what they planned to order in 1983. He adds the numbers up and produces a forecast.

Table 4-1: Customer-Based Sales Forecast

Company XYZ

Salesman Smith's Forecast by Customer

1983

		qtr 1 1983	qtr 2 1983	qtr 3 1983	qtr 4 1983	year 1983
		1	2	3	4	5
1	Customer A	35.0	45.0	60.0	40.0	180.0
2	Customer B	30.0	30.0	30.0	30.0	120.0
3	Customer C	80.0	100.0	120.0	110.0	410.0
4	Others	14.4	18.0	22.8	19.2	74.4
5	Total	159.4	193.0	232.8	199.2	784.4

Not bad for a start. But it's certainly simple enough to do on a piece of paper with a pencil, rather than on a computer spreadsheet.

Now, suppose we have several regions to consider and several salespersons in each region, each salesperson dealing with several companies. Some of the companies have different local operations and buy from two or three of the salesmen in their local areas. So, now we have to build the forecast more carefully. We have a lot more incentive to use the spreadsheet.

We're going to do that here, step by step. First, we'll do Region I, and then we'll consolidate it with the other regions. The end product is a very detailed sales forecast, ideal for tracking results as the year goes by.

Step One: Polling the Customers

The first step is to ask the customers what they expect to order. Salesman Smith already did that, and we showed the results in Table 4-1. Now we ask Salesman Jones and Saleswoman Mitchell to do the same to produce Table 4-2.

Totals, Subtotals, and the ESCAPE Function

The spreadsheet management is still quite simple. First, it's a simple input to add in the data from the sales persons' forecasts. Then we total up. We've already shown how the program can add the items for subtotals and then add the totals down at the bottom. That was in some of our earlier models.

1. MICROPLAN

In MicroPlan, you use the TOTAL (55) command to add a bunch of rows or columns that are in straight order. Line 8, for example, is produced by TOTAL. The system asks from what row to what row, and you tell it from 4 to 7. Then the final total at the bottom comes from a FORMULA (35) command, with the formula being L8+L16+L24. The TOTAL command only works when the rows or columns to be totaled are exactly next to each other.

2. THE CALC PRODUCTS

In VisiCalc, SuperCalc, and most of the other calcs, you write the proper formula into one cell, then use REPLICATE or its equivalent to spread across the rows. You would go to cell B8, for example, and type B4+B5+B6. Then you use REPLICATE B8 for C8 through F8. The totals line comes from moving to cell B26 and then entering B24+B16+B8; then a REPLICATE command can be used as above to fill in the rest of the row.

This is a good time to look at the calc programs' special ESCAPE function, which is so called because SuperCalc uses the ESCAPE key. In VisiCalc, do the same thing using your cursor arrows after starting a formula in a cell. CalcStar uses the @ key for the same function. Others do it differently. Almost all of them provide some way to move the cursor to a cell as a formula is written and have that cell written into the formula.

Table 4-2: Sales by Salesperson and Customer

Composite of Customers' Order Forecast

Company XYZ
Region I Sales, 1983
by salesperson and customer

		qtr 1 1983	qtr 2 1983	qtr 3 1983	qtr 4 1983	year 1983
		—11—	—12—	—13—	—14—	—15—
1	Region I					
2	Salesman Smith					
3	Customers:					
4	Customer A	35.0	45.0	60.0	40.0	180.0
5	Customer B	30.0	30.0	30.0	30.0	120.0
6	Customer C	80.0	100.0	120.0	110.0	410.0
7	Others	14.4	18.0	22.8	19.2	74.4
8	Subtotal	159.4	193.0	232.8	199.2	784.4
9	Salesman Jones					
10	Customers:					
11	Customer B	45.0	45.0	45.0	45.0	180.0
12	Customer D	55.0	65.0	75.0	70.0	265.0
13	Customer E	85.0	100.0	120.0	100.0	405.0
14	Customer F	20.0	25.0	35.0	25.0	105.0
15	Others	13.2	18.0	21.6	15.6	68.4
16	Subtotal	218.2	253.0	296.6	255.6	1,023.4
17	Saleswoman Mitchell					
18	Customers:					
19	Customer A	50.0	65.0	75.0	70.0	260.0
20	Customer B	120.0	130.0	140.0	150.0	540.0
21	Customer E	42.0	52.0	56.0	47.0	197.0
22	Customer G	25.0	35.0	45.0	35.0	140.0
23	Others	16.8	19.2	22.8	16.8	75.6
24	Subtotal	253.8	301.2	338.8	318.8	1,212.6
25						
26	Total sales	631.4	747.2	868.2	773.6	3,020.4
27						
28	Customer A	85.0	110.0	135.0	110.0	440.0
29	Customer B	195.0	205.0	215.0	225.0	840.0
30	Customer C	80.0	100.0	120.0	110.0	410.0
31	Customer D	55.0	65.0	75.0	70.0	265.0
32	Customer E	127.0	152.0	176.0	147.0	602.0
33	Customer F	20.0	25.0	35.0	25.0	105.0
34	Customer G	25.0	35.0	45.0	35.0	140.0
35	Others	44.4	55.2	67.2	51.6	218.4
36	Check total	631.4	747.2	868.2	773.6	3,020.4

This special feature simplifies formula entry. Try it. Build your model like ours, and get your cursor down to cell B26. Then press ESCAPE. (Or @, or whichever command your program uses; in VisiCalc you'd type simply +. We're going to call it ESCAPE.) Notice that B26 appears in the formula line. Now, go up to B25 and then B24, and you'll notice that the characters in the formula line change to match your cursor movement. When you're at B24, the line will read B24 (+B24 in VisiCalc; VisiCalc users should follow along with that extra plus sign—we won't mention it again). Now, press +. You should have the line reading B24+. Press ESCAPE, and you should see B24+B24. Move the cursor to B16, then press +. Now, you should have the formula B24+B16+. Go to B8, and you should see B24+B16+B8. Press RETURN, and you've finished the formula. This is as easy to do as it is difficult to explain. Try it.

The Check Line and Customer Totals

The spreadsheet software makes it easy to add customer totals.

1. MICROPLAN

In MicroPlan, use the FORMULA command (35) to pick the line numbers of each customer. Customer B would be L5+L11+L20, for example, written directly into the appropriate row. If a customer appears only twice you can use the ADD command (43), and the system will ask which two rows or which two columns to add.

2. CALC PRODUCTS

In the calc programs, you can write in the formulas by cells (or use the ESCAPE function above) and then use REPLICATE. We've already done a couple of these in the previous chapter, so we won't repeat it here.

The check line may be the most valuable suggestion in this book. The computer sometimes hides dumb mistakes. It's frighteningly easy to add the wrong two lines together, and the output looks so nice you never know it until you've already gone to the bank with it. That's embarrassing. In MicroPlan, the TOTAL command makes easy errors when you add your totals line back into the total—it might total lines 4 through 8, for example, instead of 4 through 7. By adding a check line like the one in these models, you'll catch at least some of those errors. If the total by salesperson doesn't check with the total by customer, there's an error there—and it isn't a computer error.

Step Two: Making It Better

Now we have a pleasant-looking forecast for Region I, but one that might be pure hogwash. We have to think about whether our customers are offering good information. Maybe they inflate projections to assure a trouble-free supply of raw materials. Maybe they're too optimistic or too pessimistic. We can't really rely on a forecast until we've considered some of these alternatives.

Looking at Past Trends

The first thing to do in this situation is to look at past data. The past doesn't necessarily predict the future, but it does help. You have to understand the past to guess about the future. If things have or haven't changed, fine; but forecast accordingly.

Table 4-3 (pages 42–43) illustrates the next logical step in the forecast. It is made from Table 4-2. We inserted some columns into the same spreadsheet, then wrote the data into the quarter-by-quarter part of it, and then let the spreadsheet help us out. In MicroPlan, you don't have to rewrite formulas because they apply to an entire row. In the other calcs, you need a few more REPLICATE commands.

Once Table 4-3 is completed, we can begin to compare it to the forecast we're building. This is simple enough when the numbers are in the computer. There are several different comparisons to make.

One of the first and simplest is to show growth rates on year-by-year and quarter-by-quarter bases. To produce a percentage growth on any quarter, use this general formula:

% growth = ((Time1/Time0) – 1)*100

So, in most of the calcs, you would probably find empty cells on the matrix and then write in the formulas to find the growth rates. REPLICATE commands simplify the work a great deal. In MicroPlan, you would be better off saving Table 4-3 on the disk first; then go to the columns and convert them to growth figures. For the percentage growth in the second quarter of 1981, for example, go first to column 2 by using the SELECT COL (34) command. Then use FORMULA (35), and write the formula:

((L2/L1) – 1)*100

This will wipe out the data in the model, changing actual numbers to percentage growth numbers. This overwriting is why you had to save the actual numbers as a model on the disk first.

You'll also discover that things work much better when you go to the last column first and then move backward through the columns as you convert to percents. Why? In the example above, you wiped out the column 2 numbers, converting them to percents, before you got to column 3.

Table 4-3: Quarterly Forecast by Salesperson and Customer

Page 1: 1981

Company XYZ
Region I Sales, 1981-82
by salesperson and customer

		qtr 1 1981 —1—	qtr 2 1981 —2—	qtr 3 1981 —3—	qtr 4 1981 —4—	year 1981 —5—
1	Region I					
2	Salesman Smith					
3	Customers:					
4	Customer A	25.0	31.0	42.0	22.0	120.0
5	Customer B	16.0	18.0	19.0	16.0	69.0
6	Customer C	54.0	66.0	83.0	50.0	253.0
7	Others	11.0	13.0	16.0	13.0	53.0
8	Subtotal	106.0	128.0	160.0	101.0	495.0
9	Salesman Jones					
10	Customers:					
11	Customer B	28.0	29.0	34.0	30.0	121.0
12	Customer D	36.0	41.0	45.0	31.0	153.0
13	Customer E	61.0	73.0	85.0	65.0	284.0
14	Customer F	11.0	14.0	19.0	13.0	57.0
15	Others	9.0	13.0	16.0	9.0	47.0
16	Subtotal	145.0	170.0	199.0	148.0	662.0
17	Saleswoman Mitchell					
18	Customers:					
19	Customer A	33.0	41.0	47.0	38.0	159.0
20	Customer B	62.0	79.0	93.0	80.0	314.0
21	Customer E	31.0	39.0	45.0	39.0	154.0
22	Customer G	15.0	21.0	25.0	18.0	79.0
23	Others	12.0	16.0	18.0	14.0	60.0
24	Subtotal	153.0	196.0	228.0	189.0	766.0
25						
26	Total sales	404.0	494.0	587.0	438.0	1,923.0
27						
28	Customer A	58.0	72.0	89.0	60.0	279.0
29	Customer B	106.0	126.0	146.0	126.0	504.0
30	Customer C	54.0	66.0	83.0	50.0	253.0
31	Customer D	36.0	41.0	45.0	31.0	153.0
32	Customer E	92.0	112.0	130.0	104.0	438.0
33	Customer F	11.0	14.0	19.0	13.0	57.0
34	Customer G	15.0	21.0	25.0	18.0	79.0
35	Others	32.0	42.0	50.0	36.0	160.0
36	Check total	404.0	494.0	587.0	438.0	1,923.0

Table 4-3 (continued)

Page 2: 1982

Company XYZ
Region I Sales, 1981-82
by salesperson and customer

		qtr 1 1982	qtr 2 1982	qtr 3 1982	qtr 4 1982	year 1982
		6	7	8	9	10
1	Region I					
2	Salesman Smith					
3	Customers:					
4	Customer A	29.0	36.0	51.0	31.0	147.0
5	Customer B	21.0	23.0	26.0	24.0	94.0
6	Customer C	60.0	64.0	75.0	59.0	258.0
7	Others	12.0	15.0	19.0	16.0	62.0
8	Subtotal	122.0	138.0	171.0	130.0	561.0
9	Salesman Jones					
10	Customers:					
11	Customer B	31.0	35.0	39.0	35.0	140.0
12	Customer D	42.0	54.0	61.0	53.0	210.0
13	Customer E	67.0	81.0	94.0	50.0	292.0
14	Customer F	15.0	21.0	28.0	19.0	83.0
15	Others	11.0	15.0	18.0	13.0	57.0
16	Subtotal	166.0	206.0	240.0	170.0	782.0
17	Saleswoman Mitchell					
18	Customers:					
19	Customer A	40.0	52.0	61.0	55.0	208.0
20	Customer B	85.0	105.0	128.0	120.0	438.0
21	Customer E	35.0	43.0	47.0	39.0	164.0
22	Customer G	18.0	25.0	30.0	20.0	93.0
23	Others	14.0	16.0	19.0	14.0	63.0
24	Subtotal	192.0	241.0	285.0	248.0	966.0
25						
26	Total sales	480.0	585.0	696.0	548.0	2,309.0
27						
28	Customer A	69.0	88.0	112.0	86.0	355.0
29	Customer B	137.0	163.0	193.0	179.0	672.0
30	Customer C	60.0	64.0	75.0	59.0	258.0
31	Customer D	42.0	54.0	61.0	53.0	210.0
32	Customer E	102.0	124.0	141.0	89.0	456.0
33	Customer F	15.0	21.0	28.0	19.0	83.0
34	Customer G	18.0	25.0	30.0	20.0	93.0
35	Others	37.0	46.0	56.0	43.0	182.0
36	Check total	480.0	585.0	696.0	548.0	2,309.0

Obviously, you get the yearly percentage growth rates by using the same formula on the year total columns. That's true in either the calc-type programs or MicroPlan.

You could set up additional rows for use, lag the original rows first, and then apply the appropriate formula. This is what we did to look at growth rates between quarters and years, with the results presented in Table 4-4.

Table 4-4: Looking at Growth Rates

Company XYZ
Region I Sales, 1981-82
by salesperson and customer

	qtr 1 1981	qtr 2 1981	qtr 3 1981	qtr 4 1981	year 1981
	----1----	----2----	----3----	----4----	----5----
38 Total lag 1		404.0	494.0	587.0	438.0
39 Total lag 4					
40 Total grth % 1	n.a.	22.3	18.8	(25.4)	n.a.
41 Total gth % 2	n.a.	n.a.	n.a	n.a.	n.a.

	qtr 1 1982	qtr 2 1982	qtr 3 1982	qtr 4 1982	year 1982
	----6----	----7----	----8----	----9----	----10---
38 Total lag 1	1,923.0	480.0	585.0	696.0	548.0
39 Total lag 4	404.0	494.0	587.0	438.0	1,923.0
40 Total grth % 1	n.a.	21.9	19.0	(21.3)	n.a.
41 Total gth % 2	18.8	18.4	18.6	25.1	20.1

The use of lags in Table 4-4 is important. Row 38 takes the sales total row from above and lags it one column. In VisiCalc, SuperCalc, and friends, simply go down to cell C38 and write in B26, then replicate across the rest of row 38. In MicroPlan, use a command called LAG (72), which then prompts for the row to lag and for how many periods to use. Row 39 lags the sales total row five columns. Row 40 takes the percentage growth from column to column, and row 41 takes the percentage growth from column to column-five-back.

Of course, we miss a few numbers this way. We get some nonsense growth rates from the fourth-quarter-to-year total. We have no year-to-year growth rates for 1981. This doesn't matter. We are only trying to get a sense of the growth involved to help us feel comfortable with our 1983 forecast. This material is only a working paper to be used in the forecast and is not to be presented to the board of directors.

What is important is highlighting trends. Notice that the business almost always goes up in the second and third quarters and down in the fourth quarter. The business grew about 20 percent in 1982, and each quarter grew about 20 percent over the same quarter the previous year.

When you're working with real data, you'll want to go over it in dozens of different ways. Look at the percentage growth by customer. Take the percent from 1981 to 1980. Watch whether the small companies grew at the same rate as the large companies. Look at whether one or two important customers are responsible for all the growth or are lagging. Whose production is increasing, whose is falling off? You want to get a good, solid feel for what is going on in this business.

Trying Some Alternate Forecasts

Now it's time to look at some alternative forecasts and to compare them with our customer-driven forecast. We may decide to keep the customer-driven one, but we'll feel better about it after having compared it with some others.

In Table 4-5, we assumed every customer is going to increase orders by exactly 10 percent in each quarter. Ten percent is the increase over the same quarter of the previous year.

We do this by building a percentage growth rate box in our model. It makes the growth rate a variable we can change at will without changing a lot of different cell formulas. This follows our "divide and conquer" rule from Chapter Two.

1. CALC PRODUCTS

In VisiCalc, SuperCalc, or other calc software, find an empty cell and label it "growth rate." Let's say this cell is B45 in this model. Go to A45 first and write in a label (so you don't forget it). Then in B45 enter 10 (for 10 percent). Then go back to wherever you want your results to appear and use B45 instead of the growth rate number. For example, go to M4, which is the same as row 4, column 11 on the model as shown. What you want in that cell is cell H4 increased by 10 percent, or multiplied by (1+(B45/100). Enter the formula:

>H4*(1+(B45/100))

Now, you can use a few REPLICATE commands to duplicate Table 4-5, the 10-percent-growth assumption.

2. MICROPLAN

In MicroPlan, you can't simply refer to a single cell. The software is row- or column-oriented. But you can take an empty column—say column 20—and use it as a percentage growth rate. Use the data pointer command, SELECT COL (34) in this case, to go to column 20: use ENTER (31), enter 1 to the prompt to enter a constant, and then enter 10 to make the constant 10. This will appear all the way down column 20. Then go back to the columns you want to grow at 10 percent, and give the FORMULA (35) command to write the percentage formula. For column 11, for example, you would want 1.1 times column 6. The formula would be

>L6*(1+(L20/100))

Table 4-5: Percentage Growth Rate Forecast

10 percent growth assumption

Company XYZ
Region I Sales, 1983
by salesperson and customer

		qtr 1 1983 ----11---	qtr 2 1983 ----12---	qtr 3 1983 ----13---	qtr 4 1983 ----14---	year 1983 ----15---
1	Region I					
2	Salesman Smith					
3	Customers:					
4	Customer A	31.9	39.6	56.1	34.1	161.7
5	Customer B	23.1	25.3	28.6	26.4	103.4
6	Customer C	66.0	70.4	82.5	64.9	283.8
7	Others	13.2	16.5	20.9	17.6	68.2
8	Subtotal	134.2	151.8	188.1	143.0	617.1
9	Salesman Jones					
10	Customers:					
11	Customer B	34.1	38.5	42.9	38.5	154.0
12	Customer D	46.2	59.4	67.1	58.3	231.0
13	Customer E	73.7	89.1	103.4	55.0	321.2
14	Customer F	16.5	23.1	30.8	20.9	91.3
15	Others	12.1	16.5	19.8	14.3	62.7
16	Subtotal	182.6	226.6	264.0	187.0	860.2
17	Saleswoman Mitchell					
18	Customers:					
19	Customer A	44.0	57.2	67.1	60.5	228.8
20	Customer B	93.5	115.5	140.8	132.0	481.8
21	Customer E	38.5	47.3	51.7	42.9	180.4
22	Customer G	19.8	27.5	33.0	22.0	102.3
23	Others	15.4	17.6	20.9	15.4	69.3
24	Subtotal	211.2	265.1	313.5	272.8	1,062.6
25						
26	Total sales	528.0	643.5	765.6	602.8	2,539.9
27						
28	Customer A	75.9	96.8	123.2	94.6	390.5
29	Customer B	150.7	179.3	212.3	196.9	739.2
30	Customer C	66.0	70.4	82.5	64.9	283.8
31	Customer D	46.2	59.4	67.1	58.3	231.0
32	Customer E	112.2	136.4	155.1	97.9	501.6
33	Customer F	16.5	23.1	30.8	20.9	91.3
34	Customer G	19.8	27.5	33.0	22.0	102.3
35	Others	40.7	50.6	61.6	47.3	200.2
36	Check total	528.0	643.5	765.6	602.8	2,539.9

The beauty of doing it this way is that now you can change your growth rates easily and quickly. In either the calc style or the MicroPlan style, you can change the growth rate constant and then tell the calc program to recalculate the matrix. You'll get a new percentage growth rate applied to the entire table.

We didn't like the 10 percent growth rate. When we compared it to the customer-driven forecast, it was off by a long way. The customers are talking about more than 3,000 units, and the 10 percent forecast means barely 2,500 units. Furthermore, since sales grew at about 20 percent in 1982 (which we know from the previous analysis), why not 20 percent again?

Table 4-6: Revised Percentage Growth Rate Forecast

20 percent growth assumption

Company XYZ
Region I Sales, 1983
by salesperson and customer

		qtr 1 1983	qtr 2 1983	qtr 3 1983	qtr 4 1983	year 1983
		11	12	13	14	15
1	Region I					
2	Salesman Smith					
3	Customers:					
4	Customer A	34.8	43.2	61.2	37.2	176.4
5	Customer B	25.2	27.6	31.2	28.8	112.8
6	Customer C	72.0	76.8	90.0	70.8	309.6
7	Others	14.4	18.0	22.8	19.2	74.4
8	Subtotal	146.4	165.6	205.2	156.0	673.2
9	Salesman Jones					
10	Customers:					
11	Customer B	37.2	42.0	46.8	42.0	168.0
12	Customer D	50.4	64.8	73.2	63.6	252.0
13	Customer E	80.4	97.2	112.8	60.0	350.4
14	Customer F	18.0	25.2	33.6	22.8	99.6
15	Others	13.2	18.0	21.6	15.6	68.4
16	Subtotal	199.2	247.2	288.0	204.0	938.4
17	Saleswoman Mitchell					
18	Customers:					
19	Customer A	48.0	62.4	73.2	66.0	249.6
20	Customer B	102.0	126.0	153.6	144.0	525.6
21	Customer E	42.0	51.6	56.4	46.8	196.8
22	Customer G	21.6	30.0	36.0	24.0	111.6
23	Others	16.8	19.2	22.8	16.8	75.6
24	Subtotal	230.4	289.2	342.0	297.6	1,159.2
25						
26	Total sales	576.0	702.0	835.2	657.6	2,770.8
27						
28	Customer A	82.8	105.6	134.4	103.2	426.0
29	Customer B	164.4	195.6	231.6	214.8	806.4
30	Customer C	72.0	76.8	90.0	70.8	309.6
31	Customer D	50.4	64.8	73.2	63.6	252.0
32	Customer E	122.4	148.8	169.2	106.8	547.2
33	Customer F	18.0	25.2	33.6	22.8	99.6
34	Customer G	21.6	30.0	36.0	24.0	111.6
35	Others	44.4	55.2	67.2	51.6	218.4
36	Check total	576.0	702.0	835.2	657.6	2,770.8

Table 4-6 presents the 20 percent assumption. Since we wrote the constant percentage growth rate into the model, we can go from the one assumption to the other very quickly. But even here, we still have fewer units than in our customer forecast; and the difference is still fairly large.

This is where we add common sense to the computer analysis. Go out and look at the market you're talking about. Call a few customers, talk to the editors of some trade magazines, go into the periodical index to see what has been written. Is the industry going to grow 20 percent again, or more, or less? Our customer-driven forecast total of 3,020 is fully 31 percent more than our 1982 sales. What seems to be going on in the industry? Is a 31 percent growth rate for 1983 realistic?

At this point, although the spreadsheet has helped, the key to our forecast is knowledge. We have to make an educated guess. We begin to see why the computer is best at doing the numbers, not the forecast.

Notice that we are in the middle of a trial-and-error process. If you like computer buzzwords, call it an *iterative process.* Go back and forth with the spreadsheet until you like what you have. If you love buzzwords, call it *interactive interation.*

After a period of study, we come back with the conclusion that the industry isn't growing 30 percent in 1983. It should rack up another 20 percent increase (not bad), but the rest is due to overoptimism, or the buyers' natural inclination to overestimate their purchases, or both factors at once. So now what do we do?

Table 4-7: Second Revised Customer Forecast

Company XYZ
Region I Sales, 1983
by salesperson and customer

		qtr 1 1983	qtr 2 1983	qtr 3 1983	qtr 4 1983	year 1983
		----11---	----12---	----13---	----14---	----15---
1	Region I					
2	Salesman Smith					
3	Customers:					
4	Customer A	0.2	1.8	(1.2)	2.8	3.6
5	Customer B	4.8	2.4	(1.2)	1.2	7.2
6	Customer C	8.0	23.2	30.0	39.2	100.4
7	Others					
8	Subtotal	13.0	27.4	27.6	43.2	111.2
9	Salesman Jones					
10	Customers:					
11	Customer B	7.8	3.0	(1.8)	3.0	12.0
12	Customer D	4.6	0.2	1.8	6.4	13.0
13	Customer E	4.6	2.8	7.2	40.0	54.6
14	Customer F	2.0	(0.2)	1.4	2.2	5.4
15	Others					
16	Subtotal	19.0	5.8	8.6	51.6	85.0
17	Saleswoman Mitchell					
18	Customers:					
19	Customer A	2.0	2.6	1.8	4.0	10.4
20	Customer B	18.0	4.0	(13.6)	6.0	14.4
21	Customer E		0.4	(0.4)	0.2	0.2
22	Customer G	3.4	5.0	9.0	11.0	28.4
23	Others					
24	Subtotal	23.4	12.0	(3.2)	21.2	53.4
25						
26	Total sales	55.4	45.2	33.0	116.0	249.6
27						
28	Customer A	2.2	4.4	0.6	6.8	14.0
29	Customer B	30.6	9.4	(16.6)	10.2	33.6
30	Customer C	8.0	23.2	30.0	39.2	100.4
31	Customer D	4.6	0.2	1.8	6.4	13.0
32	Customer E	4.6	3.2	6.8	40.2	54.8
33	Customer F	2.0	(0.2)	1.4	2.2	5.4
34	Customer G	3.4	5.0	9.0	11.0	28.4
35	Others					
36	Check total	55.4	45.2	33.0	116.0	249.6

Focusing the Forecast

What we do now is guess again. But this time we incorporate the information we have from different sources. Certainly our customers have a lot to add to our forecast. But let's use the 20 percent number to temper their guesses. Now the spreadsheet comes into play again.

Table 4-7 provides a way to look at the difference between 20 percent growth and the customer forecast. It was done with MicroPlan's consolidation module, which allows the user to subtract one entire table from another, as long as they are in an identical format. This model shows the difference between the customer forecast and the 20 percent growth forecast. In each entry, we see how far above or below 20 percent the customers' numbers actually are. A positive number means that much more than 20 percent growth, a negative number means that much less, and a blank means exactly 20 percent growth.

With any spreadsheet that allows consolidation, this is a matter of subtracting the 20 percent model from the customer forecast model. The commands will differ with each, but you will always have the customer forecast in the active workspace when you call the 20 percent into action from a file saved on the disk.

If your spreadsheet doesn't allow consolidation, you can still get Table 4-7, but it takes more steps and possibly a larger computer memory.

Memory limits the size of the matrix you use. With a large enough memory, you can put the 20 percent table in one part of the spreadsheet, the original customer-driven forecast in another, and a table of the results of the subtraction in a third. Each of the three is like a full table, 36 rows by five columns. Since most spreadsheets will allow a 36 × 15 matrix in a 64K system, this option is almost always available.

Of course, if you already have the 1982 results and the customer forecast in the active workspace, there may be a simpler way to consolidate. Take five additional columns to show the difference between customer forecast and 1.2 times the appropriate 1982 figure. If the customer forecast for first quarter 1983 is in cell M4, and the 1982 number for that same item is in cell H4, then the difference cell would have this formula:

```
>M4 – (1.2*H4)
```

Or, if you still have that percentage growth constant in cell B45, it could even be the following:

```
>M4 – ((1 + (B45/100))*H4)
```

Once you have that up on the spreadsheet, you begin to see what might be pushing up your forecast. The beauty of this method is that it makes the numbers stand out. Look again at Table 4-7. Customer C in Salesman Smith's zone is projecting a huge increase at that plant. Customer B seems to be trying to smooth out production schedules by doing more in the first quarter and less in the third quarter. Customer B is also projecting a large increase in overall purchases. Customer E looks like the buyer forgot to project the standard 15–25 percent decrease in purchases in the fourth quarter. Customer G's increase is fairly large for a small plant.

Remember that in Table 4-7 we are looking at *increases beyond 20 percent.* Since we expect the whole market to grow 20 percent, these increases are quite significant.

Get back on the phone. Call customers B, C, and E, for example, and ask them about their projected increase in orders. Customer C, it turns out, has a new plant production increase coming on-stream and will need more units. But when asked to think about it, Customer C's buyer agrees that the start-up will be slower than that, so they'll need fewer units.

Table 4-8: Revised Customer Increases

Company XYZ
Region I Sales, 1983
by salesperson and customer

	qtr 1 1983 ----11---	qtr 2 1983 ----12---	qtr 3 1983 ----13---	qtr 4 1983 ----14---	year 1983 ----15---
1 Region I					
2 Salesman Smith					
3 Customers:					
4 Customer A	0.2	1.8	(1.2)	2.8	3.6
5 Customer B	4.8	2.4	(1.2)	1.2	7.2
6 Customer C	8.0	12.0	15.0	18.0	53.0
7 Others					
	---------	---------	---------	---------	---------
8 Subtotal	13.0	16.2	12.6	22.0	63.8
9 Salesman Jones					
10 Customers:					
11 Customer B	7.8	3.0	(1.8)	3.0	12.0
12 Customer D	4.6	0.2	1.8		6.6
13 Customer E	4.6	2.8	7.2		14.6
14 Customer F	2.0	(0.2)	1.4	2.2	5.4
15 Others					
	---------	---------	---------	---------	---------
16 Subtotal	19.0	5.8	8.6	5.2	38.6
17 Saleswoman Mitchell					
18 Customers:					
19 Customer A	2.0	2.6	1.8	2.0	8.4
20 Customer B	18.0	(5.0)	(10.0)		3.0
21 Customer E		0.4	(0.4)	0.2	0.2
22 Customer G	3.4	5.0	9.0	11.0	28.4
23 Others					
	---------	---------	---------	---------	---------
24 Subtotal	23.4	3.0	0.4	13.2	40.0
25					
26 Total sales	55.4	25.0	21.6	40.4	142.4
27					
28 Customer A	2.2	4.4	0.6	4.8	12.0
29 Customer B	30.6	0.4	(13.0)	4.2	22.2
30 Customer C	8.0	12.0	15.0	18.0	53.0
31 Customer D	4.6	0.2	1.8		6.6
32 Customer E	4.6	3.2	6.8	0.2	14.8
33 Customer F	2.0	(0.2)	1.4	2.2	5.4
34 Customer G	3.4	5.0	9.0	11.0	28.4
	---------	---------	---------	---------	---------
35 Others					
36 Check total	55.4	25.0	21.6	40.4	142.4

So now we go back to those differences and modify them to reflect what the buyers told us. Table 4-8 shows you how we decided to change the excesses. Compare it to Table 4-7, and the differences will show up. We allowed some of the increases for most of the customers planning an increase. We also figured that we'll deliver as much as they want in the first quarter, but that some of those who receive a lot of units in the first quarter will want fewer than they think in the second, third, and fourth quarters. They'll have more inventory on hand and will order fewer than planned. We have to outguess them, because we're responsible for our forecast; they aren't.

Then we make another forecast. We go back and add the differences in Table 4-8 to the 20 percent forecast in Table 4-6. The result is the forecast in Table 4-9.

Table 4-9: Approaching a Final Customer-Based Forecast

Company XYZ
Region I Sales, 1983
by salesperson and customer

		qtr 1 1983	qtr 2 1983	qtr 3 1983	qtr 4 1983	year 1983
		----11---	----12---	----13---	----14---	----15---
1	Region I					
2	Salesman Smith					
3	Customers:					
4	Customer A	35.0	45.0	60.0	40.0	180.0
5	Customer B	30.0	30.0	30.0	30.0	120.0
6	Customer C	80.0	88.8	105.0	88.8	362.6
7	Others	14.4	18.0	22.8	19.2	74.4
		---------	---------	---------	---------	---------
8	Subtotal	159.4	181.8	217.8	178.0	737.0
9	Salesman Jones					
10	Customers:					
11	Customer B	45.0	45.0	45.0	45.0	180.0
12	Customer D	55.0	65.0	75.0	63.6	258.6
13	Customer E	85.0	100.0	120.0	60.0	365.0
14	Customer F	20.0	25.0	35.0	25.0	105.0
15	Others	13.2	18.0	21.6	15.6	68.4
		---------	---------	---------	---------	---------
16	Subtotal	218.2	253.0	296.6	209.2	977.0
17	Saleswoman Mitchell					
18	Customers:					
19	Customer A	50.0	65.0	75.0	68.0	258.0
20	Customer B	120.0	121.0	143.6	144.0	528.6
21	Customer E	42.0	52.0	56.0	47.0	197.0
22	Customer G	25.0	35.0	45.0	35.0	140.0
23	Others	16.8	19.2	22.8	16.8	75.6
		---------	---------	---------	---------	---------
24	Subtotal	253.8	292.2	342.4	310.8	1,199.2
25						
26	Total sales	631.4	727.0	856.8	698.0	2,913.2
27						
28	Customer A	85.0	110.0	135.0	108.0	438.0
29	Customer B	195.0	196.0	218.6	219.0	828.6
30	Customer C	80.0	88.8	105.0	88.8	362.6
31	Customer D	55.0	65.0	75.0	63.6	258.6
32	Customer E	127.0	152.0	176.0	107.0	562.0
33	Customer F	20.0	25.0	35.0	25.0	105.0
34	Customer G	25.0	35.0	45.0	35.0	140.0
35	Others	44.4	55.2	67.2	51.6	218.4
		---------	---------	---------	---------	---------
36	Check total	631.4	727.0	856.8	698.0	2,913.2

This is another case for a spreadsheet with consolidation. If you have one, you produced the spread in 4-7, then modified it to 4-8. Now you can simply add the 4-6 spread back into it to come out with 4-9. Then you are really getting the power of the spreadsheet; consider how much number pushing would be required on a calculator.

If you don't have consolidation, you may still have put a spread together that has the 20 percent and the difference numbers to get 4-7. You may also have modified 4-7 in that spread to get 4-8. If so, you can add the 4-8 matrix back into the 20 percent matrix by writing the formula that adds the appropriate cells into the customer forecast matrix.

Confusing? Think of several tables, each with the same number of rows and columns and each with the same row and column labels. All these tables are part of a single spreadsheet workspace. All might be on the same rows, with columns extending outward in a matrix that has 36 rows and 15 columns (five columns per table). Or, depending on how you fed the tables into the workspace, you might have a matrix with only five columns but 109 rows, with three sets of 36 rows, one below another. This would happen if you went to the bottom of one table and then loaded another one from the disk with complete row and column titles. Either way, you have several similar tables in the workspace. In one of them, you can have the 20 percent forecast. In another, you can have the numbers from Table 4-8. Then you can use the spreadsheet to add those tables together to produce the forecast in Table 4-9.

Don't be afraid to use the spreadsheet as a workspace. That's what it is meant for. Just keep saving your material on the disk with different file names, and re-use the tables with new formulas as a shortcut for rewriting the row and column labels all the time. Notice that in this series we have more than 10 different models, all of which were written from one simple table. Each of them was saved on the disk under a different file name.

Meanwhile, we've still got a forecast that's too high. Right? Look at it again—the 1983 total sales of 2,913 units is fully 26 percent more than the 1982 total. We need more revisions.

By now, we're getting comfortable with the large picture. We want to finish somewhere around 20 percent growth, maybe even slightly higher because of some customer investments. So we've got to make changes again.

Table 4-10 is another revised forecast. This time, we took 5 percent off each of the second, third, and fourth quarters, prorating the customer reports. We did this by getting into our table and revising along the columns.

1. MICROPLAN

In MicroPlan, we go to columns 11, 12, and 13 to multiply each, using a MULT K (53) command, by .95.

Table 4-10: Revised Forecast

Company XYZ
Region I Sales, 1983
by salesperson and customer

		qtr 1 1983 ----11---	qtr 2 1983 ----12---	qtr 3 1983 ----13---	qtr 4 1983 ----14---	year 1983 ----15---
1	Region I					
2	Salesman Smith					
3	Customers:					
4	Customer A	35.0	42.8	57.0	38.0	172.8
5	Customer B	30.0	28.5	28.5	28.5	115.5
6	Customer C	80.0	84.4	99.8	84.4	348.5
7	Others	14.4	17.1	21.7	18.2	71.4
8	Subtotal	159.4	172.7	206.9	169.1	708.1
9	Salesman Jones					
10	Customers:					
11	Customer B	45.0	42.8	42.8	42.8	173.3
12	Customer D	55.0	61.8	71.3	60.4	248.4
13	Customer E	85.0	95.0	114.0	57.0	351.0
14	Customer F	20.0	23.8	33.3	23.8	100.8
15	Others	13.2	17.1	20.5	14.8	65.6
16	Subtotal	218.2	240.4	281.8	198.7	939.1
17	Saleswoman Mitchell					
18	Customers:					
19	Customer A	50.0	61.8	71.3	64.6	247.6
20	Customer B	120.0	115.0	136.4	136.8	508.2
21	Customer E	42.0	49.4	53.2	44.7	189.3
22	Customer G	25.0	33.3	42.8	33.3	134.3
23	Others	16.8	18.2	21.7	16.0	72.7
24	Subtotal	253.8	277.6	325.3	295.3	1,151.9
25						
26	Total sales	631.4	690.7	814.0	663.1	2,799.1
27						
28	Customer A	85.0	104.5	128.3	102.6	420.4
29	Customer B	195.0	186.2	207.7	208.1	796.9
30	Customer C	80.0	84.4	99.8	84.4	348.5
31	Customer D	55.0	61.8	71.3	60.4	248.4
32	Customer E	127.0	144.4	167.2	101.7	540.3
33	Customer F	20.0	23.8	33.3	23.8	100.8
34	Customer G	25.0	33.3	42.8	33.3	134.3
35	Others	44.4	52.4	63.8	49.0	209.7
36	Check total	631.4	690.7	814.0	663.1	2,799.1

2. CALC PRODUCTS

In the calc programs, we can do the same thing by moving to another table in the same workspace (which we just talked about) and by multiplying the cell by .95. Then we use REPLICATE to fill out the columns.

Again, we see that it's more art than science. There's no magic rule that tells you to multiply by .95. It just looks like a good guess, all things considered.

That still isn't good enough. Compare what we have to the quarter-by-quarter growth rates in Table 4-4; we're still forecasting too small a decline in the fourth quarter, especially when we have the fourth quarter left to compensate for overoptimism in the previous three quarters. But, otherwise, the forecast is looking pretty good now, so we only have a small change to make.

Table 4-11: Final Forecast

Company XYZ
Region I Sales, 1983
by salesperson and customer

		qtr 1 1983	qtr 2 1983	qtr 3 1983	qtr 4 1983	year 1983
		----11---	----12---	----13---	----14---	----15---
1	Region I					
2	Salesman Smith					
3	Customers:					
4	Customer A	35.0	42.8	57.0	37.1	171.8
5	Customer B	30.0	28.5	28.5	27.8	114.8
6	Customer C	80.0	84.4	99.8	82.3	346.4
7	Others	14.4	17.1	21.7	17.8	70.9
		---------	---------	---------	---------	---------
8	Subtotal	159.4	172.7	206.9	164.9	703.9
9	Salesman Jones					
10	Customers:					
11	Customer B	45.0	42.8	42.8	41.7	172.2
12	Customer D	55.0	61.8	71.3	58.9	246.9
13	Customer E	85.0	95.0	114.0	55.6	349.6
14	Customer F	20.0	23.8	33.3	23.2	100.2
15	Others	13.2	17.1	20.5	14.4	65.3
		---------	---------	---------	---------	---------
16	Subtotal	218.2	240.4	281.8	193.8	934.1
17	Saleswoman Mitchell					
18	Customers:					
19	Customer A	50.0	61.8	71.3	63.0	246.0
20	Customer B	120.0	115.0	136.4	133.4	504.8
21	Customer E	42.0	49.4	53.2	43.5	188.1
22	Customer G	25.0	33.3	42.8	32.4	133.4
23	Others	16.8	18.2	21.7	15.6	72.3
		---------	---------	---------	---------	---------
24	Subtotal	253.8	277.6	325.3	287.9	1,144.5
25						
26	Total sales	631.4	690.7	814.0	646.5	2,782.5
27						
28	Customer A	85.0	104.5	128.3	100.0	417.8
29	Customer B	195.0	186.2	207.7	202.8	791.7
30	Customer C	80.0	84.4	99.8	82.3	346.4
31	Customer D	55.0	61.8	71.3	58.9	246.9
32	Customer E	127.0	144.4	167.2	99.1	537.7
33	Customer F	20.0	23.8	33.3	23.2	100.2
34	Customer G	25.0	33.3	42.8	32.4	133.4
35	Others	44.4	52.4	63.8	47.8	208.5
		---------	---------	---------	---------	---------
36	Check total	631.4	690.7	814.0	646.5	2,782.5

Table 4-11 presents a "final" forecast for Region I. *Final* is in quotes because it shouldn't be final for any longer than it takes to get additional data, such as the first month's sales. It should be constantly revised during the year, which is one of the reasons we put it in a spreadsheet program in the first place. For the purposes of this exercise, however, it reflects the last change we're going to make.

In the final forecast, we took the fourth quarter and multiplied it by .975. We used the same techniques explained above. Now, we have total sales for 1983 of 2,782.5 units, which is 20.5 percent more than in 1983. It's still just an educated guess, but at least it is now a good guess, one that benefits from the full process of spreadsheet analysis. It takes that general growth rate and those specific customer forecasts and merges

Table 4-12: Growth over 1982

Company XYZ
Region I Sales, 1983
by salesperson and customer

		qtr 1 1983 ----11---	qtr 2 1983 ----12---	qtr 3 1983 ----13---	qtr 4 1983 ----14---	year 1983 ----15---
1	Region I					
2	Salesman Smith					
3	Customers:					
4	Customer A	20.7	18.8	11.8	19.5	16.9
5	Customer B	42.9	23.9	9.6	15.8	22.1
6	Customer C	33.3	31.8	33.0	39.4	34.2
7	Others	20.0	14.0	14.0	11.2	14.4
		---------	---------	---------	---------	---------
8	Subtotal	30.7	25.2	21.0	26.8	25.5
9	Salesman Jones					
10	Customers:					
11	Customer B	45.2	22.1	9.6	19.1	23.0
12	Customer D	31.0	14.4	16.8	11.2	17.6
13	Customer E	26.9	17.3	21.3	11.2	19.7
14	Customer F	33.3	13.1	18.8	21.9	20.7
15	Others	20.0	14.0	14.0	11.2	14.5
		---------	---------	---------	---------	---------
16	Subtotal	31.4	16.7	17.4	14.0	19.4
17	Saleswoman Mitchell					
18	Customers:					
19	Customer A	25.0	18.8	16.8	14.5	18.3
20	Customer B	41.2	9.5	6.6	11.2	15.2
21	Customer E	20.0	14.9	13.2	11.6	14.7
22	Customer G	38.9	33.0	42.5	62.1	43.5
23	Others	20.0	14.0	14.0	11.2	14.7
		---------	---------	---------	---------	---------
24	Subtotal	32.2	15.2	14.1	16.1	18.5
25						
26	Total sales	31.5	18.1	16.9	18.0	20.5
27						
28	Customer A	23.2	18.8	14.5	16.3	17.7
29	Customer B	42.3	14.2	7.6	13.3	17.8
30	Customer C	33.3	31.8	33.0	39.4	34.2
31	Customer D	31.0	14.4	16.8	11.2	17.6
32	Customer E	24.5	16.5	18.6	11.4	17.9
33	Customer F	33.3	13.1	18.8	21.9	20.7
34	Customer G	38.9	33.0	42.5	62.1	43.5
35	Others	20.0	14.0	14.0	11.2	14.5
		---------	---------	---------	---------	---------
36	Check total	31.5	18.1	16.9	18.0	20.5

them in a way that makes good common sense. Common sense is the most important factor, no matter how sophisticated the computer model is.

Now that we have the forecast, we can look again at the growth rates. Table 4-12 takes our final forecast and breaks it into growth over 1982 for each customer of each salesperson. It makes for some interesting last looks at the results.

Notice, for example, that the forecast projects a 30 percent increase in the first quarter, followed by a less-than-20 percent increase in the following quarter. We suspect our customers are too optimistic, but we are going to give them what they want for the first quarter, and then, unfortunately, we will expect them to want less than they think in subsequent quarters. All things considered, we are now comfortable with the forecast and ready to go on to some other management problem.

Consolidating with Other Regions

Consolidation is another helpful feature of the electronic spreadsheets. Some do it better than others, but all do it a lot better than the old pencil and calculator.

We now have a good Region I forecast. Let's assume that we also have equally good forecasts for Regions II, III, and IV. We have several different ways to use them.

If we have one of the spreadsheets with a consolidation feature, then we may be able to use it to produce a final, consolidated forecast. However, that won't be easy in this case because almost all of the consolidation modules assume that all the tables to be consolidated have equal rows and columns to permit them to be added together. Each region might have a different number of salespersons or a different number of customers, or a different set of customers. These factors make equal rows and columns difficult if not impossible to achieve.

The first impulse is to standardize the forecast form. You could insist that each salesperson list four main customers plus "others," for example. You could have only three salespersons per region. But if you think about that, you'll realize it is a very difficult plan to work.

Another solution is to set up a workspace that is large enough. The workspace is the relevant limit on the size of a single table. We can't get much more than two regions into a typical 64K computer workspace, but we can probably get four or five regions plus totals into a single matrix on a 256K or 512K computer. If you have that kind of power, load each table below the other on the matrix, add down at the bottom, and you've got it. Then you can even go back, pick out the common customers (as we did in Region I), and produce a customer forecast. That is very nice, if your computer has the power to handle it.

Or, finally, you can consolidate by loading information from separate regional forecasts, each of which is saved on a disk. The process is about the same for all spreadsheet programs. Clean each region's table to leave only the total sales and the sales by customer. Then you load the streamlined tables into a new single table and add them up.

This is done in VisiCalc and SuperCalc with a LOAD command, which is /L on the command menu. The software then asks you which file to load (Answer: the file name under which you saved the spread whose total is to be added) and whether you want all or part of it (Answer: part). Identify the totals line by its cells labels (for example, A50:M50). The computer asks you where to load into the new spread, and you answer, say, A20. Then you have line 50 of one spread as line 20 of another.

Results should look something like Table 4-13, which shows the format but not the numbers for a regional totals model. Since we haven't discussed the other regions, we left them blank. At the end of this model, you could add the subtotals together for the total sales and then add customer totals from the regional breakdowns.

Table 4-13: Consolidation Format I

Final Forecast

Company XYZ

by salesperson and customer

(Note: Format Demonstration Only)

		qtr 1 1983	qtr 2 1983	qtr 3 1983	qtr 4 1983	year 1983
		----11---	----12---	----13---	----14---	----15---
1	Region I					
2	Customer A	85.0	104.5	128.3	100.0	417.8
3	Customer B	195.0	186.2	207.7	202.8	791.7
4	Customer C	80.0	84.4	99.8	82.3	346.4
5	Customer D	55.0	61.8	71.3	58.9	246.9
6	Customer E	127.0	144.4	167.2	99.1	537.7
7	Customer F	20.0	23.8	33.3	23.2	100.2
8	Customer G	25.0	33.3	42.8	32.4	133.4
9	Others	44.4	52.4	63.8	47.8	208.5
		---------	---------	---------	---------	---------
10	Subtotal	631.4	690.7	814.0	646.5	2,782.5
11	Region II					
12	Customer B	##.#	##.#	##.#		
13	Customer E					
14	Customer H					
15	Customer I					
16	Customer J					
17	Customer K					
18	Customer L					
19	Others					
		---------	---------	---------	---------	---------
20	Subtotal					
31	Region III					
32	Customer B					
33	Customer D					
34	Customer I					
35	Customer K					
36	Customer M					
37	Customer N					
38	Customer O					
39	Others					
		---------	---------	---------	---------	---------
30	Subtotal					

If you have a small computer memory or a lot of regions, you may even have to eliminate the customer-specific information in order to fit all the regional totals. That's still better than pencil and paper. The results would look like Table 4-14. This one also leaves the numbers blank because we didn't do them.

The procedure varies slightly over the various programs. In all of them, read the totals line from its file on the disk into the consolidation matrix. In most of the calc programs, this means moving the cursor to the right spot, calling the LOAD command (probably an L), and then prompting to load the totals line that you want. First, tell the computer which file you want to load, then tell it which cells to load. MicroPlan with

Table 4-14: Consolidation Format II

Final Forecast

Company XYZ

by salesperson and customer

(Note: Format Example Only)

	qtr 1 1983 ----11---	qtr 2 1983 ----12---	qtr 3 1983 ----13---	qtr 4 1983 ----14---	year 1983 ----15---
1 Region I	631.4	690.7	814.0	646.5	2,782.5
2 Region II					
3 Region III					
4 Region IV					
5 Region V					
6 Region VI					
	---------	---------	---------	---------	---------
Totals					

the added Tables module is probably smoothest because you can call the line up into the active workspace by model name and row or column number, and you can program the system so that the consolidation process is repeated automatically whenever it is needed.

Multi-Dimensional Forecasts

The spreadsheet is meant to handle complicated problems like the forecast built on several variables. So far, we've handled sales per customer, per salesperson, and per region in a single model or network of related models. We could forecast sales by many finer cuts of information. The imagination is the only limit.

We could forecast sales by products, for example. Table 4-15 shows how the sales forecast might be divided by products to be purchased by each customer. The spreadsheet process is similar. Now, instead of total sales to each customer, sales of each product to each customer are projected. These are summed to give a total by customer. Of course the spreadsheet allows us to total the sales by product as well. We can also consolidate the product totals across the different customers and different regions to provide a fully detailed forecast of future sales by product, customer, salesperson, and region.

Table 4-15: Sales by Person, Customer and Product

Company XYZ
Region I Sales, 1981-82
Salesperson, Customer & Product

		qtr 1 1983 ----11---	qtr 2 1983 ----12---	qtr 3 1983 ----13---	qtr 4 1983 ----14---	year 1983 ----15---
1	Region I					
2	Salesman Smith					
3	Customers:					
4	Product 1	8.5	8.9	13.5	9.6	36.8
5	Product 2	10.9	14.7	21.5	10.2	67.6
6	Product 3	15.4	19.6	26.2	17.4	72.1
		-------	-------	-------	-------	-------
7	Customer A	34.8	43.2	61.2	37.2	176.4
8	Product 1	10.6	11.1	13.9	10.0	54.4
9	Product 2	12.0	11.3	12.1	10.5	36.8
10	Product 3	2.6	5.2	5.2	8.3	21.6
		-------	-------	-------	-------	-------
11	Customer B	25.2	27.6	31.2	28.8	112.8
12	Product 1	13.3	11.7	14.5	12.1	36.0
13	Product 2	11.0	12.4	14.5	11.2	58.9
14	Product 3	47.7	52.7	61.0	47.6	214.7
		-------	-------	-------	-------	-------
15	Customer C	72.0	76.8	90.0	70.8	309.6
16	Product 1	4.1	6.5	8.7	8.0	39.6
17	Product 2	5.9	7.2	7.0	6.8	17.9
18	Product 3	4.4	4.3	7.1	4.4	16.9
		-------	-------	-------	-------	-------
19	Others	14.4	13.0	22.8	19.2	74.4
		---------	---------	---------	---------	---------
20	Subtotal	146.4	165.6	205.2	156.0	873.2

We could also add prices to the equation. The next exercise shows how things might begin to look when we forecast with prices as well. The product sales forecasts are done in units, and a separate part of the forecast keeps track of the prices. Once again the spreadsheet management employs the same logic but uses more variables. Units are summed as before, but now the number of units is multiplied by the price assumptions to produce the final dollar sales figure.

Table 4-16: Sales by Product with Price Variable

Company XYZ
Region I Sales, 1981-82
Sales by Product in Units

		qtr 1 1983	qtr 2 1983	qtr 3 1983	qtr 4 1983	year 1983
		----11---	----12---	----13---	----14---	----15---
1	Region I					
2	Salesman Smith					
3	Customers:					
4	Product 1	8.5	9.0	10.8	7.7	36.0
5	Product 2	5.5	7.4	10.8	4.1	27.8
6	Product 3	10.3	13.2	13.2	8.7	45.4
		---------	---------	---------	---------	---------
7	Customer A	24.4	29.5	34.8	20.5	109.2
8	Product 1	10.7	11.2	11.1	8.0	41.0
9	Product 2	6.0	5.7	6.1	4.2	22.0
10	Product 3	1.7	3.5	2.6	4.2	12.0
		---------	---------	---------	---------	---------
11	Customer B	18.5	20.4	19.8	16.4	75.1
12	Product 1	13.4	11.8	11.6	9.7	46.5
13	Product 2	5.5	6.2	7.3	4.5	23.5
14	Product 3	32.0	35.4	30.7	23.9	122.0
15	Customer C	51.0	53.4	49.5	38.0	192.0
		---------	---------	---------	---------	---------
16	Product 1	4.1	6.6	6.9	6.4	24.1
17	Product 2	3.0	3.6	3.5	2.7	12.8
18	Product 3	3.0	2.9	3.6	2.2	11.6
		---------	---------	---------	---------	---------
19	Others	10.1	13.1	14.0	11.3	48.5
		---------	---------	---------	---------	---------
20	Subtotal	146.4	165.6	205.2	156.0	673.2
21	Prices:					
22	Product 1	0.99	0.99	1.25	1.25	
23	Product 2	1.99	1.99	1.99	2.49	
24	Product 3	1.49	1.49	1.99	1.99	

Notice that adding variables to the spreadsheet adds a depth of detail that is useful in several ways. First, it provides additional information. Second—and much more important—we can now track results much more easily. In the budgeting section of this book we'll talk about *variances,* the budgeting buzzword for the difference between what is planned and what actually happens. There is no better way to track these variances than to have finely cut information in the original plan. If, for example, a price changes, it will affect the entire sales forecast. In the spreadsheet forecast that includes product specifics and price variables, simply change the price variable on a product, recalculate, and have all the rest of the forecast change. Salesperson, customer, and regional forecasts all reflect the difference immediately. If you had only the customer totals, salesperson totals, and the regional totals, this would be much more difficult.

Trees from the Forest

Sometimes your information works from the top down. Then it's easier to take the whole market first and then divide it into smaller, more manageable pieces. This is what we call the "trees from the forest" approach.

The Market Share Model

The typical market share model is a good example of how this works. Let's assume you're selling a computer program that helps people do home budgeting on a Commodore VIC-20 computer. You'd like to look at sales of this software over time, but of course you can't just ask your salespeople as we did in the preceding section, because this is a brand new market and a brand new product. So you want to build a market share model instead.

Step One is to make a good, reliable whole-market forecast. Most industries have forecasters at work somewhere in the background, either in a market research company, a stock brokerage, or an industry association. If you have a corporate budget and a corporate planning position, you're probably already working with one forecast or another. If you're on your own, look for a forecast in a magazine; use the library. Try the *Predicast* index, which lists key numbers in magazine forecasts for thousands of different product categories. Also, look at the published indexes of business periodicals.

In this case, we turn to a forecast done by a market research house, one of several that are dedicated to making computer industry forecasts. The forecast fixes the market for software on Commodore home computers in U.S. homes at just under $980,000 in 1982, with the market growing at an enormous rate. Commodore itself sold about 51 percent of this market in 1982, but as the total increases, Commodore's share is expected to decrease.

With this information we can begin to build Table 4-17: We have a line for the 1982 market, a line for the growth rate, and a third line for Commodore's declining share. Get your spreadsheet out and fill in those columns and labels, making it look like our model.

Table 4-17: Market Share Forecast

Company XYZ
Sales Forecast Based on
Market Share Calculations

	1982	1983	1984	1985	1986	1987
Home Management Software For Commodore (mil.$)	1.0	3.2	8.0	17.9	35.8	62.7
3 (growth %)		225.0	150.0	125.0	100.0	75.0
4 Commodore share (%)	51.0	40.8	32.6	26.1	20.9	16.7
5 Commodore share ($)	0.5	1.3	2.6	4.7	7.5	10.5
6 Independents share($)	0.5	1.9	5.4	13.2	28.3	52.2
7 Company XYZ share(%)		2.0	4.0	6.0	8.0	10.0
8 Company XYZ share($) (thousands)		37.7	214.5	794.2	2,267.7	5,222.6

To obtain the growth-rate-driven market forecast in lines 1 and 2 of the model, some spreadsheets offer a growth command. In MicroPlan, the GROWTH (74) command will prompt for a starting value ($.98 million) and a row in which the growth rates are to be placed. In many other calcs, you would put the starting point in cell B2 and the growth rates in cells C3 through H3. Then the formula for cell C2 would be

B2*(1 + (C3/100))

With that you can then replicate C2 through D2:H2 to get the growth rate formula all the way across.

The fourth line, Commodore (%), has the Commodore share of the market declining at about 20 percent per year. In this case, cell C4 is written as .8 times B4, and this formula is replicated across the row. Then perform a simple multiplication to get to line 5, which is row 2 times row 4 divided by 100, or B5 = B2*(B4/100). Row 6 is just row 2 minus row 5. Company XYZ's market share is an assumed percent market share that is simply entered into the spreadsheet as a number. Then the last line, row 8, is the product of taking that percent of the independent share. Cell C8, for example, is the following:

C6*(C7/100)*1000

The **1000* at the end indicates we want to speak in thousands of dollars in row 8, while the rest of the dollar figures are in millions of dollars. Using millions is a simpler way of thinking about the other figures, but by the time we get to Company XYZ, using thousands is much more convenient.

Keep track of your dollar denominations. In a simple model like this, it doesn't matter; but when things get complicated, the thousands and millions of dollars can throw you off guard. It helps to label thousands or millions in the label column.

The market share model is often quite useful. Market shares are relatively constant, and whole-market forecasts are relatively easy to find in magazines and research houses. Often the market share forecast is the best and easiest way to project even a single company's sales.

Chain Method Forecast

The chain method is a useful variant on the market share method. In this case, you have a series of related known facts, and you draw from that series an ever-sharper picture of your targeted piece of information. The example does this with popcorn: We are considering acquiring the popcorn concessions at some movie theaters in a city of 2 million people, and we'd like to forecast sales over the next three years. The most obvious forecast, and maybe the best in a case like this, is a simple straight-line forecast based on past sales. But in this example we can't do this because the former operator kept very poor records. Also, we want to produce some objective measure of reasonable sales expectations on our own, rather than use someone else's numbers, because the people selling the concessions may have ulterior motives in overestimating the sales. So, we use a chain forecast like the one in Table 4-18.

Table 4-18: Chain Method Forecast

Company XYZ
Sales Forecast Based on
Chain Method (Popcorn Sales)

	1983	1984	1985
Population	2,000,000	2,040,000	2,080,800
Disposable Income	8,000,000,000	8,160,000,000	8,323,200,000
1% spent on entertai	80,000,000	81,600,000	83,232,000
5% spent on cinema	4,000,000	4,080,000	4,161,600
10% spent on popcorn	400,000	408,000	416,160
Market Share	20	22	24
Sales Forecast	80,000	89,760	99,878

The chain starts with a population figure and a population growth rate. Our city is growing at about 2 percent per year, and has 2 million people at present. This is shown in row 1 of the model.

The next series of numbers comes from available economic information. You might look at economic indicators in the local library or ask in the reference section for some key numbers. Trade associations can be very helpful. You may even have to estimate—and if you do, it's far better to estimate by using the chain method than by just starting from scratch with no information.

Our model assumes $4,000 disposable income per person, of which 1 percent is spent on entertainment per year. We multiplied the 2 million people by $4,000 in line 2 and then took 1 percent of that (multiply by .01) in line 3. Then we assume that 5 percent of the entertainment money goes to the movies, giving us line 4; and of that, we say, 5 percent is spent on popcorn. That gives us our popcorn forecast in line 5.

Now that we have some popcorn numbers, we use the market share model again. Line 6 assumes our concession's share of the total, and line 7 multiplies that by the whole market figure to produce a final estimate of our popcorn sales.

Notice how we handle percentages normally. We write in the percent number, not its decimal equivalent. That means 20 percent appears on the table as 20, not .20. Usually, this will simplify use of the model when changes are necessary; it will also make a printout that is easier to read and a model that you can explain more easily to someone else. But it also makes a greater chance for error, which you get if you forget to divide the number by 100 in your actual formulas. This means that when you have 20 percent in cell B6, and you are taking 20 percent of row 5, your formula is not B6*B5; it is (B6/100)*B5. If you use the percents in this way, don't mix them up.

The chain forecast looks simple enough to do by hand on paper and not by computer on a spreadsheet program. Sometimes it is. But normally there are estimates that have to be polished through trial and error; and then there are good reasons to look at what would happen if some of the key percentages were to change. What if disposable income drops by a percent, or people spent 10 percent instead of 5 percent of their entertainment money on the movies? Ask the model.

The Whole-Market Forecast

The whole-market forecast looks at the entire market for a given product or service, not just at one company's sales. Sometimes this can be done much as one of the above sales forecasts is done. Sometimes different tools are in order. Much depends on the kind of market and the information available.

Some General Tips

The Product Life Cycle

Almost all products go through different stages of development, and those stages are reflected in the growth rates shown in Figure 7. The important points are the takeoff and the time when the market approaches saturation.

Figure 7
Product Life Cycle

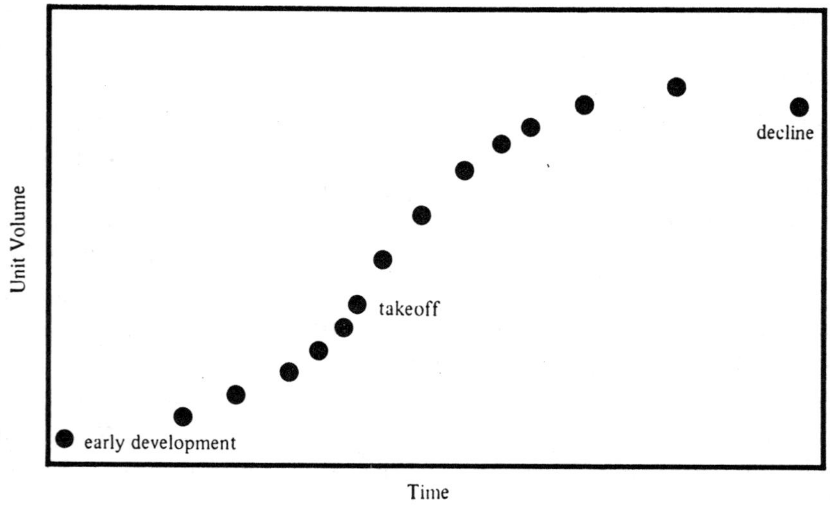

In the early development stage, growth rates may be high, but very few units are involved. This is a new market just beginning to reach its potential consumers' minds and is even further from their pocketbooks. At this point, a few magazine articles begin to address this new technology. Innovators begin to look for the product, and distribution channels are set up.

Takeoff is when the market turns upward. Pioneer buyers have spread the word, and the general public begins to buy. This is what happend when, for example, mass merchandisers began to sell a lot of $150 home computers in 1982, or when color television sets took off in the 1960s. This is the stage all those people who invested in the early market are waiting for. Growth rates are still attractive, and volume has skyrocketed.

Growth rates decline when the market approaches saturation. At this point, most of the buyers who want the product have it. The market turns into a low-growth and replacement market, just as the markets for stoves and refrigerators did.

Using the Life Cycle in Forecasts

There are three keys to using the product life cycle in your market forecasts. First, don't forget that takeoff resembles a snowball when it comes, and the situation changes enormously. Second, don't forget that once markets get going, saturation will develop eventually. Third, don't forget that each product has a different life-cycle; some fast, some slow, and some quite unlike the normal pattern.

Takeoff is the trickiest stage. There are markets that never take off at all; some companies spend years waiting for the snowball to get started, and it never does. There are also markets that take off at odd moments, at times you would not normally expect, or after long periods of apparent smoldering. The home computer boom was predicted as early as 1978, but it didn't happen until 1982. Some companies went broke waiting for it; others went into business markets and were not even there when it finally happened.

After takeoff, it's too easy to forget that market growth rates will eventually approach saturation and decline. Some of the color television people projected increasing growth through the 1970s and were caught off guard when the market moved up to about 10–15 million units per year and then stopped. The video game market drew a crowd of new entrants in 1982 and then virtually stopped growing.

The speed of a life-cycle is also hard to predict. The video game industry boomed and faded like a typical fad. The home computer industry will probably last longer before saturating the market; then it will become a replacement market. Much depends on what the product does for its buyers and on who those buyers are; take your own best guess. Sometimes the standard idea-adaptation research (below) will help.

Mature markets are by far the easiest to forecast. These have slow growth rates and little change from year to year. In these markets, the old-fashioned forecasting methods—such as taking the average growth rate of the last five years and projecting it into the next five years—work reasonably well.

Idea-Adaptation Research

Social scientists have studied adaptation of new ideas by many different groups. There are studies about doctors using a new drug, studies about farmers using a new farming technique, etc.

Most of these studies show a common pattern in adaptation. A new idea is used first by a group of 2 to 3 percent of the larger group, called innovators. The innovators prove the idea works, but they have relatively little influence on the group as a whole. The idea takes off when it is taken up by the so-called opinion leaders, who are a second group of roughly 13 percent of the larger group. These are people smart enough to see what those innovators are doing and influential enough to spread this activity to the larger group.

This common pattern fits perfectly with the product life-cycle pattern. Figure 8 shows how the curve repeats itself with different labels.

Figure 8
Idea Adaptation

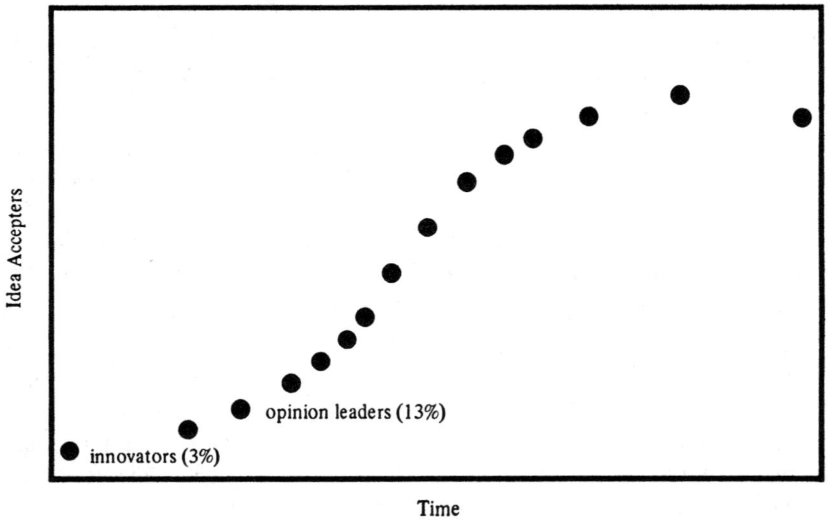

Sometimes you can use this research to estimate the speed of the product life-cycle. If less than 10 percent of the potential user group has the product, then the life-cycle may be still quite young and have a lot of growth left. It may also be ready to take off.

The Spreadsheet Model

You can use some of this knowledge in your spreadsheet models for market forecasts. Assume a total potential market for the product you are forecasting and project the installed base for each year as a percentage of the total potential market. Then compare the output of that with the normal life-cycles and adaptation research; in many systems, you can even graph the output to see whether it presents a familiar pattern.

Like many other techniques discussed in this book, this one alone will not provide any magical answers. It should be used in conjunction with other analyses and additional information, all of which comes together with your own common sense to produce a satisfactory best guess.

A Sample Market Forecast

Let's look at a professional forecast done on a spreadsheet using some of these analysis techniques. The forecast was done in early 1983 for Creative Strategies International (CSI), a leading computer industry market research and consulting house. It projected the 1983 through 1987 markets for integrated or second-generation computer software applications products such as Apple's Lisa or VisiCorp's VisiOn. Using the analysis steps explained below, it was done mainly on a microcomputer spreadsheet.

We'll look at this forecast in detail. It shows how a professional, published forecast uses the same kind of judgmental spreadsheet analysis we've been discussing. It used a good combination of research, estimation, common sense, and spreadsheet trial and error.

Step One: Total Potential Market

First, we look at what appears to be a good set of numbers for the total potential market: microcomputers sold between 1978 and 1987. These numbers, shown in Table 4-19, are taken straight from those that CSI published early in 1983 as part of a regular update service on microcomputer markets.

Table 4-19: Microcomputer Unit Shipments

1978-1987

(thousands)

	1978	1979	1980	1981	1982
Home	64	61	103	222	800
Education	14	31	55	98	225
Small business	18	40	72	129	309
Large business	21	47	79	149	412
Govt/other	4	12	21	36	90
Total U.S.	121	191	330	634	1836
Non U.S.	17	124	325	694	1329
Total	138	315	655	1328	3165

	1983	1984	1985	1986	1987
Small business	598	1046	1673	2510	3513
Large business	799	1198	1677	2264	2830
Total U.S.	3218	5290	7806	10917	14021
Non U.S.	2544	4579	7326	11355	17032
Total	5762	9869	15132	22272	31053

source: Creative Strategies International

Microcomputers: Markets, Strategies & Opportunities

These numbers address segments of the market and come with a complex set of definitions not included here. Only business systems, obviously the main market for this new kind of software, are shown for future years.

The microcomputer shipment forecast, by the way, was also produced on a spreadsheet model that looks strikingly similar to our salesperson/product/region/units/price model in the preceding section. It details past and present shipments by vendor, model, average price, and market segment. Then, with those facts in the spreadsheet, the forecast projects into the future using an analysis of total potential market and present penetration trends.

We produced Table 4-20 with our spreadsheet software but did it almost entirely by entry of data. Numbers were output from the hardware forecast model and were then entered into a new model for this forecast. The only assistance from the computer was in summing the numbers. The totals had been part of the first model; by having the computer calculate them again, we benefited from an additional check for error. And of course, once we had the data in our new model, we used it to create the new forecast.

Table 4-20: 16-bit Microcomputers Forecast

(percent, thousands)

	1983	1984	1985	1986	1987
16-bit %	20	30	40	45	50
16-bit units	1152	2961	6053	10022	15527
16-bit installed	1449	4061	9121	17989	32030

Legend:

16-bit %: 16-bit based systems as percent of total microcomputer shipments

16-bit units: unit shipments of 16-bit based systems in thousands

16-bit installed: installed base of 16-bit based systems in thousands according to CSI formula:

Shipments this year + .75(last year) + .6(previous) + .4(previous) + .2(previous)

source: Creative Strategies International

Microcomputers: Markets, Strategies and Opportunities

In a perfect world, we could have used the microcomputer hardware forecast model to create our new second-generation, integrated model. There should be no reason for retyping. But the first model was done in VisiCalc on an Apple III, and this new one was done in SuperCalc on a homemade CP/M computer. So, we retyped the data . . . and thought once again how much we all lose because of a small-computer Tower of Babel.

Step Two: Focusing on High-End Units

Step Two redefines our total potential as a subset of the first potential. The new-generation, integrated software will run only on more powerful 16-bit or 32-bit microcomputers. Therefore we have to focus more directly on those micros as a percentage of the total. Table 4-20 shows the results.

Notice that we are already using the general rules for spreadsheet analysis. We have separated the numbers for 16-bit micros from those for other kinds of micros, and we've divided our market into five subsegments. "Divide and conquer" gives us more power to focus our analysis as we go on.

The installed base treatment in Table 4-20 is a very good example. Notice that the retirement assumptions are spelled out on the table because they are very important to the installed base. The forecast assumes a decline in shipments in successive years: 75 percent, then 60 percent, then 40 percent, and so on of the shipments in the base year. The calc program handles this very well with a formula that is then replicated. Let's look at the real model in Table 4-21:

Table 4-21: Market Forecasting Worksheet #1

:	A	F ::	G ::	H ::	I ::	J ::	K ::
1:							
2:		1981	1982	1983	1984	1985	1986
3:	Home	222	800	1259	2204	3306	4629
4:	Education	98	225	333	574	775	1007
5:	Small business	129	309	598	1046	1673	2510
6:	Large business	149	412	799	1198	1677	2264
7:	Govt/other	36	90	179	268	375	507
8:		---	-----	-----	-----	-----	-----
9:	Total U.S.	634	1836	3218	5290	7806	10917
10:	Non U.S.	694	1329	2544	4579	7326	11355
11:		---	-----	-----	-----	-----	-----
12:	Total	328	3165	5762	9869	15132	22272
13:	Non U.S. business	424	771	1403	2398	3645	5367
18:	16-bit systems (%)	2	12	20	30	40	50
19:	16-bit units	20	380	1152	2961	6053	11136
25:	16-bit installed bas	20	395	1449	4061	9121	17989

We cut parts of the model out of the illustration. Early years are in columns B through E, which aren't shown. The last year is also cut out because it doesn't fit as easily on a page as on a computer screen. Some rows are left out because they aren't related to this discussion.

This kind of editing is simple. We printed from the model onto a file on a floppy disk. Then we took the file into our word processing program for editing.

Now, looking at the model, consider the formulas for the installed base rows, which was row 25 in the model. In the simple SuperCalc notation, row 25 formulas are as follows:

A25	="16-bit installed base
B25	=B19
C25	=C19+(.75*B19)
D25	=D19+(.75*C19)+(.6*B19)
E25	=E19+(.75*D19)+(.6*C19)+(.4*B19)
F25	=F19+(.75*E19)+(.6*D19)+(.C*D19)+(.B*C19)
G25	=G19+(.75*F19)+(.6*E19)+(.4*D19)+(.2*C19)
H25	=H19+(.75*G19)+(.6*F19)+(.4*E19)+(.2*D19)
I25	=I19+(.75*H19)+(.6*G19)+(.4*F19)+(.2*E19)
J25	=J19+(.75*I19)+(.6*H19)+(.4*G19)+(.2*F19)
K25	=K19+(.75*J19)+(.6*I19)+(.4*H19)+(.2*G19)
L25	=L19+(.75*K19)+(.6*J19)+(.4*I19)+(.2*H19)

The actual input of the formula was in cell L25, and we then replicated back to cell B25. Most calc programs let us replicate automatically back to 1978 and compensate automatically for the lack of previous years' history by assigning zeroes. So, for cell C25, SuperCalc gives you what we have above—C19+(.75*B19)—rather than an error message in which the computer complains that it doesn't have enough cells to go back to.

MicroPlan is once again different from the others and in this case is less efficient. In MicroPlan, you could reproduce these installed base assumptions using the LAG command (72) and about a dozen extra rows. First, you set up a series of rows in which shipments are lagged by one period, two periods, three periods, etc. Call the 72 command and answer the prompt with the number of periods desired.

Then set up another series of rows in which those lagged shipment years are multiplied by your retirement assumptions. The one-year lagged shipments are multiplied by .95, the two-year shipments by .85, and so on. Use the MULT K (53) command. Then finally set up a row to sum the shipments plus the product of that last multiplication, and you should have the same installed base numbers. It's clumsy, yes, but it does work.

Step Three: Some Checking along the Way

A professional forecast is like a crossword puzzle. Many different streams of information are checked and rechecked against one another, and conflicts are resolved many times as they arise. Finally, the forecast seems to handle all the rough edges, and you go to print with it.

This checking and rechecking begins early in the process. In Table 4-22, we find a way to check the 16-bit numbers we just produced in Table 4-21.

Table 4-22: Hypothetical Business Market Projection

unit shipments in thousands

(business market shipments only)

	1982	1983	1984	1985	1986	1987
Altos	20	36	62	95	139	198
Apple	214	250	350	500	700	1000
Commodore	177	332	551	830	1203	1660
Convergent	7	13	23	36	54	77
Cromemco	29	34	47	68	95	136
Digital	8	17	31	53	87	137
Dynabyte	6	11	18	29	43	62
Fortune	8	15	25	38	54	75
Zenith	30	56	93	141	204	281
Hewlett Packard	64	120	199	300	435	600
IBM	142	302	576	1012	1720	2803
Intertec	28	50	77	109	147	188
Non-linear	9	17	28	42	61	84
North Star	18	34	56	84	122	169
Olivetti	35	66	109	164	238	328
Osborne	80	134	196	256	319	377
Otrona	3	6	9	14	20	28
Sord	40	75	124	188	272	375
Tandy	101	189	314	473	686	947
Televideo	5	10	16	26	38	55
Vector Graphic	10	18	29	43	60	80
Wicat	2	4	6	9	14	19
Xerox	40	75	124	188	272	375
Other	416	936	1576	2300	3157	3938
Total	1492	2800	4642	6995	10141	13991

source: Creative Strategies International

NOTE: Hypothetical vendor-specific projections are presented as a test for reasonableness only. Actual 1983-1987 shares depend on business strategies and implementations. Above represents an approximation only.

The numbers in the 1982 column are taken from the CSI update service information and are reliable estimates of each major maker's shipments of microcomputers to business markets in 1982. The sum should match what our first set of numbers gave for business markets in 1982, especially after we allow for a large number of shipments made to non-U.S. markets.

To explore this table, let's look at the full model that produced it:

Figure 9
Microcomputer Model

:	A	B	C	D	E	F	G	H	I	J	K	L
1:												
2:		1977	1978	1979	1980	1981	1982	1983	1984	1985	1986	1987
3:	Home	19	64	61	103	222	800	1259	2204	3306	4629	5786
4:	Education	1	14	31	55	98	225	383	574	775	1007	1259
5:	Small business	1	18	40	72	129	309	598	1046	1673	2510	3513
6:	Large business	1	21	47	79	149	412	799	1198	1677	2264	2830
7:	Govt/other	1	4	12	21	36	90	179	268	375	507	633
8:	Total U.S.	—	—	—	—	—	—	—	—	—	—	—
9:	Total U.S.	23	121	191	330	634	1836	3218	5290	7806	10917	14021
10:	Non U.S.	2	17	124	325	694	1329	2544	4579	7326	11355	17032
11:	Total	—	—	—	—	—	—	—	—	—	—	—
12:	Total	25	138	315	655	1328	3165	5762	9869	15132	22272	31053
13:	Non U.S. business	2	12	84	209	424	771	1403	2398	3645	5367	7648
14:	(percent of total	75	71	68	64	61	58	55	52	50	47	45
15:	Total business sys	4	51	171	360	702	1492	2800	4642	6995	10141	13991
16:	Altos						20	36	62	95	139	198
17:	Apple						214	250	350	500	700	1000
18:	Commodore						177	332	551	830	1203	1660
19:	Convergent						7	13	23	36	54	77
20:	Cromemco						29	34	47	68	95	136
21:	Digital						8	17	31	53	87	137
22:	Dynabyte						6	11	18	29	43	62
23:	Fortune						8	15	25	38	54	75
24:	Zenith						30	56	93	141	204	281
25:	Hewlett Packard						64	120	199	300	435	600
26:	IBM						142	302	576	1012	1720	2803
27:	Intertec						28	50	77	109	147	188
28:	Non-linear						9	17	28	42	61	84
29:	North Star						18	34	56	84	122	169
30:	Olivetti						35	66	109	164	238	328
31:	Osborne						80	134	196	256	319	377
32:	Otrona						3	6	9	14	20	28
33:	Sord						40	75	124	188	272	375
34:	Tandy						101	189	314	473	686	947
35:	Televideo						5	10	16	26	38	55
36:	Vector Graphic						10	18	29	43	60	80
37:	Wicat						2	4	6	9	14	19
38:	Xerox						40	75	124	188	272	375
39:	Other						416	936	1576	2300	3157	3938
40:	Total						1492	2800	4642	6995	10141	13991
41:	Altos	0	0	0	0	0	20	40	75	90	100	100
42:	Apple	0	0	0	0	0	0	5	20	40	70	100
43:	Commodore					0	0	0	10	40	70	100
44:	Convergent					100	100	100	100	100	100	100
45:	Cromemco					8	15	22	35	50	75	90
46:	Digital					100	100	100	100	100	100	100
47:	Dynabyte					10	20	40	75	90	100	100
48:	Fortune					100	100	100	100	100	100	100
49:	Zenith					10	15	22	35	50	75	90
50:	Hewlett Packard					5	20	40	75	90	100	100
51:	IBM					100	100	100	100	100	100	100

52:	Intertec	0	15	22	35	50	75	90
53:	Non-linear	0	0	0	20	50	75	90
54:	North Star	0	0	0	25	50	75	90
55:	Olivetti		100	100	100	100	100	100
56:	Osborne		0	30	50	70	75	80
57:	Otrona		0	0	0	20	40	50
58:	Sord		0	0	15	20	35	50
59:	Tandy		5	10	30	50	70	90
60:	Televideo		30	60	75	85	90	95
61:	Vector Graphic		20	60	90	100	100	100
62:	Wicat		100	100	100	100	100	100
63:	Xerox	0	0	0	25	50	75	100
64:	Other		20	35	45	60	75	90
65:	Total							
66:	Altos		4	15	47	85	139	198
67:	Apple		0	13	70	200	490	1000
68:	Commodore		0	0	55	332	842	1660
69:	Convergent		7	13	23	36	54	77
70:	Cromemco		4	7	17	34	71	122
71:	Digital		8	17	31	53	87	137
72:	Dynabyte		1	4	14	26	43	62
73:	Fortune		8	15	25	38	54	75
74:	Zenith		5	12	33	70	153	253
75:	Hewlett Packard		13	48	149	270	435	600
76:	IBM		142	302	576	1012	1720	2803
77:	Intertec		4	11	27	55	110	169
78:	Non-linear		0	0	6	21	46	76
79:	North Star		0	0	14	42	92	152
80:	Olivetti		35	66	109	154	238	328
81:	Osborne		0	40	98	179	240	301
82:	Otrona		0	0	0	3	8	14
83:	Sord		0	0	19	38	95	188
84:	Tandy		5	19	94	237	480	852
85:	Televideo		2	6	12	22	35	52
86:	Vector Graphic		2	11	26	43	60	80
87:	Wicat		2	4	6	9	14	19
88:	Xerox		0	0	31	94	204	375
89:	Other		83	328	709	1380	2368	3544
90:	Total		325	930	2191	4441	8077	13137

The first 15 lines are taken from the hardware forecast we mentioned above. The only subtlety is in lines 13 and 14, which take a percentage of non-U.S. shipments as non-U.S. business systems. These are added to the large and small business segments to produce the total business units in line 15.

The 1982 business systems numbers by brand name come from the CSI database. They were entered into the cells from G16 to G38 as simple data.

The "other" in row 39 is what we call a "plug." It picks up the difference between the total business units in row 15 and the total of rows 16 through 38. In calc language, that's

>G15 – SUM(G16:G38)

Look at it. Does it seem right that other vendors should have 416,000 units out of a total of nearly 1.5 million? If it doesn't look right, we can go back and redo the forecast, which would once again show how good spreadsheet analysis is a matter of try-and-try-again, combining information with common sense.

In fact, we made several runs through this before deciding on the final that's shown. Our first iteration came out with only 100,000 units in the "other" category. This total was way too low. After all, this is worldwide shipment, and we have almost ignored the important Japanese and European vendors in the markets. We went back, adjusted our total numbers, and then produced a forecast in which more than half a million units went to "others." That was too high. So finally we settled on the figures shown, which seemed just right.

Remember the story of Goldilocks and the Three Bears? How she tested and tested the bowls of porridge, finding one too hot, one too cold, and finally one that was just right? That's what we do with the spreadsheet.

Once we have 1982 looking right, we go forward into future years. This is much easier to do when the baseline is solid. It is also a spreadsheet trick. We will use the total business market numbers we have in row 15 and the company numbers in G16 through G38 to move forward in time.

For each company listed, use either the market growth rate or some percentage related to it. If Apple, for example, is going to grow at the market growth rate, go to cell H17 and use this formula:

```
>G17*(H16/H15)
```

This formula multiplies 1982 Apple units (G17) by the 1983 growth rate (H16/H15) to produce 1983 Apple units. If we wanted Apple to grow 5 percent faster than the market, we'd use the following:

```
G17*((H16/H15)+.05)
```

Or, for companies growing more slowly than the market, we'd subtract rather than add some number at the end of the formula. One growing 5 percent more slowly than the market would be represented by the following:

```
G17*((H16/H15)−.05)
```

Thus, we used this method to guess at individual company growth rates. There were some changes made before we settled on the final table as shown. When we did make a change, we were satisfied that it was a reasonable representation.

Then we divided again. Table 4-23 is the formal printout of the section of the model from G41 through L68, which takes those business shipments and assigns their percentages of 16-bit systems. "Divide and conquer" comes into play because it is so much easier to investigate and estimate these percentages than it is just to produce a market total. Each vendor had to estimate the percentage of 16-bit units in the base year. For those who wouldn't help with the estimates, we consulted product literature, distributors, and software suppliers to produce in-house estimates.

Table 4-23: 16-bit Business Units as Percent of Total

by Vendor

1982-1987

	1982	1983	1984	1985	1986	1987
Altos	20	40	75	90	100	100
Apple	0	5	20	40	70	100
Commodore	0	0	10	40	70	100
Convergent	100	100	100	100	100	100
Cromemco	15	22	35	50	75	90
Digital	100	100	100	100	100	100
Dynabyte	20	40	75	90	100	100
Fortune	100	100	100	100	100	100
Zenith	15	22	35	50	75	90
Hewlett Packard	20	40	75	90	100	100
IBM	100	100	100	100	100	100
Intertec	15	22	35	50	75	90
Non-linear	0	0	20	50	75	90
North Star	0	0	25	50	75	90
Olivetti	100	100	100	100	100	100
Osborne	0	30	50	70	75	80
Otrona	0	0	0	20	40	50
Sord	0	0	15	20	35	50
Tandy	5	10	30	50	70	90
Televideo	30	60	75	85	90	95
Vector Graphic	20	60	90	100	100	100
Wicat	100	100	100	100	100	100
Xerox	0	0	25	50	75	100
Other	20	35	45	60	75	90

source: Creative Strategies International

NOTE: Hypothetical vendor-specific projections are presented as a test for reasonableness only. Actual 1983-1987 shares depend on business strategies and implementations. Above represents an approximation only.

After completing this, we applied the percentages to the unit numbers in the preceding table. The business numbers in G16 through L39 were multiplied by the percentages in G41 through L67, giving us the 16-bit business unit numbers in G69 through L90. These are the numbers shown in the formal printout in Table 4-24. Now we have a piece of information to compare to our earlier projection of 16-bit units as a percentage of total units.

At this point, we've also got a series of tables in a single spreadsheet workspace: the original shipment table, the business units by company, percents as shown in Table 4-23, and the 16-bit business units as shown in Table 4-24. All this has just about filled our 64K computer memory.

Now, save this whole table on the disk. This is important, because we're about to destroy it. We'll preserve the 16-bit units in the lower table section, change the percent

Table 4-24: Hypothetical 16-bit Systems Shipments by Vendor

(business markets only)

1982-1987

(thousands)

	1982	1983	1984	1985	1986	1987
Altos	4	15	47	85	139	198
Apple	0	13	70	200	490	1000
Commodore	0	0	55	332	842	1660
Convergent	7	13	23	36	54	77
Cromemco	4	7	17	34	71	122
Digital	8	17	31	53	87	137
Dynabyte	1	4	14	26	43	62
Fortune	8	15	25	38	54	75
Zenith	5	12	33	70	153	253
Hewlett Packard	13	48	149	270	435	600
IBM	142	302	576	1012	1720	2803
Intertec	4	11	27	55	110	169
Non-linear	0	0	6	21	46	76
North Star	0	0	14	42	92	152
Olivetti	35	66	109	164	238	328
Osborne	0	40	98	179	240	301
Otrona	0	0	0	3	8	14
Sord	0	0	19	38	95	188
Tandy	5	19	94	237	480	852
Televideo	2	6	12	22	35	52
Vector Graphic	2	11	26	43	60	80
Wicat	2	4	6	9	14	19
Xerox	0	0	31	94	204	375
Other	83	328	709	1380	2368	3544
Total	325	930	2191	4441	8077	13137

source: Creative Strategies International

NOTE: Hypothetical vendor-specific projections are presented as a test for reasonableness only. Actual 1983-1987 shares depend on business strategies and implementations. Above represents an approximation only.

numbers, and then apply the percents against the 16-bit units to produce new applications environments in the top table's cells, G16 through L40. We'll have to write the new numbers right over the old ones in those cells.

This is a good time to talk about saving your spreadsheets. As you go through a series like this, save a model on your disk at about every step to protect against computer failure, memory jams, or a decision to return to an older, better model. If you must, save part of the model off before using another part.

Table 4-25 estimates the percent of those 16-bit systems that will run new applications environments. To create this table, take the numbers presented in the previous table and use SuperCalc's PROTECT function to keep them from changing with every

Table 4-25: Hypothetical Integrated/New Generation
Business Market Shipments
as Percent of Total 16-bit business Shipments
by Vendor

1983-1987

	1983	1984	1985	1986	1987
Altos	0	10	25	35	50
Apple	100	100	100	100	100
Commodore	0	50	75	90	100
Convergent	0	30	45	60	80
Cromemco	0	10	25	35	50
Digital	0	5	15	25	40
Dynabyte	0	5	15	25	35
Fortune	0	15	35	50	60
Zenith	0	5	15	25	40
Hewlett Packard	0	20	40	50	60
IBM	5	30	45	55	65
Intertec	0	0	10	30	45
Non-linear	0	20	35	50	60
North Star	0	40	55	75	90
Olivetti	0	20	45	60	75
Osborne	0	20	40	60	80
Otrona	0	0	40	75	90
Sord	0	10	20	35	50
Tandy	0	25	45	60	75
Televideo	0	30	50	65	80
Vector Graphic	0	20	35	50	65
Wicat	5	40	75	90	100
Xerox	0	25	45	60	75
Other	0	20	35	50	60

source: Creative Strategies International

NOTE: Hypothetical vendor-specific projections are presented as a test for reasonableness only. Actual 1983-1987 shares depend on business strategies and implementations. Above represents an approximation only.

new recalculation. To do this, give the slash, P for PROTECT, and then cells G69:L90 when the computer asks you to identify which ones. Otherwise, when you change the percentages in G40:L67, you'll automatically change the G69:L90 unit numbers that are affected by the percent.

Notice again the use of different tables in one model. A while back we had three tables: the business unit shipments, the percent of 16-bit units, and the 16-bit units. The business units are data cells, and the percent cells are applied to them to get the 16-bit units as result cells. All three tables occupy sets of cells in part of a single spreadsheet model. Now we will change the percents so that they represent the percents of the 16-bit units that are new-generation applications environments; we want to get a new set of units, a set that is the sum of the 16-bit units times those percents, and put that set where the original business units are.

1. CALC PRODUCTS

To do this with most calc programs, including VisiCalc, SuperCalc, CalcStar, and the other leaders, we can't simply write new numbers into the cells, because those cells have some formulas assigned to them. Business units were derived from formulas based on market growth rates, as we explained in Table 4-22. The 16-bit units are the sum of those business units times the percent formulas. So, if we write just the new percent numbers, we will get strange—and useless—results.

There are a number of different ways to guard against re-use of tables. In many calcs, the PROTECT function blocks off ranges of cells so that further calculations can't be made on them; it disconnects their formulas. This is the best way to handle the problem: Protect the 16-bit units, change the percents, and then make the original business unit cells into the sum of 16-bit units times percent formula.

If you don't have a PROTECT, you may have a SAVE option that lets you save the numbers in the cells but not the formulas assigned to them. VisiCalc does this by giving first an S (storage) and then a # to get the special numbers-only SAVE function. Thus, you can save without formulas, load the numbers-only file you just saved, and start again. The cells will have the same numbers in them, but the spreadsheet will think they were entered as numbers and will do no data manipulation on them unless you write in new formulas.

If neither option is available, you might just enter numbers cell by cell in the 16-bit table. This wipes out the formulas, and you end up with the equivalent of protected cells. It takes only a few extra minutes. Then write the percent numbers in and change the formulas on the original business unit cells to make them into new-generation applications environment cells.

2. MICROPLAN

MicroPlan handles this trick better. It has several options. You can protect the new 16-bit unit numbers by changing the MicroPlan RANGE to exclude those rows from any further calculations. Or use the NULLIFY (39) command to wipe out the formulas row by row: Go to a row, give the command, and answer Y to the Y/N prompt. If you have the MicroPlan Tables module, save a whole model on a disk and then multiply a defined part of that model, right off the disk, back into the model you're working on. To do this, give a 13 to go to the Tables menu. Use the commands in that menu to identify the rows of the saved table you want and then multiply those rows by the rows in the active table you want—the 16-bit rows. For that, of course, you must put percents in their decimal form instead of their percent form (that means .50 instead of 50, for example).

By whichever method, eventually you manage those percents against those 16-bit units to come up with Table 4-26. There are estimated to be thousands of business computers using new-generation applications environments.

Table 4-26: Revised Hypothetical Integrated/New Generation
Business Market Unit Shipments

by Vendor

(thousands)

1983-1987

	1983	1984	1985	1986	1987
Altos	0	5	21	49	99
Apple	13	70	200	490	1000
Commodore	0	28	249	758	1660
Convergent	0	7	16	32	62
Cromemco	0	2	8	25	61
Digital	0	2	8	22	55
Dynabyte	0	1	4	11	22
Fortune	0	4	13	27	45
Zenith	0	2	11	38	101
Hewlett Packard	0	30	108	217	360
IBM	15	173	455	946	1822
Intertec	0	0	5	33	76
Non-linear	0	1	7	23	46
North Star	0	6	23	69	137
Olivetti	0	22	74	143	246
Osborne	0	20	72	144	241
Otrona	0	0	1	6	13
Sord	0	2	8	33	94
Tandy	0	24	107	288	639
Televideo	0	4	11	22	42
Vector Graphic	0	5	15	30	52
Wicat	0	2	7	12	19
Xerox	0	8	42	122	281
Other	0	142	483	1184	2126
Total	28	556	1948	4725	9297

source: Creative Strategies International

NOTE: Hypothetical vendor-specific projections are presented as a test for reasonableness only. Actual 1983-1987 shares depend on business strategies and implementations. Above represents an approximation only.

Meanwhile, aside from the details of the spreadsheet software, look at how well we've managed our information content. Instead of estimating the new-generation numbers from the beginning, we've found a way to move by several simple-step estimates toward a final estimate. This is almost always a better way to make an estimate. Once again, the "divide and conquer" rule appears; some people say this is the same thing as analysis.

By the time we get to Table 4-27, we need a summary. We've done several different things with our forecast. This table summarizes some of the numbers produced by the other tables; it is produced by printing parts of the model onto disk files and then by calling them into a word processing file for consolidation.

Table 4-27: Forecast and Important Assumptions

16-bit and New Generation/Integrated Software

1982-1987

(percent, thousands)

	1982	1983	1984	1985	1986	1987
16-bit business system units	325	930	2191	4441	8077	13137
New generation business units	0	28	556	1948	4725	9297
16-bit systems as % of total units	12	20	30	40	50	60
16-bit systems all markets units	380	1152	2961	6053	11136	18632
New generation as % of total units	0	.25	25	50	65	80
New generation on all new systems	0	29	740	3026	7238	14905
New generation as % add-on to old units	0	1	8	13	15	20
New generation add-on sales	0	4	106	398	734	1224
New generation unit sales total		33	846	3424	7972	16129

source: Creative Strategies International

As we pull the numbers together, we refine the forecast. The table includes the newly produced numbers for new-generation applications environments on business computers. Using these as a key to the estimate, we then assume a percentage of total units that are new-generation operating environment units. We look for a number that makes business new-generation units a large but declining portion of the total new-generation units.

This part of the forecast takes us further into the realm of the educated guess, which is not made lightly. Such a guess requires following an industry closely for several years, being fully aware of trends and developments, and then conducting a long series of interviews with all vendors and distributors of related products: computers, software, and other add-ons. The best estimate is a combination of research and judgment.

The forecast in Table 4-27 is based on the trend toward cheaper and more powerful home and educational systems with better software. Originally, the business systems will absorb most of the new-generation software, but, in time, the other systems will also use it.

Now, as we move to Table 4-28, we'll sail along. The hard parts of the analysis are done, and now we can manipulate the information to make it more useful to managers. The volume comparison is another composite of earlier tables with a few percent and comparison lines thrown in.

Table 4-28: Volume Comparisons: 16-bit, Business, New Generation

(percent, thousands)

	1982	1983	1984	1985	1986	1987
16-bit units installed base	395	1449	4061	9121	17989	32030
Old Generation Systems installed base	395	1416	3184	4891	6118	4909
New Generation Systems installed base	0	33	877	4230	11870	27121
16-bit business as % of all business units	86	81	74	73	73	71
New Generation business as % of 16-bit business units		3	25	44	58	71
New Generation Business as % of Total New Generation		96	75	64	65	62

source: Creative Strategies International

The new-generation applications environment installed baseline uses a formula based on our earlier installed base formula for business units (although the retirement assumptions change). Compare this to the 16-bit installed baseline produced earlier and use a simple subtraction to get old-generation and new-generation.

All other percent lines in Table 4-28 are produced by dividing the percent item by the total item, then by multiplying by 100. For example, to get 16-bit business units as a percent of total business units, just divide the 16-bit business units for that year by the total business units for that year and multiply by 100.

1. MICROPLAN

In MicroPlan, this can be done with a FORMULA (35) command, then (assuming the total is in row 10, and the 16-bit is in row 20) with the following:

>(L20/L10)*100

2. CALC PRODUCTS

In the calc programs, this would be done first for column B:

(B20/B10)*100

Follow this with a REPLICATE command (remember, that's COPY in some calc programs) across the rest of the row.

Table 4-29: New Generation Bundling and Cost/Price Assumptions

(percent, thousands, dollars)

	1983	1984	1985	1986	1987
Total New Generation Unit Shipments (thousands)	33	846	3424	7972	16129
Percent New Generation Units Sold Bundled w/Hardware (percent)	70	50	55	60	65
New Generation Units Sold Bundled w/Hardware (thousands)	20	370	1665	4343	9689
New Generation Units Sold Separate from Hardware (thousands)	13	476	1760	3629	6441
Price per System Bundled w/Hardware (dollars)	800	400	250	150	100
Price per System Sold Separately (dollars)	2000	600	250	200	150
Systems Software as Percent of Total System Cost (percent)	30	30	28	25	22
Hardware as Percent of Total System Cost (percent)	40	45	50	55	60
Applications Software as Percent of Total System Cost (percent)	30	25	22	20	18

source: Creative Strategies International

The other percentage rows just duplicate that one. For that matter, you could forget the *100 and use decimal form (.50 instead of 50, etc.), but we like percents better.

Table 4-29 presents some important assumptions. It covers bundling and systems components.

Bundling affects the market value. Without going into detail here, it is based on the probability that much of this new-generation software will be sold along with computers for a single price. This practice is called "bundling," which affects system prices and the total market revenues.

The rest of the assumptions are quite simple. We need price assumptions, which we simply enter into the model as educated guesses produced by a long process of research, interviews, and judgments. Then we must make other percentage assumptions to distinguish between hardware costs, system software costs, and so on. The spreadsheet makes it simple, and the logic is much like what we've already discussed. The table is mainly data entry, although, as you might guess, we plan to use those assumptions to produce some unit numbers in the following tables.

Table 4-30: Market Value of New Generations Software Systems

(millions of dollars)

	1983	1984	1985	1986	1987
New Generation Systems Full retail value (ignoring bundling)	66	508	856	1594	2419
Retail market (systems sold separately)					
Systems software	8	86	123	181	213
Special hardware	10	129	220	399	580
Applications software	8	71	97	145	174
total	25	286	440	726	966
Captive market at bundled price	16	148	416	651	969
Actual market (retail plus captive)	41	434	856	1377	1935

source: Creative Strategies International

Table 4-30 multiplies the assumptions out in the logical order to produce the revenue components of the market. This is a simple matter once we've laid down the assumptions and have the unit numbers ready. Because millions of dollars take up a lot of space in the columns, we usually take the product of price times units and divide that by 1000 so we have dollars in the millions. This looks like the following, if we're taking row 40 times row 60:

>(B40*B60)/1000

Then we replicate across the row to finish it up. In MicroPlan, employ the FORMULA (35) command at whichever row you want to use and then take the following:

>(L40*L60)/1000

Table 4-31: Projected Add-on Software

For New Generation Systems

(dollars, millions of dollars)

	1983	1984	1985	1986	1987
Software add-on assumptions: (dollars)					
First year add-ons	250	150	100	75	50
Second year	150	100	75	60	40
Third year	75	60	50	40	25
Fourth year	50	40	30	20	15
Resulting Add-on Software Forecast (millions of dollars)	8	130	408	838	1224
Total New Generation Software Systems Market Value at Retail Including Add-ons (millions of dollars)	74	638	1264	2432	3643

source: Creative Strategies International

The last table in the series, Table 4-31, assumes that these same software systems will generate some add-on software purchases. Research indicates that these add-on purchases decline through the active life of a small computer system. So, using the spreadsheet facility, we estimated these purchases as you see on this table. Then we take the spreadsheet back up to our unit shipment and installed baselines (which are still sitting around in the workspace model) to collect the data for this formula:

```
ADD/ONS = ((1ST YEAR)*(SHIPMENTS*RETIREMENT)) +
          ((2ND YEAR)*(SHIPMENTS*RETIREMENT)) +
          ((3RD YEAR)*(SHIPMENTS*RETIREMENT)) ETC.
```

This is the same kind of problem we handled earlier with the installed base. On our SuperCalc and/or VisiCalc model, we can simplify the process by replicating the installed base formulas from that part of the model. Then we give an EDIT command and add in our new cells from the software add-on assumption. So,

```
>(G40*.95)+(F40*.9)−(E40*.8)+(D40*.7)
```

becomes

```
>(G60*(G40*.95))+(G61*(F40*.9))+(G62*(E40*.8))+(G63*(D40*.7))
```

With that last trick, we add things up again and have a forecast for a new applications environment. This forecast was published and was used professionally by dozens of major companies in the industry. All we've skipped here is the process of long repetitions of "what-if" runs of the model, seeing whether assumptions look reasonable, and of course researching and interviewing to build up the factual base on which those assumptions stand.

A Strategic Interactive Model

So far, we've assumed that a sales forecast is a simple guess at future sales. We haven't looked at the impact of our own actions. Presumably, sales will be higher if we advertise more or cut prices: They'd be lower if we advertise less or raise prices. This is worth considering in our forecasting model.

Our version of an interactive model is still quite simple. These things can—and sometimes do—get enormously complicated. Consider if you will the fact that our advertising and promotion increases will drive up the total advertising and promotion in the market and therefore will increase total unit sales, which then means our additional units may not even increase our percentage of the market share. Furthermore, you could spend a lifetime investigating the exact relationships among advertising, promotion, price, and how they all affect sales. To make the model even more complicated, assume that our increase in advertising will trigger reactive increases from competitors and that our price cut will trigger cuts. Then you can take profits away from everyone without getting any benefit.

Table 4-32 was made by a simple interactive sales forecasting model. Row 4 is taken from our earlier forecast of the market for Commodore VIC-20 software packages. Row 5 is an estimated average market unit price, which gives us row 6, the market units, by dividing row 4 by row 5. Row 7, called competitive flack, estimates what the rest of the market is spending on advertising and promotion.

Table 4-32: An Interactive Sales Forecast

: A ::	B ::	C ::	D :
2:	1982	1983	1984
3:	--------	--------	--------
4:Whole market ($)	980000	3200000	8000000
5:Assumed unit price	30	25	20
6:Whole market (units)	32666	128000	400000
7:Competitive flack	98000	320000	800000
8:Our price	28	25	15
9:Our flack	50000	100000	200000
10:Our unit share (%)	10.00	14.02	20.18
11:Our units	3266	17942	80732
12:Revenue	91448.00	448550.00	1210980.00
13:Fixed cost	200000	200000	200000
14:Unit cost	5.00	3.00	3.00
15:Unit profit	23.00	22.00	12.00
16:Gross profit	75118.00	394724.00	968784.00
17:Profit - flack	-174882.00	94724.00	568784.00

Row 6 uses the INTEGER function, a feature of VisiCalc, SuperCalc, and most other calc programs. The formula for B6, for example, is

>INT(B4/B5)

The INTEGER function rounds the result of (B4/B5) to the nearest whole number. That rounding function, on occasion, is nice for simplifying tables; otherwise, you get nonsensical fractions of units being sold.

With that, we go to our own company. Most of what we put in here is simple input, but there are a couple of nice lines. Row 10 makes our unit market share a reflection of our price versus the market price, our previous year's market share and our flack versus the rest of the market's flack. The formula might someday be the result of exhaustive research; many more mature industries work with models of this sort, produced by comprehensive statistical analysis. In this case, it's another estimated guess, maybe even half-game. The formula for C10 is

>B10−((B10−((B9/(B7+B9))*100))*(.5*(B9/(B7+B9))))+(C5−C8)

D10 was produced by replicating C10.

The best way to understand these formulas is to build that model and try it. You'll find that your market share changes one way or another as you change price and advertising strategies.

You can also take the formula apart if you wish. It starts out with B10, your previous year's market share. Everything else that happens either adds or subtracts from B10, because the assumption is that if you had 10 percent of the market last year, you'll still have a percentage this year even if you don't advertise at all and even if you raise prices. The second phrase of the formula, (B10−((B9/(B7+B9))*100), takes the difference between last year's market share (B10 again) and last year's share of total flack (B9 divided by B7+B9 times 100); if your company's flack was a higher share than its market share, then the model says market share will go up. Why? Because B10 minus that will be negative, and you're still subtracting all this from the main B10, so you subtract a negative number from B10 and add to your total.

Of course, you don't get a one-to-one relationship with your advertising dollar. Building your market share costs money, and if you double your share of total advertising, normally you won't double your market share in a single year. Our formula assumes that you get about half of that back in market share. That is in the third phrase, (.5*(B9/(B7+B9)), which multiplies what we would have been adding or subtracting by .5 to diminish its importance. This reflects the fact that nothing changes all that fast. Then the fourth phrase, (C5−C8), gives us additional market share (or takes it away) for the difference between our price and the average market price.

The rest of the model reflects our business results as they follow from our marketing strategy. Row 11 converts market share to units, and row 12 converts units to revenue using our price strategy in row 8. Our fixed cost is $200,000.

The unit cost is an introduction to the conditional or IF functions in the calc programs. Almost all the calcs have them. The formula for B14 is

```
>IF(B11>12000,3,5)
```

This is a perfect example of using the IF function. This formula says that if the first phrase is true—B11 is more than 12000—then the second phrase is used: If it is false, then the third one is used. So, if our volume is greater than 12,000 units, the average unit cost is $3.00, and if it is less than that, the average unit cost is $5.00. The $3.00 and $5.00 are simple entries, but the IF function allows us to put formulas between the columns, as in

```
>IF(B11>12000,(B3*B4)/B5,(B4*B3)/B6)
```

In this case, this is a nonsensical formula, but one that still shows how to use formulas in the IF function. This means that if B11 is more than 12000, you use (B3*B4)/B5, and if it isn't, then the acting formula is (B4*B3)/B6. In this case, we want to show that our unit cost is lower if we operate above a certain volume. This is important to the strategy.

The rest of the model simply takes what we spend and subtracts this from what we make to produce a forecast of profits resulting from different marketing strategies. Table 4-33 shows what happens when we change our strategic input. You could write this model into your computer and come up with an infinite variety of different strategic scenarios, each with its different output. Try it.

Table 4-33: Strategic Interactive Model, Scenario 2

: A	B	C	D
2:	1982	1983	1984
3:	--------	--------	--------
4:Whole market ($)	980000	3200000	8000000
5:Assumed unit price	30	25	20
6:Whole market (units)	32666	128000	400000
7:Competitive flack	98000	320000	800000
8:Our price	28	21	21
9:Our flack	25000	200000	200000
10:Our unit share (%)	10.00	15.05	18.55
11:Our units	3266	19263	74206
12:Revenue	91448.00	404523.00	1558326.00
13:Fixed cost	200000	200000	200000
14:Unit cost	5.00	3.00	3.00
15:Unit profit	23.00	18.00	18.00
16:Gross profit	75118.00	346734.00	1335708.00
17:Profit - flack	-149882.00	-53266.00	935708.00

Correlation

Correlation is a fancy statistical word for what happens when two sets of numbers move up or down together in some recognizable pattern. Most people expect production to increase when investment increases, and the stock market index usually increases when the gross national product increases. Tire sales usually increase when auto sales increase because a large share of the tire makers' product goes onto new cars.

Sometimes correlation works in reverse. In most markets, volume increases when price decreases and vice versa. The stock market index usually goes down when interest rates go up and vice versa. These relationships are called negative correlations and can be just as valuable as positive ones.

Correlation can get complicated fast. In its most sophisticated versions, correlation is the foundation of very complicated economic models made up of thousands of equations and variables. People spend years studying these relationships and ways to manage information based on them.

We don't have to get that complicated here. Simple correlations can help you forecast. The market share model is a correlation forecast: It makes sales equal to the whole market times some percentage number. Many other simple uses of correlation can be valuable in sales forecasting.

The main idea is finding some easily available number that leads to a more difficult number. The best example is a whole-market forecast that leads you to a company sales forecast, like the market share model. Whole-market forecasts are usually available in business magazines, trade associations, and research firms.

The forecast in Tables 4-34 and 4-35 shows one simple example of working with correlation: It uses whole-market indicators and related products to understand what goes on with Product ABC.

The first part, Table 4-34, is based on history. We see how Product ABC sales, industry sales, widget sales, and one expert forecaster have performed. Industry sales and widget sales are historical, and the expert's row is what she predicted would happen to industry sales.

Table 4-34: Correlation Analysis

Company XYZ

Sales History
and Related Indicators

	1978	1979	1980	1981	1982
Product ABC sales (thousands units)	312.00	455.00	543.00	470.00	455.00
Industry Sales	4320.00	5560.00	6800.00	5750.00	5200.00
Widget Sales	2020.00	1600.00	1350.00	1450.00	1835.00
Expert Forecast	4000.00	5500.00	6250.00	5500.00	5250.00
ABC/Industry	0.07	0.08	0.07	0.08	0.08
ABC/Widget	0.15	0.28	0.40	0.32	0.24
Regression on widgets	447.00	894.36	-0.27		
Regression on Industry	447.00	-44.82	0.08		
Regression on Expert	447.00	-92.90	0.10		
Widgets > 894-.27W					
Industry > .08I-44.82					
Expert > .1E - 92.90					

There are some apparent patterns. Product ABC sales come to about 7 or 8 percent of the whole market, and obviously they go up when the market goes up and down when it goes down. They seem to move in reverse of the widget sales—when widgets go down, ABC goes up and vice versa. The forecaster is close to industry sales but tends to underestimate. In 1982, however, she overestimated; it's possible she's noticed her mistake and is compensating for the earlier misses.

We want to get somehow at those patterns for our own use. One simple way shows up in the rows in which we divide our sales by industry sales and then by widget sales. In the first division, we find our 7-to-8 percent market share coming out. In the second, we don't seem to have a helpful pattern, despite the way the widgets and ABC move in reverse.

Table 4-35: Forecast Based on Correlation

Company XYZ
Sales Forecast
Based on Correlations

Future	1983	1984	1985
Industry	5000.00	5500.00	6000.00
Widgets	1400.00	1200.00	1050.00
Expert	5250.00	6000.00	7000.00
Product ABC Forecasts:			
Industry-based	355.18	395.18	435.18
Widget-based	516.00	570.00	610.50
Expert-based	432.10	507.10	607.10
Final forecast:	450.00	500.00	600.00

In the following lines, we explore CalcStar's regression facility, which should and will be more common in calc programs very soon. In the meantime, you can duplicate the regression function on a financial calculator or on a piece of graph paper. In calcs that do have regression functions, you want to find how Product ABC sales vary when the other indicators vary. To put the widget regression into row 12, move the cursor to B12 and give the command for the regression on widgets, which would be

>+REGR(B6>F6,B3)

B3 is Product ABC sales and B6>F6 is the series for the widget sales. This produces the mean value of B3>F3 (our ABC Product sales history) in cell B12. It also puts the widget regression into the computer memory. Then we move to B13 and type

>+PROJ(0)

This gives us the number in B13, which is the constant portion of the equation we're going to get. We'll explain in a minute. Move to B14 and type

>+SLOPE()

We get the slope portion of the equation. Now, we have the basics of a simple formula. Product ABC sales are roughly equal to

894.36 – (0.27*WIDGETS)

The goal of any simple regression is a formula that includes a constant and a slope. The classic form is

FORECAST = CONSTANT NUMBER + (SLOPE*INDICATOR)

If you were to graph the sales of ABC and the widget in a graph, with widgets going up and down and ABC going right to left (take a look at Table 4-34), you'd find that the straight line going through them crosses zero at about 900—or, with a computer, 894.36. Using the CalcStar regression function, run the regression, get the slope, and then get the constant using the PROJ and SLOPE commands.

In the following two lines, we ran the same regression commands on the industry and the expert rows to get formulas for forecasting Product ABC sales using those indicators. The results are written in the rows below:

Based on industry results:

ABC=.08*INDUSTRY−44.82

Based on the expert forecast:

ABC=.1*EXPERT−92.90

Now, we have a choice of magic formulas with which to forecast sales using industry forecasts. Table 4-35 gives us some industry forecasts to use. It includes our industry association forecast of the industry, a professional widget forecast, and the expert's forecast.

We use these forecasts and our formulas to suggest possible Product ABC sales forecasts. The first is in row 7 of the model. It was done by putting the following into B7:

>(.08*B2)−44.82

Then it was done by copying (CalcStar's version of replicating) into the other two rows. The appropriate formulas are used, as explained above, for the forecast based on the widgets and the industry expert.

We now have three competing forecasts among which to choose; an alternative is to produce a fourth. Once again, we're at a forecast's judgment phase, in which we assimilate different sources of information and apply common sense to produce the final forecast.

In this case, we will probably use the expert forecast version because it looks like the best reflection of a low-growth 1983. Both the industry association and the expert expect low growth in that year, and the expert's formula comes close to that. It also falls between the other two. Better still, our own forecast in the final row takes the best from the different formulas to arrive at something that feels like a good composite. The final forecast also has the advantage of looking unscientific. It's better that way.

Forecasting Summary

Remember that all of this is more art than science. Don't copy our model unless it fits well; make your own. There is no prescribed way to form a model, except using as much information as possible and a lot of guessing. Try to combine different methods into one forecast and compare the results. Just keep trying until your model feels right.

FIVE

Budgets

Budgets are probably the least loved business analysis tools. Even the word ''budget'' sounds like disapproving accountants and denied requests; ''It's not in the budget'' is one of the world's most familiar excuses.

But, despite their bad reputation, budgets are always useful tools and are almost always absolutely essential to the proper running of a business. Budgets are used for planning and for tracking performance against plans. A good budgeting system can make a huge difference to the running of a company.

Furthermore, as the power of computers increases the business system's emphasis on planning its numbers, budgets and budget analysis will become more involved and more detailed. With the spreadsheet programs, they can be built more simply and managed more easily than ever before.

Budgets for Planning and Tracking

Budgets have two main purposes. First, they can be a valuable tool for planning. Second, they are the simplest and most obvious way to track results against a plan. A business that is ''on budget'' is going according to plan.

Budgets for Planning

Budgets are plans. They show how much money is going to be spent by whom, when it will be spent, and what it will buy. They also show how much money is supposed to be received, where it is coming from, and when it is expected.

The cash budget, or cash-flow budget, is probably the best example. A cash budget is usually a spending plan that matches spending to revenues and keeps track of the cash left over. If the cash budget shows a deficit, spending is cut, revenue is picked up, or someone must get a loan to make ends meet. The cash budget reschedules spending where it can to keep borrowing to a minimum by matching the outgo with the income. It plans ahead. Toymakers, for example, have to budget their use of Christmas cash to allow for the next year's production cycle. Mattress makers plan cash requirements around summer sales peaks. The treasurer or controller of a large corporation must budget cash requirements for all divisions and subsidiaries.

Sales budgets and investment budgets are also used for planning purposes. The sales budget is used by the financial manager to plan cash flow and by the production management to plan product flow to match sales. The investment budget plans capital expenditures to match cash requirements with expansion and new investments. The investment budget should reflect corporate strategy; investments are one of the key influences on the long-term presence of a company. The capital expenditures budget can be the single most important tool for developing a corporate strategy.

Budgets for Tracking Performance

Budgets are also used for tracking performance. The difference between budgeted sales and actual sales gives a sales manager or a general manager a good, quick, and simple way to follow a company's performance between accounting statements. The same is true for comparisons of budgeted expenditures or most other budgeted items versus actual expenditures.

The difference between budgeted and actual results is called a variance. Variance analysis, the art of interpreting variances, is the subject of a lot of respected academic and accounting literature. There are positive variances (more profit) and negative variances (less profit). An item such as direct labor costs could have both positive and negative variance at the same time, if, for example, production took fewer hours than budgeted (a positive variance) but at greater hourly cost than budgeted (negative variance). This can become as subtle and obscure as the medieval art of counting angels on the head of a pin.

But variance analysis doesn't have to be subtle or obscure to be important. Most often, a manager wants to know where and how performance varied from budget, and, most importantly, why it varied. Are costs rising faster than expected? Is a new competitor hurting sales? Is labor productivity changing, or new management systems increasing the spending on staff positions? The heart of variance analysis is management: What is going on, and why?

Budgets and Responsibility

A budget should fit its purpose. This depends on such variables as company structure, company goals, reporting responsibilities, and chains of command.

Budgeted entities are often divided into three or more kinds of units, depending on the variables mentioned above. There are cost centers, revenue centers, and profit centers. Cost centers are such units as marketing, planning, accounting, and others that do not generate any revenues. Revenue centers are sales units, regional sales units, etc. Profit centers are such units as divisions of a corporation or regions that produce the goods the corporation sells; they are responsible for both revenues and costs. There are even ROI centers, which are responsible for all the above, plus return on investment.

The budget for a cost center plans expenditures and measures the unit's ability to complete assigned tasks within budgeted expenditure levels. The budget for a revenue center plans revenue levels and may or may not plan for the expenditures (such as sales order processing in a sales office) associated with those revenues. A profit center budget fixes both revenues and expenditures and plans on the difference as profit or loss. An ROI center budget compares profits to the total investment that produced them.

Spreadsheet Budgeting Tips

You have to do it right. Otherwise, you might as well get down the green eyeshades and the accounting paper and do it the old way. Some of the general tips from Chapter Two deserve special mention within the context of budgeting:

Always Leave a Trail

Your budget was saved under the file name BUDGET. You called it up, changed it, and saved it under the file name BUDGET. On the save, however, you received an operating system error saying that the file had not been saved correctly. You just lost a lot of work.

Remember that sinking feeling? Three or four hours of work lost to the machine. But now you know how to protect yourself next time: Save the modified version as BUDGET2. You'll still have BUDGET saved.

Moral: Save your work right. Keep a couple of earlier generations on the disk. Use file names to organize: BUDGET1, BUDGET2, and BUDGET3 are nice to have around. Even if you're short on disk space, keep at least one previous version for reference and backup. We've mentioned this before, but it is worth repeating.

Leave Room for Error

In some calcs, you must declare a matrix size before you start building a model. Afterward, you can change the size only through a tedious process of reading row after row into a new matrix. Think ahead and leave enough room for future flexibility. If you think the budget requires 50 rows and 10 columns, set it up at 75×20. If you don't, you'll someday wish you did.

In most calcs, you can insert rows and columns to your heart's content or until your system's memory runs out, whichever comes sooner. Here, the problems of later expansion are not as severe. But some calcs are much more limited than others, so be careful. You can be two-thirds through a budget and have memory run out.

There is a way around this, if you plan ahead. In most of the calcs, you can save portions of your work on disk. Build your budget so that pieces of it might be saved for a later time when a consolidation model can bring them all together. For example, different expenditure types (such as production versus sales versus administrative) might be prepared as separate files. Totals can be brought onto a fourth model and added up. This is awkward, but it is better than using a pencil and eraser.

To do this, you must plan compatible TOTALS lines. You can't have the departmental costs include overhead in one department but not in another. You can't start with January in one budget and with March in another; if you do, at the very least you will have to be a lot more careful.

Build from Foundations Up

Break numbers down into their fundamental parts to increase your model's flexibility. Use the spreadsheet power to make your estimated revenue the product of price times units, for example, instead of a simple numeric input. Then, if you decide to change price or unit projections, the computer will help. This is once again a variation on our "divide and conquer" rule.

Any of the major spreadsheet programs gives you formula options. You can make an item a simple input or a product of some other input. You input a simple number or a formula; the choice is important.

1. CALC PRODUCTS

For example, if the cursor is at G10, you can input either a simple number or a formula: Input E10*F10, and the G10 item will be equal to the E10 item multiplied by the F10 item. This could easily be revenue (G10) equals units (E10) times price per unit (F10). After one cell is prepared in this manner, the REPLICATE (in VisiCalc and SuperCalc) or the COPY (in CalcStar) command is used to copy the same formula across a full row.

2. MICROPLAN

MicroPlan handles this with the FORMULA command, which makes an entire row or column subject to a formula. For example, with the cursor at row 10, the MicroPlan FORMULA (35) command would allow you to input L8*L9 to get the same results.

The more detailed the model, the more flexible it is for future changes. For example, you might make unit direct cost a function of materials plus direct labor, not a simple number. Or, you might break materials down into component parts and direct labor into operations. Or, in another operation, you might make direct labor cost a product of wage rates times hours worked. Make revenue price times units less discounts less tax. With all of these variations preset, future changes will be easier to absorb.

Details depend on the specifics of each budget. Carefully consider which items might change and which items might not. Build flexibility into the structure of the spreadsheet model.

There is an important trade-off. As the level of detail increases, flexibility increases but so do complexity, model-building time, and the probability of error. If you want a half-hour cost estimate, you might be better off leaving the detail for some other occasion. If you are going to re-use (and probably modify and improve) a given budget model over a period of time, greater complexity is desirable. Time taken to build the model should be proportional to time to be saved in later use.

Choose Your Foundations Well

Base your model on the variables that will be most useful. Choose those that are going to affect the greatest number of other variables and those that are most likely to change.

For example, use units in a manufacturing budget and see what happens: Revenue, direct labor, direct materials, overhead, and other items are driven by units. When the unit numbers change, so should the others, and if the model is built right, they will. If the model pivots on number of laborers, or hours worked, or some other variable, you'll have to input more by hand, and you'll enjoy it less. Consider using rows and columns to store variable items such as inflation factors, direct labor hours per unit of production, and cost per direct labor hour. Even when these are constants, the REPLICATE, COPY, and MicroPlan row-oriented commands will work more simply if the constant is repeated across an entire row. Then tomorrow, when the situation changes, it'll be easier to reflect those changes in your model.

Think about Structure

Some structures are better than others. Remember which subtotals and consolidations might be convenient. All spreadsheet programs work better if you can add adjacent rows for subtotals (rows 10–15, for example, sum to cost of goods sold). But you have to plan whether you want to subtotal cost of goods sold, say, or total labor costs. In one case, place direct labor with direct materials. In another, put direct labor along with indirect labor, supervision, management, and so on.

Inserting rows is tricky when you are dealing with subtotals. For example, when you add a new row for general and administrative expenditures—you just realized you forgot to figure in leasing a nice computer—be careful that the subtotal below is still valid. Many calc programs require a recalculation command (the exclamation point in VisiCalc and SuperCalc) before the subtotals are adjusted.

This becomes even more important in the more advanced spreadsheets, which allow consolidation. If the model program is going to take cost of goods sold for several different product lines, each of which has a separate budget, then the budgets should be structured so that the cost-of-goods variable is the same in each one. MicroPlan can be programmed to add the cost-of-goods line from each of several separate budgets to come up with a combined cost of goods. But you have to plan for this. Also, in CalcStar and SuperCalc you can manipulate larger matrices by saving matrices as separate files and bringing them into and out of the computer workspace. Each year might be a separate model, or each department might be a separate model, and you can usually store separate rows on your disk in a way that allows you to consolidate totals. But your totals have to be consistent between the different files: You can't locate January in column C in one department and in column D in another.

Some Simple Budget Models

In Chapter Two, we looked at a simple start-up company budget. The logic of a corporate budget is quite similar. Usually, however, more sophisticated reporting is required. Often, there is a need for distinguishing between different kinds of expenditure items (such as controllable versus noncontrollable items) or between fixed and variable expenses.

A Departmental Budget (Cost Center)

The simplest departmental budget is the cost center budget. Table 5-1 presents a small company's manufacturing plant budget, based on standard cost items.

Table 5-1: A Simple Cost Center Budget

	January	February	March	April
Direct costs:				
Units produced	200	250	400	300
Direct materials	17,000.00	21,250.00	34,000.00	25,500.00
Direct labor	3,000.00	3,750.00	6,000.00	4,500.00
Subtotal	20,000.00	25,000.00	40,000.00	30,000.00
Factory overhead				
Indirect labor	1,500.00	1,500.00	1,500.00	1,500.00
Maintenence	500.00	500.00	500.00	500.00
Equipment depreciation	350.00	350.00	350.00	350.00
Utilities	250.00	255.00	260.00	265.00
Insurance	200.00	200.00	200.00	200.00
Plant supplies	150.00	187.50	300.00	225.00
Building depreciation	100.00	100.00	100.00	100.00
Property taxes	75.00	75.00	75.00	75.00
Miscellaneous	50.00	50.00	50.00	50.00
Subtotal	3,175.00	3,217.50	3,335.00	3,265.00
Cost of goods	23,175.00	28,217.50	43,335.00	33,265.00

Notice how this budget is built: It begins with a production budget, adds direct costs determined by the units produced, and only then adds predictable indirect costs. At least one indirect cost item, factory supplies, depends on the number of units produced.

Once you've defined your rows and columns on the spreadsheet, the formulas are very simple. Most of the rows are filled by multiplying the unit production number by some standard cost number. Then totals are added up. Whether you are replicating with a standard calc package or building with MicroPlan or Multiplan, the mechanics are very simple.

The production budget is usually set by management. The monthly production figure is intended to coordinate between sales expectations and acceptable inventory levels.

Direct costs depend on how many units are produced. The budget assumes each unit will cost $85 in direct materials and $15 in direct labor. The direct labor estimate is probably made up of one hour of labor at $15 an hour. Direct costs are called standard costs because they assume the same amount of materials and the same amount of labor for each unit. Later, actual results will be compared to the estimated standard cost; a variance analysis will focus then on the difference.

To enter that onto the spreadsheet, of course, you have the direct materials row multiply the unit row by 85. The direct labor row multiplies the unit row by S15.

Indirect costs are estimated, using either accounting calculations (for depreciation, property taxes, etc.) or past experience. Utilities run at $250 per month and are increasing slightly, so start in the spreadsheet at $250 (a simple input variable) and add $5 per month. Maintenance runs at $500 per month, so we enter that in the appropriate row. Factory supplies cost 75 cents per unit produced, so that row is .75 times the unit row. These are average figures drawn from the past few months. Cost accountants estimate standard costs using a range of different techniques.

Standard cost budgets can be very sophisticated. The standard cost estimates could be estimates produced on demand by a production engineer, could be simple and rough estimates, or could be the product of long and detailed statistical analysis. Even started as a quick estimate, the standard cost per unit can be refined through experience until it is a valuable tool for planning and for tracking performance.

Fixed and Variable Costs

Many budgets break down cost items into fixed and variable costs. Fixed costs such as depreciation and property taxes are incurred regardless of plant production levels. Variable costs such as direct labor and materials depend on production levels.

Table 5-2 is a fixed/variable cost budget for the factory shown in Table 5-1. This is a very simple revision of the spreadsheet analysis and is only a matter of reshuffling rows and changing headings. Otherwise, it is very much like the previous table. In all major spreadsheet programs, restructuring is best done from the ground up and should be anticipated from the beginning; the fixed/variable cost budget is built in this manner. But the spreadsheets also allow flexibility for converting an existing cost budget to a more convenient structure. MicroPlan uses its row-and-column REORDER (23 for rows, 28 for columns) command to restructure. Subtotal and total commands (55) must be reset after the restructuring, or the program gets confused. In VisiCalc and SuperCalc, insert a row, replicate from the earlier row, and finally delete the earlier. CalcStar does the same thing with the COPY command.

Table 5-2: Fixed and Variable Costs Budget

(Plant Budget)

	January	February	March	April
Variable costs:				
Direct materials	17,000.00	21,250.00	34,000.00	25,500.00
Direct labor	3,000.00	3,750.00	6,000.00	4,500.00
Indirect labor	1,500.00	1,500.00	1,500.00	1,500.00
Maintenence	500.00	500.00	500.00	500.00
Utilities	250.00	255.00	260.00	265.00
Plant supplies	150.00	187.50	300.00	225.00
Miscellaneous	50.00	50.00	50.00	50.00
Subtotal	22,450.00	27,492.50	42,610.00	32,540.00
Fixed costs:				
Equipment depreciation	350.00	350.00	350.00	350.00
Insurance	200.00	200.00	200.00	200.00
Building depreciation	100.00	100.00	100.00	100.00
Property taxes	75.00	75.00	75.00	75.00
Subtotal	725.00	725.00	725.00	725.00
Cost of goods	23,175.00	28,217.50	43,335.00	33,265.00

Usually, variable costs are the only costs that increase or decrease along with production volume. Fixed costs are the costs that would be left over if the plant shut down for a month or two. Maintenance, indirect labor, and utilities appear in this example not to be following production volume, but they would go away entirely if the plant were shut down for a month and would go up or down if plant volume stayed high or low for a few months.

Some accounting systems distinguish between fixed and variable costs because this helps management make decisions about cost control, production volume, and pricing. Variable costs are usually controllable at the plant level, while fixed costs aren't. Hence, a plant manager can be held responsible for controlling variable, but not fixed, costs. Sometimes a special order at an off time can be taken at less than full price but more than variable cost to smooth production schedules and absorb fixed costs. Occasionally a company will purposely price an item below its full production cost but above its variable cost because this helps pay fixed costs without absorbing capacity needed for more profitable items.

The fixed- versus variable-cost breakdown can also lead to more sophisticated business analysis. It determines a product's marginal income, which is revenue less variable costs. Marginal income is used to determine contribution margins for each of several products. This can lead to sophisticated techniques for determining the best product mix, regional contributions, and other aids to long-term planning.

Controllable and Non-Controllable Costs

Some systems distinguish between controllable and non-controllable costs. The difference may be as simple as the difference between fixed and variable costs, as defined in the last section. It might also depend on corporate structure and the decision-making power held by different people in management. Or it might depend on the nature of the business. Table 5-3 is an example of how management might fix a production manager's budget by distinguishing between controllable and non-controllable costs. In this hypothetical example, the production manager doesn't purchase or store materials and is not responsible for indirect labor or maintenance.

Table 5-3: Controllable and Non-controllable Costs Budget

(Production Budget)

	January	February	March	April
Controllable costs:				
Direct labor	3,000.00	3,750.00	6,000.00	4,500.00
Plant supplies	150.00	187.50	300.00	225.00
Miscellaneous	50.00	50.00	50.00	50.00
Subtotal	3,200.00	3,987.50	6,350.00	4,775.00
Non-controllable costs:				
Direct materials	17,000.00	21,250.00	34,000.00	25,500.00
Indirect labor	1,500.00	1,500.00	1,500.00	1,500.00
Maintenence	500.00	500.00	500.00	500.00
Equipment depreciation	350.00	350.00	350.00	350.00
Utilities	250.00	255.00	260.00	265.00
Insurance	200.00	200.00	200.00	200.00
Building depreciation	100.00	100.00	100.00	100.00
Property taxes	75.00	75.00	75.00	75.00
Subtotal	19,975.00	24,230.00	36,985.00	28,490.00
Cost of goods	23,175.00	28,217.50	43,335.00	33,265.00

Here again, the spreadsheet manipulation is obviously simple. Reshuffling rows and changing headings give us a new format for the same basic budget. That, of course, is one of the best reasons for putting the budget into the spreadsheet model in the first place. More than one manager uses the microcomputer spreadsheet to reshuffle the same simple set of numbers to meet the demands of several different reporting formats.

Table 5-4 presents the plant manager's budget in a system that distinguishes between controllable and non-controllable costs. The plant manager is responsible for the production manager's performance as well as that of the support staff; therefore, more of the production costs are treated as controllable costs.

Table 5-4 still saves the plant manager from responsibility for material costs. Presumably the assembly process is so simple that waste and scrap are irrelevant, and another department purchases and stores assembly components. Otherwise, the plant manager would have to control direct material costs.

Comparing the models for Tables 5-3 and 5-4 shows how much this kind of budget depends on the specific situation. Controllable and non-controllable costs are not necessarily the same as fixed and variable costs. A restaurant chain, for example, budgets local unit managers for "controllable costs" that include rent, labor, promotion,

Table 5-4: Alternate Controllable and Non-controllable Costs Budget

(Plant Budget)

	January	February	March	April
Controllable costs:				
Direct labor	3,000.00	3,750.00	6,000.00	4,500.00
Indirect labor	1,500.00	1,500.00	1,500.00	1,500.00
Maintenence	500.00	500.00	500.00	500.00
Utilities	250.00	255.00	260.00	265.00
Plant supplies	150.00	187.50	300.00	225.00
Miscellaneous	50.00	50.00	50.00	50.00
Subtotal	5,450.00	6,242.50	8,610.00	7,040.00
Non-controllable costs:				
Direct materials	17,000.00	21,250.00	34,000.00	25,500.00
Equipment depreciation	350.00	350.00	350.00	350.00
Insurance	200.00	200.00	200.00	200.00
Building depreciation	100.00	100.00	100.00	100.00
Property taxes	75.00	75.00	75.00	75.00
Subtotal	17,725.00	21,975.00	34,725.00	26,225.00
Cost of goods	23,175.00	28,217.50	43,335.00	33,265.00

and maintenance but don't include food purchases or utilities. The owners say individual units can't control their food costs because the purchases are made by the head office, and because shipment amounts are determined by a formula based on daily sales; they can't control their utilities because usage is determined by hours, daily sales volume, and local rates. So the controllable costs don't include the major variable cost item (food purchases) and do include the major fixed costs item (rent).

Standard Costs

Some budgets are based on standard production costs. The standard cost of production consists of standard cost of materials, standard quantity of materials, standard cost of direct labor, and standard hours of direct labor. A standard cost of overhead is based on production levels measured in direct labor hours worked or some other convenient indicator. Overhead can be divided into fixed overhead and variable overhead, each of which is supposed to have a standard cost.

Standard cost budgets lend themselves to spreadsheet computer applications. In these budgets, production costs are the product of multiplying projected unit production volume by the standard cost of each unit, including variable overhead, and adding standard fixed overhead. This kind of operation is simple with the spreadsheet.

Standard cost systems must track the difference between expected standard costs and actual production costs, noting the causes of whatever difference occurs. Normally, standard costs are often updated. If the standard cost of an input is $1.00 per pound, and price increases move that up to $1.10, then the price increase is recorded as the cause of a variation from standard, and the standard is revised to the higher price. This is also quite simple with any of the commercial spreadsheet programs.

The Customized Budget

There are no fixed rules for setting up even a simple cost center budget. Each one should be customized to match the exact needs of the situation. Look at what your budget should be doing for you and set it up whichever way seems most useful. The examples here should give you some idea of how many different ways you can budget a single operation.

Complex budgeting systems can be built as combinations of related simple systems. Most spreadsheet application languages allow you to budget in convenient units such as departments or groups and then to consolidate all the units in a combined corporate budget. Use your tools well.

Spreadsheets and Budgets

The cost center budgets above show how simply and naturally the spreadsheet tools and formats work with the normal process of budgeting. Most of the formulas involved are quite simple, and totals are added up in a straightforward manner.

Budget Variance

Variance is the frequently forgotten other half of budgeting. Without ways of tracking results and of seeing the difference between budgeted and actual results, budgeting is little more than an academic exercise. Variance is the difference between budgeted and actual: for example, between actual sales and budgeted sales, between actual direct labor and budgeted direct labor or between actual costs and budgeted costs. Variance analysis looks at what caused a difference, and good management looks at what that means to the business.

Many businesses, especially the small, entrepreneurial kinds, ignore or forget the other half of budgeting. Budgets are proposed, discussed, accepted, and forgotten. Sometimes, even when a budget is strictly followed, business might have been better if variance analysis had highlighted some special problems or opportunities. It might have shown rising costs, for example, of a material component that could have been replaced easily with a cheaper one. Or rising maintenance costs that could have been reduced economically by new equipment or a new process. By highlighting changes and problems, variance analysis makes finding a solution more likely.

Variance analysis ranges from simple and straightforward to sophisticated and complex. Some cost-accounting systems separate variances into many different types and categories. Sometimes a single result can be broken down into many different variances, both positive and negative. The most sophisticated systems separate to great detail unit and price factors on materials, hours worked, cost per hour on direct labor, and fixed and variable overhead variances. Though difficult, this kind of analysis can be invaluable in a complex business.

The example used in Tables 5-5 and 5-6 is relatively simple. It was done almost instantaneously on a spreadsheet program. Rather than break variance into many different components, it gives a manager an instant reading on exactly what went differently than planned in the budget.

Table 5-5 presents hypothetical actual results for the period that was budgeted in Table 5-1. Please refer to the original budget in Table 5-1.

Table 5-5: Simple Cost Center Budget Actual Results

	January	February	March	April
Direct costs:				
Units produced	193.00	234.00	409.00	327.00
Direct materials	17,543.00	21,027.00	38,119.00	24,603.00
Direct labor	2,857.00	3,659.00	6,034.00	4,171.00
Subtotal	20,400.00	24,686.00	44,153.00	28,774.00
Factory overhead				
Indirect labor	1,500.00	1,740.00	1,620.00	1,500.00
Maintenence	104.00	302.00	897.00	55.00
Equipment depreciation	350.00	350.00	350.00	350.00
Utilities	243.00	247.00	281.00	257.00
Insurance	200.00	200.00	200.00	200.00
Plant supplies	112.00	119.00	248.00	209.00
Building depreciation	100.00	100.00	100.00	100.00
Property taxes	75.00	75.00	75.00	75.00
Miscellaneous	29.95	83.50	19.50	77.00
Subtotal	2,713.95	3,216.50	3,790.50	2,823.00
Cost of goods	23,113.95	27,902.50	47,943.50	31,597.00

Looking at Table 5-5 means little without comparison to the original budget. The format is the same, and the numbers are in the same order of magnitude. But few readers actually refer back to Table 5-1 to compare the original to the actual. Unfortunately, many businesses also forget to compare the original to the actual. Especially if business is going well—the operation shows a profit, and cash flow is satisfactory—comparisons with the original budget are made poorly or not at all.

Table 5-6 shows what really happened. It was produced by subtracting the actual results from the budget numbers, leaving a negative number when the actual was lower and a positive when the actual was higher. Those, of course, are the variances. The spreadsheet program should make this operation a matter of setting up a table and subtracting.

Table 5-6: Simple Cost Center Budget Variance Analysis

	January	February	March	April
Direct costs:				
Units produced	(7.00)	(16.00)	9.00	27.00
Direct materials	543.00	(223.00)	4,119.00	(897.00)
Direct labor	(143.00)	(91.00)	34.00	(329.00)
Subtotal	400.00	(314.00)	4,153.00	(1,226.00)
Factory overhead				
Indirect labor	-	240.00	120.00	-
Maintenence	(396.00)	(198.00)	397.00	(445.00)
Equipment depreciation	-	-	-	-
Utilities	(7.00)	(8.00)	21.00	(8.00)
Insurance	-	-	-	-
Plant supplies	(38.00)	(68.50)	(52.00)	(16.00)
Building depreciation	-	-	-	-
Property taxes	-	-	-	-
Miscellaneous	(20.05)	33.50	(30.50)	27.00
Subtotal	(461.05)	(1.00)	455.50	(442.00)
Cost of goods	(61.05)	(315.00)	4,608.50	(1,668.00)

The calc programs are getting better all the time, and most of the newer offerings—Lotus 1-2-3, Multiplan, SuperCalc 3, VisiCalc Advanced, etc.—now have consolidation routines that will let you subtract actual results from budgeted results if both tables are in the same format. The results are the variances. MicroPlan's tables module serves the same function. Without this routine, you must put both budgeted and actual results into the same model and then subtract the actual from the budgeted by writing the formulas row by row.

According to this table of results, the total cost of goods was less than budgeted during three of the four months and more than budgeted during one month. The negative variances (in parentheses) are good news because they mean you didn't spend as much as you budgeted yourself. The positive variance is cost that went over budget. The largest single variance was the positive $4,000 variance in materials in March.

Looking at the table, already the manager is asking some very important questions:

— Why was production different from scheduled?
— Why was direct material cost so high in March?
— Why the overtime for indirect labor?

The variance table provides management with a lot of significant information. Without this data, some of those important questions might have gone unasked. The relationship between different items—is the high maintenance cost in March related to the higher production volume, for example—might have never been discussed.

Variance analysis is still incomplete, however, because it is hard to tell whether costs matched standard costs per unit. Since production schedules weren't met, variances might be caused simply by lower unit volume. Management probably wants to know the results per unit.

Table 5-7 shows how the direct materials and labor costs differed from the standard costs, which were used to build the budget in Table 5-1.

Table 5-7: More Detailed Variance Analysis

Part I
Simple Cost Center Budget
Standard Unit Direct Costs

	January	February	March	April
Direct materials per unit	85.00	85.00	85.00	85.00
Direct labor per unit	15.00	15.00	15.00	15.00
Direct costs per unit	100.00	100.00	100.00	100.00

Part II
Actual Results
Unit Direct Costs

	January	February	March	April
Units produced	193.00	234.00	409.00	327.00
Direct materials	90.90	89.86	93.20	75.24
Direct labor	14.80	15.64	14.75	12.76
Subtotal	105.70	105.50	107.95	87.99

Part III
Actual Results
Direct Cost Variances

	January	February	March	April
Units produced	(7.00)	(16.00)	9.00	27.00
Direct materials	5.90	4.86	8.20	(9.76)
Direct labor	(0.20)	0.64	(0.25)	(2.24)
Subtotal	5.70	5.50	7.95	(12.01)

The presentation in Part III of Table 5-7 makes the variances easier to read. Direct material costs were higher on a per-unit basis than expected, while direct labor costs were slightly lower than expected. A still more detailed analysis would look at whether material costs were higher because greater quantities were used or because material prices changed. Labor costs were lower because fewer labor hours were used than budgeted or because each labor hour cost less than budgeted.

The per-unit breakdown is produced by the spreadsheet program. Total cost of each item per month is divided by the number of units produced in that month.

Table 5-8: Single Product Profit Center Budget

	January	February	March	April
Sales:				
(units)	180.00	250.00	300.00	350.00
Value	45,000.00	62,500.00	75,000.00	87,500.00
Direct costs:				
(units)	200.00	250.00	400.00	300.00
Direct materials	17,000.00	21,250.00	34,000.00	25,500.00
Direct labor	3,000.00	3,750.00	6,000.00	4,500.00
Subtotal	20,000.00	25,000.00	40,000.00	30,000.00
Factory overhead				
Indirect labor	1,500.00	1,500.00	1,500.00	1,500.00
Maintenence	500.00	500.00	500.00	500.00
Equipment depreciation	350.00	350.00	350.00	350.00
Utilities	250.00	255.00	260.00	265.00
Insurance	200.00	200.00	200.00	200.00
Plant supplies	150.00	187.50	300.00	225.00
Building depreciation	100.00	100.00	100.00	100.00
Property taxes	75.00	75.00	75.00	75.00
Miscellaneous	50.00	50.00	50.00	50.00
Subtotal	3,175.00	3,217.50	3,335.00	3,265.00
Cost of goods	23,175.00	28,217.50	43,335.00	33,265.00
Corrected C.o.G. Sold	20,857.50	28,217.50	32,501.25	38,809.17
Gross Margin	24,142.50	34,282.50	42,498.75	48,690.83
Less:				
General & Administrativ	4,500.00	6,250.00	7,500.00	8,750.00
Marketing & Sales	6,750.00	9,375.00	11,250.00	13,125.00
Interest	-	-	-	-
Taxes	5,157.00	7,463.00	9,499.50	10,726.33
Net Profit	7,735.50	11,194.50	14,249.25	16,089.50

	January	February	March	April
Sales:				
(units)	180.00	250.00	300.00	350.00
Value	45,000.00	62,500.00	75,000.00	87,500.00

Variance analysis can go into much greater detail. In the example above, the gross variance is $400, as follows:

Budgeted cost:	$20,000 (200 units * $100 per unit)
Actual cost:	$20,400 (193 units * $105.70 per unit)
Gross variance:	$ 400 unfavorable

This gross variance can be broken down as follows:

Production variance:	$ 700 favorable ((200 − 193)*100)
Material variance:	$1,139 unfavorable ((85 − 90.9)*193)
Labor variance:	$ 39 favorable ((15 − 14.8)*193)
Total (gross)	$ 400 unfavorable

This sort of presentation gives a manager a better view of the causes of the unfavorable variance. In this case, the culprit is higher material costs per unit. The manager now knows what the trouble is and can look for a reaction. Maybe the standard cost should be raised because material costs have risen, and maybe purchasing can improve its purchase prices.

Profit Center Budget

The simple cost center budget can turn into a profit center budget. But the cost budget remains. A sales budget projects unit sales, and an administrative budget projects general and administrative expenses (commonly known as G&A), marketing expenses, and sales expenses. There are different ways to treat interest, taxes, and net profit.

The profit center budget resembles a full company budget. It includes sales, cost of goods sold, G&A, and the other normal components of corporate income. A profit center budget looks a lot like a company income statement made in advance; it is, in fact, quite similar to the "Pro Forma Income Statement," which will be discussed in detail in Chapter 7.

Table 5-8 presents a profit center budget built for the same model business presented in the other sections of this chapter.

Much of the profit center budget's construction is like that of the cost center budget already presented. But there are some important differences worth noting.

The sales budget is based on a sales forecast much like the forecasts discussed in Chapter Four. Usually, the sales forecast comes before the production budget is established (in this case, in Table 5-1). Production is set to guarantee inventory for sales and a comfortable inventory level. Notice that March production builds inventory for April, when production levels are down because of vacations (a hypothetical situation).

Production costs are taken straight from the cost center budget presented earlier. These run from direct costs to the sum, called cost of goods in Table 5-1.

The "Corrected C.o.G. Sold" line makes an accounting conversion from the sum of production costs incurred to the cost of goods sold. Without this line, the costs of goods built for inventory look like costs of goods sold, and profits are artificially cut. This is easiest to see in the comparison between March and April: Without the proper accounting, March's 300 units would appear to have been budgeted at much more than April's 350 units ($144.45 per unit in March compared to $95.04 per unit in April, if units sold are divided into total production costs). After the numbers are properly converted, units sold in March are supposed to cost $108.34 each, while those sold in April cost $110.88 each. The latter are slightly more expensive because, since production was higher in March, fixed costs are spread over more units.

The formula for conversion, in this example, is quite simple. The corrected cost of goods sold is equal to

(PRODUCTION COSTS)/(UNITS PRODUCED)*(UNITS SOLD)

A sophisticated accounting system might offer some refinements to this formula. But this formula is practical, simple, robust, and simple to use on any spreadsheet formula. It gives a very useful estimate.

Now, look at some other profit center items:

Gross margin is defined by most accountants as sales less cost of goods sold. This is a convenient number for judging the profitability of a business. If the gross margin is less than 40 percent of sales, most business analysts say, there is either some very special type of business going on or there is a business facing very low profitability. In most healthy businesses, gross margins run 50 percent or more of sales. Otherwise, there is little room left for additional expenses, taxes, and profits.

General and administrative expenses are set in this budget example at 10 percent of sales. In most real budget situations, they would have been budgeted item by item, as the production costs were. The budget would include salaries for key people, support salaries, and additional budget items. For example, this part of an actual start-up business plan had the following items in its general and administrative expenses budget:

CEO (salary)
VP Finance (salary)
VP Administration (salary)
    Office staff
    Office supplies
    Equipment lease
    Rent
    Travel
    Miscellaneous
Total

Since the procedures for building this budget are so much like those already illustrated for the production costs budget, the total in our example was simply estimated at 10 percent of total sales, a reasonable average figure.

Marketing and sales expenses were estimated for this example at 15 percent of total sales. As with the general and administrative expenses, these would normally be built on a cost budget structure but are estimated here at a normal level. The sales and marketing budget of an actual business plan includes the following items:

VP Marketing (salary)
- Salesforce (salaries)
- Commissions
- Promotion/advertising
- Staff
- Rent
- Travel
- Order entry
- Product management
- Technical support
- Miscellaneous

Marketing and sales total

For a going business, interest expenditures can be estimated quite well using past results and estimated balance of money owed. For this example, however, interest expenditures were estimated at zero.

Taxes and net profits are simple with the spreadsheet program. Taxes are estimated at 40 percent of profits before taxes. Net profit is equal to gross margin less general and administrative expenses, less marketing and sales expenses, less interest and taxes.

The result is a profit center budget. Estimated expenses are subtracted from estimated sales to produce an estimated profit per month. Now the profit center has a set of targets and goals. If the budgeting process is successful, the people responsible for meeting the budget believe in the targets, in the goals, and in the chances of successfully turning the budget business into actual results.

Cash Budget

The cash budget, also called cash-flow projection or pro forma cash-flow statement, is another of those business tools that seems as if it were made for a spreadsheet program. Without the computer, a cash-flow management system requires what feels like endless struggling over green accounting paper. Each change in one week will affect the starting and ending balances in all following weeks. That, in turn, might change the financing requirements, which will change the interest payments, which will change profits, which will change tax payments, and so on. It's a lot easier with a computer.

Cash, of course, is by a good margin the most important commodity a manager manages. Cash management is the first and most important task without which nothing else is going to work. Paychecks must be made out, and creditors must be paid, or the business won't go on. If the cash budget works, management has time to borrow funds when needed to cover the business during a dry period; if the cash budget doesn't work, a dry period can kill a going business very quickly, even a business for which dry periods are a normal part of the business cycle, not a sign of trouble.

The cash budget projects income and expenditures at the time they actually affect the cash flow rather than at the time they show up on the books. In normal business operations, there can be very important differences between the two times.

Take a single product as an example. Materials are ordered two months in advance, are received when ordered, and are paid for 30 days later. Direct labor is applied in production and is paid for during the same pay period. A product is produced and goes either into inventory or to a customer. A sale is recorded when the product is shipped, and shipping costs are incurred at the same time. If 30 days elapse since receipt of the material, the material is supposedly paid for already. Shipping costs are likely to be paid when incurred. Meanwhile, an invoice goes along with the shipment to the customer, and payment is probably expected in 30 days. Sometimes payments are received in 90 days; when a small business ships goods to a large business on which it depends for significant volume, it will often wait 45 to 90 days for its money.

The income and expenditure related to a given product follow a cycle. This is illustrated in a hypothetical single product case in Table 5-9. The product is produced and sold in February. Materials were ordered in January but are delivered in February and are paid for in March. Meanwhile, labor, overhead, and management costs are paid in February, the month the product is manufactured. Marketing costs are incurred in February, the month of the sale, but are actually paid in March, 30 days later. Although the product is shipped, and the sale recorded in February, payment actually is made in April.

Here we see the importance of cash flow. The business made a healthy $75 on $250 of sales, a 30-percent profit. But without a working cash budget and the management that goes with it, this business might have gone sour. At the end of March, it was $175 behind in its payments.

The proper cash management solves the problem. This company should borrow money in February and March to carry it over until payments come in April. Even at 20 percent per annum, interest on $200 for two months is less than $10.

Cash budgets follow this same logic. They predict the revenue stream and the expenditure stream. They plan for periods when expenditures exceed revenues.

Cash Budget Leads and Lags

The key to the cash budget is timing. Table 5-9 shows how important timing can be. A 60-day revenue lag turns a profitable operation into a potential disaster.

Table 5-9: Single Product Cash Budget Example

	January	February	March	April
Sales:	-	250.00	-	-
Revenue:	-	-	-	250.00
Expenditures:				
Direct materials	-	-	85.00	-
Direct labor	-	15.00	-	-
Mfg. overhead	-	12.50	-	-
General & administ	-	25.00	-	-
Marketing/sales	-	-	37.50	-
subtotal	-	52.50	122.50	-
Net cash results	-	(52.50)	(122.50)	250.00
Cumulative cash	-	(52.50)	(175.00)	75.00

Timing is built into the cash budget as a revenue lag. The revenue lag is the amount of time that passes, on the average, between making a sale and receiving payment. Most small businesses offer their customers 30-day credit and a discount for paying cash within 10 days. If all customers pay within the allotted 30 days, the business's finance manager is happy, and the revenue lag is 30 days. Unfortunately, that's unusual. In most businesses, 45 days is about average, and 60 days is not uncommon.

With just a bit of ingenuity, you can build a revenue lag into your spreadsheet program cash flow. Many of the spreadsheet packages, built for financial analysis, include commands to "lag" a row or a column by a given number of payment periods. In Table 5-9, for example, the computer was told to produce revenue by lagging sales two periods. In the simpler spreadsheets, you can still tell the computer that the entry in one row is equal to the entry in another row a couple of columns back.

Even the trickier lags, such as 45 or 75 days, are possible. Depending on which spreadsheet language you're using, you may have to be more or less creative. But a 45-day lag, for example, can be produced by setting up one row with a one-month lag and another with a two-month lag, by dividing both by two, and then by adding them together. This goes as follows:

```
Row 1 = sales(month)
Row 2 = sales(month-1)
Row 3 = sales(month-2)
Row 4 = .5*(Row 2 + Row 3)
```

Row 4, in this case, contains the projected revenues for sales in row 1 with a 45-day lag. The months should be running across the columns.

A "lead" is the opposite case. A small business might find itself forced to pay cash for some key material required in the manufacturing cost. The cash leaves the business at a given time, say one month, before the product is sold. This means the spreadsheet has to take the estimated materials per units sold and accelerate payment to one month ahead of the sale. This is called a lead. To set one up, many spreadsheet languages provide a simple command, some require a formula that pulls information from the following column, and some have other ways.

A Model Cash Budget

All of this comes together in the cash budget. All items in the original budget are adjusted for the actual cash effect of each. The revenue lag is estimated. Accounts payable probably has a lag of 30 days. Tax payments are estimated by the dates the taxes will actually be paid, regardless of when the obligation to pay starts. Materials payments are figured for the days of actual payment, regardless of when the bills are due. The results look something like Table 5-10, a sample cash budget.

Table 5-10: Model Cash Budget

	January	February	March	April
Sales:				
(units)	180.00	250.00	300.00	350.00
Value	45,000.00	62,500.00	75,000.00	87,500.00
Revenue:				
Sales	-	-	45,000.00	62,500.00
Other	100,000.00	-	-	-
Subtotal	100,000.00	-	45,000.00	62,500.00
Direct costs:				
(units)	200.00	250.00	400.00	300.00
Direct materials	-	17,000.00	21,250.00	34,000.00
Direct labor	3,000.00	3,750.00	6,000.00	4,500.00
Subtotal	3,000.00	20,750.00	27,250.00	38,500.00
Factory overhead				
Indirect labor	1,500.00	1,500.00	1,500.00	1,500.00
Maintenence	500.00	500.00	500.00	500.00
Equipment depreciation	-	-	-	-
Utilities	-	250.00	255.00	260.00
Insurance	-	200.00	200.00	200.00
Plant supplies	-	150.00	187.50	300.00
Building depreciation	-	-	-	-
Property taxes	-	-	-	300.00
Miscellaneous	50.00	50.00	50.00	50.00
Subtotal	2,050.00	2,650.00	2,692.50	3,110.00
Total production	5,050.00	23,400.00	29,942.50	41,610.00
General & Administrativ	4,500.00	6,250.00	7,500.00	8,750.00
Marketing & Sales	6,750.00	9,375.00	11,250.00	13,125.00
Interest	-	-	-	-
Taxes	-	-	-	22,119.50
Capital expenditure	-	-	-	-
Total expenditure	16,300.00	39,025.00	48,692.50	85,604.50
Net cash results	83,700.00	(39,025.00)	(3,692.50)	(23,104.50)
Cumulative cash results	83,700.00	44,675.00	40,982.50	17,878.00

Note how the company in Table 5-10 solved the problem of financing revenue lags: Did you see the extra $100,000 in January as "other" revenue? That's capital, equity capital investment to get the business going.

Now, the cash budget begins to get interesting. What if you can't get $100,000 in equity investment? How about a bank loan to finance receivables—Table 5-11 shows what happens when a bank puts in the financing. No one has to put up $100,000, and no one has to sell a piece of the company to get that $100,000, either (for the moment, we'll put aside what the bank says about lending that kind of money to a company with no equity). But the change from equity to bank financing changes the cash flow (and the profits) by adding a new expenditure, interest payments.

Table 5-11: Model Cash Budget

	January	February	March	April
Sales:				
(units)	180.00	250.00	300.00	350.00
Value	45,000.00	62,500.00	75,000.00	87,500.00
Revenue:				
Sales	-	-	45,000.00	62,500.00
Other	100,000.00	-	-	-
Subtotal	100,000.00	-	45,000.00	62,500.00
Direct costs:				
(units)	200.00	250.00	400.00	300.00
Direct materials	-	17,000.00	21,250.00	34,000.00
Direct labor	3,000.00	3,750.00	6,000.00	4,500.00
Subtotal	3,000.00	20,750.00	27,250.00	38,500.00
Factory overhead				
Indirect labor	1,500.00	1,500.00	1,500.00	1,500.00
Maintenence	500.00	500.00	500.00	500.00
Equipment depreciation	-	-	-	-
Utilities	-	250.00	255.00	260.00
Insurance	-	200.00	200.00	200.00
Plant supplies	-	150.00	187.50	300.00
Building depreciation	-	-	-	-
Property taxes	-	-	-	300.00
Miscellaneous	50.00	50.00	50.00	50.00
Subtotal	2,050.00	2,650.00	2,692.50	3,110.00
Total production	5,050.00	23,400.00	29,942.50	41,610.00
General & Administrativ	4,500.00	6,250.00	7,500.00	8,750.00
Marketing & Sales	6,750.00	9,375.00	11,250.00	13,125.00
Interest	2,000.00	2,000.00	2,000.00	2,000.00
Taxes	-	-	-	19,719.50
Capital expenditure	-	-	-	-
Total expenditure	18,300.00	41,025.00	50,692.50	85,204.50
Net cash results	81,700.00	(41,025.00)	(5,692.50)	(22,704.50)
Cumulative cash results	81,700.00	40,675.00	34,982.50	12,278.00

Note the difference in Table 5-11. Revenue looks the same, with the same $100,000 in the first month; but there are interest payments now and a $100,000 debt that must be paid back eventually to the bank. Profits will be reduced by the amount of interest paid, and taxes are also reduced by 40 percent of the amount of interest paid (assuming a 40-percent tax rate, remember?).

By now, you are beginning to see how many different ways you can adjust the cash flow once you have the numbers on your computer screen. Now, let's look again at this borrowing business.

Table 5-11 is unrealistic—few, if any, banks will lend $100,000 to a new business without equity capital. So maybe a realistic scenario is required. Let's assume:

1. There is $30,000 in equity investment; and
2. the bank will finance up to 70 percent of accounts receivable.

Then we have the situation shown in Table 5-12, with a $30,000 equity payment at the beginning and accounts receivable financing as needed to cover necessary payments. Interest payments are smaller, and profits (and taxes) are higher.

Table 5-12: Model Cash Budget C

	January	February	March	April
Sales:				
(units)	180.00	250.00	300.00	350.00
Value	45,000.00	62,500.00	75,000.00	87,500.00
Revenue:				
Sales	-	-	45,000.00	62,500.00
Other	30,000.00	31,500.00	10,000.00	15,000.00
Subtotal	30,000.00	31,500.00	55,000.00	77,500.00
Direct costs:				
(units)	200.00	250.00	400.00	300.00
Direct materials	-	17,000.00	21,250.00	34,000.00
Direct labor	3,000.00	3,750.00	6,000.00	4,500.00
Subtotal	3,000.00	20,750.00	27,250.00	38,500.00
Factory overhead				
Indirect labor	1,500.00	1,500.00	1,500.00	1,500.00
Maintenence	500.00	500.00	500.00	500.00
Equipment depreciation	-	-	-	-
Utilities	-	250.00	255.00	260.00
Insurance	-	200.00	200.00	200.00
Plant supplies	-	-	-	-
Building depreciation	-	-	-	-
Property taxes	-	-	-	300.00
Miscellaneous	50.00	50.00	50.00	50.00
Subtotal	2,050.00	2,500.00	2,505.00	2,810.00
Total production	5,050.00	23,250.00	29,755.00	41,310.00
General & Administrativ	4,500.00	6,250.00	7,500.00	8,750.00
Marketing & Sales	6,750.00	9,375.00	11,250.00	13,125.00
Interest	-	630.00	830.00	1,130.00
Taxes	-	-	-	21,535.50
Capital expenditure	-	-	-	-
Total expenditure	16,300.00	39,505.00	49,335.00	85,850.50
Net cash results	13,700.00	(8,005.00)	5,665.00	(8,350.50)
Cumulative cash results	13,700.00	5,695.00	11,360.00	3,009.50

Of course, there are some tricks built into the spreadsheet. For example, a row not shown on the table adds up the accounts receivable and multiplies by .7 to watch the total financing available:

ACCOUNTS RECEIVABLE = SALES (COL − 1) + SALES(COL − 2)
MAXIMUM FINANCING = .7* (ACCOUNTS RECEIVABLE)
= .7*(SALES(COL − 1) + SALES(COL − 2))

Another row, not shown on the table, keeps track of the financing balance:

BALANCE = BALANCE(COL = 1) + NEW FINANCING

And the following holds for all columns except the first:

NEW FINANCING = OTHER REVENUE

With this done, the interest payment can be calculated automatically. We assume a 2-percent-per-month financing charge.

INTEREST = .02*BALANCE

Depending on the size of the spreadsheet system, you can run the interest payments back into the pro forma income statement to calculate the new tax payment due in April. It will be smaller by an amount equal to the tax rate times the interest payments. In this case

TAX = (PREVIOUS TAX) − (.4*(830 + 630)) = 21,535.50

And now we have an on-file cash budget that can be called off a memory disk at any time for review and update. Many small companies are now maintaining their cash budgets using a spreadsheet system, updated daily, weekly, or monthly. With this kind of system, the manager can get a look at the cash position almost instantly, and the finance people can keep the cash position and the financing plan entirely up-to-date at almost all times. In many spreadsheet systems, managers can access the budget and the actual figures at the same time, subtract the budget from the actual, and see the variance between the two. In short, cash management is easier and more effective.

SIX

Investment Analysis

You've just inherited a lot of money, had the necessary celebrations, bought the new house and the Ferrari you've always wanted, and you still have a lot left over for investment. What do you do with it? The stock market is obvious. Banks are competing for high-yield interest deposits. You could go into real estate or venture capital investment or . . . it's time for investment analysis.

Or you've been promoted to head of your department at work, and you need the company to put $100,000 into new equipment. You're sure it will save twice that much over the next five years. How do you show your boss? That involves capital budgeting, which is a variation of investment analysis.

Despite the occasional stroke of genius, which is usually just good luck, the business of investment analysis is one that involves a lot of hard calculations. The range of available investments makes a market as varied as your local supermarket—from savings accounts to money markets to stock markets to real estate to oil wells to tax shelters to who knows what else. The careful investor has to look hard and well at the alternatives and compare the value of each in terms of cost, apparent probable return, and level of risk.

Investment analysis is a tool for sorting through these different possibilities, for looking at each objectively. Its goal is to quantify cost, return, and risk in some objective way. Once you have the alternatives and their proper numbers, then you can truly compare.

But there is a catch. Investment analysis quantifies probable future results—but no one is certain about the future. As with so many other analytical computer tools, investment analysis is one in which the numbers are objective and can be run by the system, but the heart of the analysis is plain guesswork. You still guess what will happen to the stock market, the real estate market, or whatever investment you are analyzing. Again, the computer and the spreadsheet program are beautiful for doing the numbers, but they are only as good as the guesses on which the numbers are based. The most sophisticated investment analysis—and Wall Street has hundreds of fancy analysts with expensive equipment for backup—is at best an educated guess.

Here, of course, is where your spreadsheet analysis comes in. Once again, the key to good guesswork is what we call scenario analysis or "what-if" games. After you run up a set of probable numbers on that real estate deal, ask yourself what happens if the whole market falls 15 percent, or if rents go down 20 percent, or if mortgages go up to 21 percent per year. The spreadsheet system is again ideal for this kind of double checking.

Principles of Investment Analysis

Different kinds of investments compete with each other for each investor's dollar. The jargon is at times baffling. But in the end, every investment should be measured by the cash that goes into it and the cash expected out of it, by the time it takes to get that cash out, and by the apparent risk involved. There are several standard investment measurements that attempt to incorporate one or more of these important concepts.

Cash In and Out

It seems simple: You measure an investment by the actual cash put into it and the cash taken out of it. But it isn't simple—many people often become confused after forgetting this very basic first principle.

Table 6-1 presents three hypothetical investments. Investment 1 is a real estate purchase, Investment 2 is a stock purchase, and Investment 3 is Hollywood speculation. Each is evaluated according to actual cash flow during the five presumed years of investment, *net of taxes*.

Table 6-1: Principle of Cash Analysis

	Year 1	Year 2	Year 3	Year 4	Year 5	Total
Cash analysis						
Investment 1	(50,000)	(1,200)	(800)	(400)	80,000	27,600
Investment 2	(50,000)	1,250	1,437	1,653	62,900	26,340
Investment 3	(25,000)	50,000				25,000

Investment 1 is the purchase of a rental house for $150,000. The down payment is $50,000, and the investor takes a $100,000 loan at 16 percent per annum, amortized over 15 years. Monthly cash flow is figured (using the spreadsheet) as follows.

Payment	(1,500.00)
Tax effect	750.00
Rent	675.00
Maintenance, etc.	(25.00)
Monthly net	(100.00)

The tax effect is the estimated amount of taxes the investor will save by investing in the house. It is caused by the fact that the interest component of the monthly payments is tax deductible; and the house, since it is being used as a business investment, can be depreciated, adding another deduction against taxes.

In year 5, the investor resells the house for $187,500 and the $100,000 loan is repaid, leaving $87,500 less assumed taxes (a 20-percent capital gains tax on $37,500, which would be $7,500), or $80,000.

Investment 2 is a stock market investment, 1,000 shares of stock at $50 per share. In year 2, the company produces earnings per share of $5 and dividends per share of $2.50, which result in $1.25 per share net of the investor's taxes on the income. Profits and dividends grow by 15 percent per year over the next few years, and the stocks are eventually sold for a profit, from which a 20-percent capital gains tax is deducted.

Investment 3 is a bit unusual. The investor bought ten $5,000 shares of a new B-grade movie, the producers of which offered financing shares to small investors. Though these shares cost a total of $50,000, the investor sheltered $50,000 from taxes and therefore saved $25,000 in tax money, so the net cash effect was only $25,000. The movie was a hit, so the return was $10,000 per share—which was taxable, so the net in the table is only $50,000 instead of $100,000.

Note that the treatment of these investments in Table 6-1 demonstrates the first principle of investment analysis: *Only the cash matters.* The real estate deal could have involved a house costing only $50,000 to one costing $250,000; if payments are the same, then the house price is irrelevant. If down payment is not required, the cost of a $100,000 house financed 30 years at 13.27 percent and the cost of a $250,000 house financed 30 years at 2.74 percent interest are essentially the same: $1,000 per month for 30 years. The full price tag is far less important than the interest rate. The cash effect is identical.

The Time Value of Money

Given a choice, most people would rather have $10 today than $10 next month. Most people would prefer $100,000 now to $100,000 next year. Most people, in fact, would prefer $100,000 now to $105,000 or even $110,000 next year. This choice reflects the time value of money.

Basically, a dollar today is worth more than a dollar a year from now. Money now is worth more than the same amount of money will be worth later. A while ago, when inflation was running at 10 percent per year, this was fairly obvious; money now will buy more goods than money later. But the principle of the time value of money is important even if there is no inflation. Money now gives you options now, flexibility now, and—even in a zero-inflation economy—interest earnings now, even if you don't spend it until next year.

The time value of money has been reflected through the decades in a theoretical "real interest rate," which is the going rate less inflation. Part of the interest you pay or the interest you receive is direct compensation for inflation; part is compensation for the time value of money. This second part is the real interest rate, which is often determined by estimating the current rate of inflation and by subtracting that from the current going rate of interest. If, for example, the rate of inflation in the United States runs about 2 to 3 percent while the prime rate (what banks charge their best customers) runs about 11 to 12 percent, then the real interest rate is nine percent. This is an unusually high rate of interest, by the way. Many experts blame it on uncertainty about future developments; uncertainty logically increases the time-value-of-money effect by increasing the relative value of money now instead of money later. But this is the subject of another kind of analysis.

Analysts adjust for the time value of money by discounting future cash flows at whatever rate they think is a fair estimate of time value. If that is 10 percent, then next year's cash flows are divided by 1.1. The following year's are divided by 1.21 (1.1×1.1), the next year's by 1.33 (1.21×1.1), and so on. The investments in Table 6-1 are discounted at a 10-percent rate in Table 6-2. Notice that, when they are discounted in this way, the relative attractiveness of one or another changes radically as you look at the totals column. Suddenly, the one that yields the least profit is the most attractive, because it yields that profit quickly. And the one that yields the most profit is least attractive, because you have to wait five years to get at that money.

Table 6-2: Discounted Cash Flow

(10 percent discount rate)

	Year 1	Year 2	Year 3	Year 4	Year 5	Total*
Investment 1	(50,000)	(1,091)	(661)	(301)	54,641	2,588
Investment 2	(50,000)	1,136	1,188	1,242	49,177	2,743
Investment 3	(25,000)	45,455				20,455

* Net Present Value

This discounted cash flow is called the present value, and the total is equivalent to the *net present value*. We'll have more to say about that in a bit, as we discuss different investment measurements and how to work them with a spreadsheet. The important point right now is that something must be done to account for the difference in the time the cash comes in.

Importance of Risk

The third important principle of investment analysis is that return should be proportionate to risk. More risk should yield more money. If you put $100 into a bank savings account, you're satisfied with $110 in a year. If you put $100 into a brother-in-law's latest invention, you want $1,000 back, because you figure that's worth risking $100 for. If you invest $100 on a sure-thing horse in a race, you're happy to get $150 back. If you bet on a long shot, you want a big payoff.

Good investment analysis respects risk. Professionals have some complex systems for measuring risk and for reflecting how risk affects their investment judgment. Unfortunately, there is no single accepted way to do this, nor are there any methodical background numbers like the NPV and IRR numbers for measuring return on investment.

For example, look at the comparison of different investments in Table 6-1 and the results of those investments in Table 6-2. The third investment seems the only possible alternative in this analysis.

But something is missing in the analysis. The third investment is very risky, and the numbers say nothing about that. What if the $50,000 is lost entirely? Are we weighing the fact that good investment analysis will lead us immediately to something as flaky as financing movies? No. Actually, we say that the difference in potential yields reflects the difference in risk. As we go on we'll suggest several ways to account for that very important difference: We may, for example, discount the third investment at 25 percent instead of 10 percent. In this case, its discounted total value is only $15,000 instead of more than $20,000. Or maybe it's so risky that we should discount it at 50 percent; then its final total is only $8,333. However we do it, we have to consider the difference in risk. We'll say a lot more about that later.

Measurements: the Investment Yardsticks

There are at least four standard measurements of return on investments. These are the simple ROI, the payback period method, the net present value, and the internal rate of return. All are used by different people to compare different investments. Some people will argue that one or another is better, but we say that the two simpler ones (ROI and payback period) are not as good. We'll show you some spreadsheet models, however, for all of them.

The Simple ROI

Return on investment is an extremely confusing phrase because it means so many things to different people. It's one of those phrases that people recognize and define for themselves.

Despite some ambiguities, ROI is used quite often to measure corporate performance. Managers are judged by the ROI on projects they manage; whole divisions of large companies are rated by ROI. This all leads to lengthy debates about the terms, definitions, and accounting systems.

In its simplest form, ROI is return on capital invested. The cash-only principle applies, and return is presented in percentage form. A $50,000 bond yielding $5,000 per year has a 10-percent ROI. A business worth $2 million producing $200,000 profits per year has a 10-percent ROI.

Table 6-3 presents simple ROI for the investments in Table 6-1. To calculate ROI on VisiCalc, simply insert and label the required extra rows and then have each cell take the cell above it as a percentage of the initial investment. For example, cell C6 is

$$-100*(C5/B5)$$

Then replicate C6 through D6 . . . G6 to get the ROI on Investment 1. Do the same for Investments 2 and 3.

Table 6-3: Simple ROI

	A	B	C	D	E	F	G
1		Year	Year	Year	Year	Year	
2		1	2	3	4	5	Total
3		---------	---------	---------	---------	---------	---------
4							
5	Investment 1	(50,000)	(1,200)	(800)	(400)	80,000	27,600
6	ROI		-2.4	-1.6	-0.8	160.0	55.2
7	Investment 2	(50,000)	1,250	1,437	1,653	62,900	26,340
8	ROI		2.5	2.9	3.3	144.0	52.7
9	Investment 3	(25,000)	50,000				25,000
10	ROI		100.0				100.0

Of course, there are a lot of reasons that ROI is not a good objective measurement. It doesn't consider the time value of money, and it doesn't consider risk. Furthermore, it leads to very difficult ambiguities about the value of the investment. For example, in determining the ROI on a manufacturing plant, should you consider the initial investment, the replacement value, or the price you'd get if you sold the plant? How do you handle depreciation on the investment? Which would you rather have for your $50,000—a $50,000 profit now or $10,000 per year for the rest of your life? The first sounds like a 100-percent ROI, and the second sounds like a 20-percent ROI.

On the other hand, ROI is a simple measurement that many people understand. When the ambiguities are cleared out by corporate definitions, it works reasonably well as a basis for comparison. So, while it may not be the best, it's probably the most common measurement.

The Payback Period

The payback period is another common, simple investment yardstick. Despite its many flaws, it is still a quite common corporate decision-making apparatus.

The payback period is the time it takes to repay an investment. A $1,000 investment that yields $100 per year pays itself back in 10 years.

VisiCalc and many other calcs have a true/false flag that's useful in setting up payback period analyses. We use it in Table 6-4. The initial investment is in cell B3. The yearly return estimate is in row 4, all across the row. The cumulative payback is in row 5, where the formula cumulates the total by adding each year's return to the previous year's total. Each cell in row 6 has a formula stating that the row 5 cumulative investment is equal to or greater than the cell B3 initial investment. For example, the cell C6 formula is

(C5=>(−1*B3))

Interestingly enough, VisiCalc and many other calcs return a TRUE if the statement is true and FALSE if it's false. So all you do for payback period is run that test across the row, and the first cell that comes up with a TRUE flag marks the year when payback is reached.

Table 6-4: Demonstrating Payback Period

	B	C	D	E	F	G	H
1	year	year	year	year	year	year	year
2	1	2	3	4	5	6	7
3Initial	-50000						
4Return		-2000	0	5000	15000	25000	30000
5Cum. return		-2000	-2000	3000	18000	43000	73000
6Payback?	FALSE	FALSE	FALSE	FALSE	FALSE	FALSE	TRUE

Simple? Yes. That's its virtue and its main drawback. It entirely ignores what happens after the initial payback. Some investments might barely pay themselves back, while others go on forever. Would you rather invest $1,000 to get $1010 the next year (payback is only one year) or get $200 per year for the next 20 years? Payback analysis says the first is the best. It isn't.

Net Present Value

The net present value measurement is one of the most effective and most respected. It is the sum of the discounted cash flow of an investment.

By summing the discounted cash flow, you consider all three of the principles of investment analysis. Your cash flow is based on cash only, the discount considers the time value of money, and the rate at which you discount should reflect the risk involved.

Spreadsheet application programs do this kind of analysis for you fairly easily. Some have discounted cash-flow analysis built right into the language, as a command given to apply a discount rate to a cash flow. MicroPlan does, Multiplan does, but

SuperCalc and VisiCalc don't (though their new, upgraded versions do). If yours doesn't, the formula for discounted cash value in the Nth year is

Value in Year N = Cash/((1 + Rate)raised to the N power)

or, in year 3 of Investment 1:

$$-661=(-800)/(1.1^{23})$$

The last entry, $(1.1^{2}3)$, means 1.1 raised to the third power, which is 1.1 multiplied by itself as follows:

$$1.1^{23}=1.1\times 1.1\times 1.1=1.21$$

Table 6-5 puts Tables 6-1 and 6-2 together to show you how to do this on VisiCalc, which doesn't have a built-in net present value function. SuperCalc works the same way. The key to this model is row 13, which contains an NPV function that we just built. The formula for cell C13 is

+B13/(1 + (B14/100))

This, combined with the discount rate input into cell B14, gives us the NPV number. When that's done, we replicate to cell F13 using B13 as a relative number (VisiCalc asks us this—just answer R when it lights up B13) and B14 as a NO CHANGE number. That gives us an NPV number all across that row.

Table 6-5: Net Present Value

	A	B	C	D	E	F	G
1	Model 6-3						
2							
3		Year	Year	Year	Year	Year	
4		1	2	3	4	5	Total
5		---------	---------	---------	---------	---------	---------
6	Investment 1	(50,000)	(1,200)	(800)	(400)	57,500	5,100
7	Investment 2	(50,000)	1,250	1,437	1,653	62,900	17,240
8	Investment 3	(25,000)	50,000				25,000
9	Investment 1	(50,000)	(1,091)	(661)	(301)	39,273	(12,779)
10	Investment 2	(50,000)	1,136	1,188	1,242	42,962	(3,473)
11	Investment 3	(25,000)	45,455				20,455
12							
13	NPV LINE	1.00	0.91	0.83	0.75	0.68	
14	DISCOUNT:	10.00					

The formula for cell D13 is

+C13/(1 + (B14/100))

This is part of the magic of the REPLICATE command.

Now, go back to row 9 and put in the discounted cash-flow numbers. Start with cell B9, and make that cell

+B6*B13

Then replicate from B9 to C9...F9, with B6 and B13 being relative and you have the discounted cash-flow number for Investment 1. Then replicate from B9 to B10 and B11, with B6 being RELATIVE and B13 being NO CHANGE. (You can't just replicate B9 into B10...F10 because the values get confused; try it and see what happens.) Then replicate from B10 to C10...F10, with all values being RELATIVE, and from B11 to C11...F11, again with all values being RELATIVE. Your TOTALS lines in VisiCalc are all like G9, which is

@SUM(B9...F9)

The totals in cells G9...G11 are NET PRESENT VALUES for each investment. The first two are negative, and the third is positive.

Table 6-5 is a self-teacher of the idea of discounted cash value. Go back to cell B14, change the assumed discount rate, press the exclamation point to recalculate, and watch what happens. Notice how net present value declines as the discount rate increases and vice versa. Take the $50,000 payoff in Investment 3 and delay it by two years to see what happens to the net present value. The spreadsheet is a great way to understand what the discounted cash flow idea is saying about money now and money later.

Whether or not you use discounted cash flows to this extent, there is an important principle behind them. Money now is worth money later. An investment yielding $50,000 in one year is better than one yielding $10,000 per year for five straight years. The time value of money is an important consideration.

The NPV number is very important and not nearly as theoretical as it is practical. The time value of money isn't that theoretical. In this example, if we assume for a moment that tax-free government bonds yield 10 percent per year interest, then the NPV is suddenly converted to a direct comparison between the yield of each investment and the yield of a risk-free investment in government bonds. The investor would make more in bonds than in either Investment 1 or Investment 2. In this case, he or she should ask, "Why bother?" Suddenly, the discounted cash-flow analysis converts NPV to a real measure of the worth of an investment compared to a competing investment.

Many companies use discounted cash-flow analysis and the NPV figure to analyze equipment purchases, new product investments, and capital budgets. Often, the company sets the discount rate at a certain level and demands that cash-flow analysis on proposed programs produce a positive NPV.

Internal Rate of Return

Internal rate of return (IRR) works very much as the net present value does. It also considers the cash flow and the time value of money, and it makes for easy consideration of levels of risk associated with different investments.

IRR is the discount rate at which the net present value of an investment is zero. You find it by trial and error; even the computer finds it by trial and error. The better computer programs find the IRR by changing the discount rate many times until the NPV is zero.

If you build the model used in Table 6-5, you can see one quick way to find an internal rate of return. First, do it for the first investment. Go back to the model and change the discount rate from 10 percent to 9 percent. Then check your NPV, which is in the total column. The NPV should increase from $2,588 to $4,591. Since we want it down to zero, that's the wrong direction to go. Try changing the rate to 12 percent, and the NPV should go to −$1,152, which is less than zero. Now we know the IRR of this investment is somewhere between 10 and 12 percent. At 11 percent it's still positive, and at 11.5 percent it's already negative, so that narrows it down. If you continue, you'll discover that the IRR is about 11.4 percent for the first investment. Don't try to make the NPV exactly zero because you can spend all day over a couple of decimal points; 11.4 percent is close enough . . . it's actually something like 11.362.

Do the same thing for the second and third investments. You should come up with 11.5 percent for the second and 100 percent for the third.

Many more advanced spreadsheet programs include an IRR function. MicroPlan was one of the first to have one; Multiplan, Advanced VisiCalc, and many others now have them. If you plan to buy a program but don't want to do all that trial-and-error IRR, ask to see the financial functions.

IRR is an excellent comparative measure. While the NPV gives you another good comparison, the NPV of a larger investment will be larger normally, even though its yield per dollar might be lower. IRR gives a very good measure of how much return you get on an invested dollar after discounting for the time value of money.

When used well, IRR works in close association with risk. Higher IRR should be associated with more risk in most cases. Use a lot of judgment on this one: Is risky IRR of 100 better than safe IRR of 11.4? How about risky IRR of 25 versus safe IRR of 15? What if IRR 25 needs just a little money, and the safe one needs a lot? (Hint: Invest in both—we'll see about portfolio analysis later.)

A Word of Caution on Measurements

Investment measures such as NPV and IRR look very scientific. Especially when you see them being cranked from your computer printer, there is a temptation to treat them as if they were solid, objective facts.

DON'T!

Remember, all those official-looking little numbers are the product of many very questionable assumptions. Your cash-flow analysis is full of estimates and projections. Treat these numbers brusquely, for what they're worth, as a guide to thinking: They should give you the right questions, not the right answers. When IRR for one investment is 11.3 and for another it's 11.4, the two IRRs are objectively about equal. Even if the IRRs are 12 percent and 14 percent, your methods aren't normally scientific enough to justify choosing the 14 percent automatically. Weigh your choices very carefully—the analysis tells you they are about equal.

Risk Analysis

Risk is one of the toughest issues in investment analysis. The cash flows, costs, even the tax effects fit into good, hard numerical formulas. Risk doesn't. But at the same time, it is perhaps the most important concept in successful investment.

Impact of Risk

Investors talk about risk/return relationships. We've seen them in the investment discussion. Simply put, you want more return for more risk.

The balance of risk is what turns some investors into professionals and some into speculators. It's one of the key differences between the stock market and Las Vegas. Professionals will take some high-risk deals if the potential returns are enough to justify the risks, but they will look for a way to balance those high-risk deals with lower-risk deals that keep some of the money in a fairly safe place.

Risk in this sense is defined as a range of possible returns. A wide range of returns is a risky investment. A narrow range is safer. If you invest $1,000 in the spin of a roulette wheel, you can either lose everything or win $35,000. If you invest the money in a bank at 10 percent you get $1,100 back. The first range is very broad, the second extremely narrow. These extremes are high and low risks.

Quantifying Risk

The financial world is rich in sophisticated analytical models for quantifying risk. Unfortunately, anything that works is almost certainly based on educated guesses about what might happen.

Expected Value

The expected value of an investment is a number that can be calculated using a spreadsheet and a series of estimates based on the analyst's guesses about what might happen. Table 6-6 shows how to make an expected value of a pair of different investments.

The key to this set of numbers is what the professionals call "subjective probability assessments," which is what we've been calling educated guesses. After studying all the possibilities on Investment 2 here, we decide that there is about a one-in-ten (.10) chance that the thing is going to blow up on us, costing us $18,000 in addition to the original investment. There's about a four-in-ten (.40) chance that we'll get a $2,000 return, a one-in-four (.25) chance that we'll get $5,000, a .15 chance that we'll get $15,000, and a .10 chance that we'll get $25,000.

Table 6-6: Calculating Expected Value

	A	B	C	D	E	F
1		INV 1			INV 2	
2	PROB	YIELD	ADJUSTED	PROB	YIELD	ADJUSTED
3	.10	3000	300	.10	-18000	-1800
4	.25	4000	1000	.40	2000	800
5	.30	5000	1500	.25	5000	1250
6	.25	6000	1500	.15	15000	2250
7	.10	7000	700	.10	25000	2500
8	EXECTED VALUE NO. 1:		5000	EXPECTED VALUE NO. 2:		5000

The expected value is $5,000, which sits in cell F8. It is the sum of cells F3 through F7, which are each the product of multiplying one of those probabilities by its corresponding dollar yield. For example, cell F3 is D3*E3. For those who like fancy mathematical formulas, the expected value is equal to

LAST CASE
PROBABILITY*YIELD (MISSING P)
FIRST CASE

This says nothing more than what we just explained with the spreadsheet model.

You can also go right back into your spreadsheet investment analysis model to incorporate expected values instead of estimated cash flows. For each estimated cash-flow entry, set up the expected value model to produce your expected value and put it into the right cell.

Probabilities

These chances to which we refer are *probabilities*. Probabilities are numbers between 0 and 1 that are used to represent the chance that something will happen. A .5 probability is like the toss of a coin; you have one chance in two of guessing the outcome. A probability of 1 is a certainty, such as the sun's rising tomorrow. A .99 probability is close to a sure thing, and a .01 probability is a long shot, one in a hundred. For those who like one in a million, that is .000001.

Risk/Return, Expected Value, and Risk Preference

Now, look at the difference between Investments 1 and 2 on that expected value model. They have the same expected values but an enormous difference in risk. Investment 2 has a much wider range of possibilities and is therefore much riskier.

Which one is better? That depends on what you want. Investment theory says that if you always invested in things like Investment 2, you'll end up making about $5,000 per investment over the long term. The same would happen with Investment 1. There is nothing except style to tell whether you like the high-risk or low-risk way of investing.

Notice, however, that Investment 2 matches Investment 1 in expected value *only* because the potential payoff is much higher. If the rich side of Investment 2 were $7,500 and $10,000 instead of $15,000 and $25,000, then its expected value would be only $2,375, less than half that of Investment 1. This is because of the built-in relationship between risk and return. More risk should mean more return. That's the only reason that things are equal in this case.

Risk Analysis

Risk analysis in investments has been the subject of many doctoral theses. There are some very complicated formulas, some elegant ones, and even some practical ones. Scores of professional analysts gather around one method or another, and professors of finance write books and papers on various models. You'll hear occasionally of the capital-asset pricing model, the beta value of an investment, variance, co-variance, and other buzzwords used in this world. In this book, we'll stick to more practical and much more common techniques, such as risk analyses using NPV and IRR methods.

NPV Risk Analysis

The net present value analysis can incorporate risk in two different dimensions: First, the cash flow values for each year's yield can be changed to expected values for each year; second, different investments should be assigned different discount rates to reflect their different levels of risk.

Changing the cash-flow values to expected values is conceptually very simple. It does, however, take some time to add the extra numbers into the spreadsheet matrix. Furthermore, many analysts question the wisdom of estimating at that scientific level when you are talking about cash flows years from now. There is good reason to believe that by giving a single future cash-flow estimate, you are naturally presenting yourself with an instinctive guess at expected value—an idea that makes a lot of sense.

The differential discount rate requires commonsense judgment. In a variation on our comparative investments in Tables 6-1, 6-2, and 6-5, for example, we might have assigned different discount rates to each investment to arrive at the model in Table 6-7.

The different discount rates reflect the differences in risk perceived among the proposed investments. The speculation investment should be discounted at 50 percent because it represents a very high risk. The real estate investment is also a higher risk than banking money, at least during the recent long-term depression of housing sales in the United States. Finally, the stock market investment is considered the least risky (now there is a questionable assumption) and is therefore discounted at only 5 percent.

Analysis tells us that the stock market investment is the best one. The highest NPV is roughly equivalent to the best investment.

The discount rates make so much difference that we can change them to play with end results. Corporate analysts do just that to win approval when chips are down: They change the discount rate, and the numbers change with it.

Table 6-7: NPV Risk Analysis

	A	B	C	D	E	F	G
1							
2							
3		Year	Year	Year	Year	Year	
4		1	2	3	4	5	Total
5		---------	---------	---------	---------	---------	---------
	Expected values:						
6	Investment 1	(50,000)	(1,200)	(800)	(400)	80,000	27,600
7	Investment 2	(50,000)	1,250	1,437	1,653	72,000	26,340
8	Investment 3	(25,000)	50,000				25,000
	Discounted expected values						
9	Investment 1	(50,000)	(1,043)	(605)	(263)	45,741	(6,171)
10	Investment 2	(50,000)	1,136	1,188	1,242	59,234	13,156
11	Investment 3	(25,000)	33,333				8,333
	Discount rates:						
12	Investment 1	15.00					
13	Investment 2	5.00					
14	Investment 3	50.00					
	NPV lines:						
15	Investment 1	1.00	0.87	0.76	0.66	0.57	
16	Investment 2	1.00	0.95	0.91	0.86	0.82	
17	Investment 3	1.00	0.67	0.44	0.30	0.20	

IRR and Risk Analysis

Using an IRR system for investment analysis, simply keep in mind the difference in risk when comparing the IRR. There are a lot of different methods.

For example, we worked with a bank that had to gauge many different investments and used an IRR method that assigned each proposed investment to a risk category from 1 to 5. Those in the highest risk category were approved only when the IRRs were over 25 percent. Those in the lowest were approved with IRRs over 5 percent.

A large company asks all division heads to present an IRR analysis to justify proposed new investments over a specified dollar amount. The company as a whole has an IRR of about 20 percent, according to some fancy financial analysis; so an investment that looks like its IRR is better than 20 percent should improve the performance of the company as a whole. But high-risk investments, company management says, must have an IRR of more than 30 percent, or they will not be approved.

Though some people have raised this to the level of science, using complicated analytical techniques, there is actually much guesswork involved. IRR is useful in considering alternatives and in asking the right questions.

Portfolio Effect

There has also been a great deal of sophisticated analysis done on the portfolio effect in investments. The basic idea is that spreading your investments across a diversity of different kinds of investment reduces the risk associated with the whole portfolio.

In the stock market, for example, there is less risk in a portfolio of 100 stocks than in just one stock. Since the stock market itself has substantial risk in the up-and-down of the market as a whole, there is still less risk in a portfolio that includes stock market investments, real estate, commodities, new companies, government bonds, money market funds, savings bonds, plus maybe an old-fashioned savings account and some money under the mattress for good measure.

How does this apply to a spreadsheet? It is a reminder to use your numbers well and to recognize what they can and can't do.

Stock Market Applications

The stock market is the investment analyst's mecca. The best elements of investment analysis were born, tested, and proved over generations at the stock market before becoming accepted by the professionals without argument. Tomorrow's accepted theories will be run through the stock-market gauntlet first and then will be taught in the finance courses at the universities.

Despite generations of sophisticated analysts looking for some new way to get ahead, the basics remain the same. The principles of stock market analysis are still cash-only, the present value of future funds, and the measure of risk and return.

Many people forget these basics when they get into the stock market. So, keep your spreadsheet handy and do your own analysis of what's going on. By the time you finish the numbers yourself, you'll understand what the trade-offs are.

Stock Market Valuation

How much is a stock worth? Some say it's an average of 10 times the earnings, and some stocks go up to 30 and 40 times their earnings. Others go up by a sales ratio, one or two times the sales. Then they all get confused by mixing up last year's earnings or this year's earnings.

We have a suggestion along these lines. A share of stock, as with any other investment, is worth the present value of its future cash flow. This is one of the simplest and best ways to value a stock; the method has been tested over decades and has lasted longer than a lot of competing theories.

It also works well in a spreadsheet. Let's consider the stock investments in Table 6-8. For each, we list the dividends we expect to receive and the price we expect to sell the stock for in five years. We don't list the price at which we buy, because we want to establish a theoretical price.

When we finish the model, we have a simple tool for evaluating what the price *ought to be* for certain stocks. Of course, we have to get the financial information available on the company to forecast dividends and stock price five years from now. But we are still in the wonderland of guessing and estimating. At least now we have a framework for assigning values to these stocks. The share's NPV is the same as what we say it is really worth.

Table 6-8: Sample Stock Valuation

	A	B	C	D	E	F	G
1							
2							
3		Year	Year	Year	Year	Year	
4		1	2	3	4	5	Total
5		---------	---------	---------	---------	---------	---------
		Expected values (of 500 share block):					
6	Stock 1	500	600	800	1,000	10,000	12,900
7	Stock 2	1,000	1,250	1,500	1,800	20,000	25,550
		Discounted expected values @ 10 percent					
9	Stock 1	500	545	661	751	6,830	9,288
10	Stock 2	1,000	1,136	1,240	1,352	13,660	18,389

Theoretical share price = NPV/500

stock 1 = $18.58/share
stock 2 = $36.78/share

Compare what you think it's worth to what the market price is. If the share is selling for more than it's worth, don't buy it, of course. If it's selling for less than it's worth, then it's a good buy. First, go back and look at the analysis again—why does everyone else think it's worth less? Are they right?

Ratio Analysis

Financial ratio analysis is another rich field full of doctoral theses and professional research. It offers valuable practical help in looking at investments. The goal in investment analysis is to predict future yields, and financial ratios can tell you a lot about a company. They can help point up the company's strengths or weaknesses, compare the company to others in the same industry, or highlight the company's performance and allow time to spot improvements or declines.

Ratios are taken from accounting statements. The most important accounting statements are the balance sheet, which lists a company's assets and liabilities, and the income statement, which shows how the company made a profit or loss in a given time period. Both statements are discussed in detail in the following chapter, which shows you how to make them for your own existing or proposed business. If you are not familiar with the accounting forms and how to read them, you should read the next chapter before continuing this one.

Important Ratios

There are some thick books on ratio analyses. For our spreadsheet version, we'll look at some of the more important ones. The worth of an analysis is not determined by how arcane the ratio is; most professionals still prefer the tried and true ratios we'll discuss.

Current Ratio

Current ratio is used most by analysts to tell quickly how a company stands on the most important commodity: money. Current ratio is current assets divided by current liabilities:

$$\frac{\text{current assets}}{\text{current liabilities}}$$

The higher the ratio, the better. Less than 1 means you don't have enough money to pay your bills. More than 2 means you might invest that money in something better than current assets. You won't find many companies beyond a current ratio of 2 because that means the company has twice as many current assets as current liabilities.

Acid Test

The acid test does the same thing as the current ratio but without inventories. Inventories are sometimes accounting fiction: junk that's called assets. So some time back in stock-market history the analysts came up with the "acid test" on current position:

$$\frac{\text{current assets} - \text{inventories}}{\text{current liabilities}}$$

If inventories are worthless, this method still gives us an idea of how the current position looks.

Collection Period

The collection-period ratio tests accounts receivables for age. The older they are, the worse they are; old accounts receivables may never be collected. Here is the collection-period ratio:

$$\frac{\text{accounts receivable} \times 360}{\text{sales}} = \text{X days}$$

Technically, the bottom line above should be annual credit sales or non-cash sales and may be added for refinement. For an industrial company selling almost everything on 30-60-90-day or 30-day terms, the sales and the annual credit sales are about the same.

The collection period is usually quoted in days: 30, 60, or 90. People also use the receivable turnover ratio, which is annual sales divided by receivables and which is equivalent to 365 divided by the number of days in the collection period:

$$\frac{\text{annual sales}}{\text{receivables}}$$

Analysts use the collection period to check how the financial management performs the tasks of handling accounts receivable and granting credit. Except in special cases, high collection periods and low receivable turnovers indicate some problems with the accounts receivable.

Inventory Turnover

Inventory turnover is another way to get at the nature and history of inventories. Inventories are a good indicator of how well a company is doing—if it builds products that turn into inventory and don't get sold, it is going to have some problems.

Turnover ratio relates the level of inventory to annual purchases, which are often measured as "cost of goods sold." The inventory turnover measure is

$$\frac{\text{cost of goods sold}}{\text{average inventory}}$$

This produces a number that is often referred to as *inventory turns*. Five turns is quite good, for example, and one is rather bad, but these figures depend on the type of business. Grocery stores have very high inventory turnover, while heavy construction equipment has a very low turnover. Slow-moving inventory is more likely to be obsolete or full of problems than fast-moving inventory is.

Debt Ratios

Many analysts look first at a company's debt ratios for a quick view of its financial position. There are many debt-ratio rules concerning finance.

The debt-to-equity ratio, for example, is one of the most important indicators. It is almost equivalent to what is called *leverage*. Take Table 6-9, for example.

Table 6-9 is a simple model. Cells D1 and D2 must be equal to total assets, B1, according to one of the first rules of accounting. EBIT (earnings before interest and taxes) is

$$+B4-(B5+B6)$$

B6 stands for general and administrative, sales and marketing, and research and development expenditures. Interest (B7) is assumed at 10 percent of debt, and taxes are

$$.5*(B7-B8)$$

Return on equity is net profit (B9) divided by equity (D2).

When you put this model on the screen and start playing with the numbers, you can immediately see the difference in debt/equity ratios. Check that in the two scenarios we include: In the first, you invest $800 in equity to make $152.50 profit, which is only a 19-percent return on equity (return on equity is net profit divided by equity); in the second scenario, you invest only $200 to make $122.50 profit, which is a 61-percent return on equity. This is why the second company is said to be highly leveraged—by borrowing money, it can increase the potential profit just as a lever increases a person's strength.

Table 6-9: Looking at Debt/Equity

Scenario 1: low debt/equity

	A	B	C	D
1				
2	ASSETS	1000	DEBT	200
3			EQUITY	800
4	SALES	1250		
5	COGS	625	DEBT/EQ	.25
6	G&A ETC.	300		
7	EBIT	325		
8	INTEREST	20		
9	TAXES	152.5		
10	NET	152.5		
11	RETURN ON			
12	EQUITY	.19		

Scenario 2: high debt/equity

	A	B	C	D
1				
2	ASSETS	1000	DEBT	800
3			EQUITY	200
4	SALES	1250		
5	COGS	625	DEBT/EQ	4
6	G&A ETC.	300		
7	EBIT	325		
8	INTEREST	80		
9	TAXES	122.5		
10	NET	122.5		
11	RETURN ON			
12	EQUITY	.61		

Leverage works both ways; the highly leveraged company is also much more vulnerable to changing conditions and financial problems.

You can use the same model to see what debt/equity ratios mean to a company that isn't making much profit. We tried it on our own—with $1,000 sales, the conservative company makes $27.50 profit and breaks even at $945, while the aggressively leveraged variation loses $2.50 and breaks even at $1,005.

There are a number of different versions of debt/equity ratios. Some analysts prefer debt/net worth or debt/total capitalization, which are almost the same thing. While it doesn't really matter which is used, be careful about making comparisons across the definitions. Don't compare a debt/equity ratio with a debt/total capitalization ratio, because the latter will include some long-term debt on the bottom of the equation.

Profit Margins

Gross profit is sales less the cost of goods sold. In the accounting sense, cost of goods sold is the material, labor, and overhead costs associated with the goods that were sold in a given time period. The gross profit margin is the ratio of gross profits to sales:

$$\frac{\text{sales} - \text{cost of goods sold}}{\text{sales}}$$

Gross profits must be around 30 or 40 percent for a normal manufacturing company to pay for administrative, marketing, and research and development expenses from the gross before it becomes earnings before interest and taxes (EBIT). Then the company pays interest and taxes; if the gross profit margin isn't fairly high, then there are no profits left.

Net profit margin does about the same thing but with net profits. On net margins, a good profit can vary from less than 2 percent (good grocery stores do about 1.5 percent) to 20 or 30 percent for boom companies. Since the net profit margin measures profits against sales rather than profits against investment, it is not a measure of investment desirability. A supermarket can turn in profits of 1.5 percent of sales and produce more profit per invested dollar than a software business turning in a net of 40 percent of sales.

Return on equity or return on investment is probably the best measure of profitability of an investment. It measures how much you get back per dollar invested. We already did this in the previous section:

$$\frac{\text{net profit}}{\text{owners' equity}}$$

If your investment in a company does no better than bank interest, you probably shouldn't be investing in that company. This is how to consider return on equity.

There are many complicated and sophisticated variations for those who prefer refined formulas. You could do rate of return on common stock equity. For example:

$$\frac{\text{net profits} - \text{preferred stock dividends}}{\text{net worth} - \text{par value of preferred stock}}$$

This takes the effect of preferred stock out of the equation. Whichever formula you use, the important thing is to use it consistently as you compare a company to other companies or to its own past performance.

Return on assets or profits to assets is another important measure of how a company is going. Just as profit-to-sales ratio depends a great deal on the nature of the industry, so does return on assets. A steel company returns less on assets than a book publisher because the steel company has to own a multibillion-dollar plant, and the book publisher doesn't.

Return on assets is figured as you might guess:

$$\frac{\text{net profits}}{\text{assets}}$$

Spreadsheets and Ratios

You don't need a spreadsheet to do these ratios. But it can make things much more convenient. We find ourselves setting up a spreadsheet model that includes the common ratios as part of the financial portions of a business plan. Then, as we change financial plans with changing business conditions, we get an automatic, immediate reading of important resulting ratios.

For someone doing a lot of financial analysis, a spreadsheet model might simplify handling of ratios by asking for some standard input and by providing ratios. In the debt/equity model above, for example, you can fill in any company's numbers and automatically produce the debt/equity and return-on-equity ratios.

Most spreadsheet software allows you to read numbers from the accounting output into the spreadsheet, so you can program a system to give you automatic ratio analysis. VisiCalc will do this with DIF files; MicroPlan, SuperCalc, and others have special functions that allow you to do this.

Trend Analysis

Ratios are for comparison. They don't tell you very much by themselves. A 5:1 debt/equity ratio is excellent in some cases and a sign of near bankruptcy in others. The same is true for most of the other ratios. So the importance of ratios is company-to-company and past-to-present comparisons.

Many investment information and counseling businesses provide standard ratios to be used as bases for comparison among businesses. The ratios of a minicomputer manufacturing company should be compared to those of its competitors and to a composite of the industry. For example, minicomputer companies spend about 7 to 8 percent of revenues on research and development, about 30 to 40 percent on cost of goods sold, and about 20 to 30 percent on sales and marketing. Their turnover and debt/equity ratios depend a lot on individual performance, but they will have more in common with each other than with companies from other industries.

Put these things side by side on a spreadsheet. If you're looking in detail at a company, put it onto the spreadsheet side by side with the industry average and with its top four competitors. This makes comparison much easier. Once you have this spreadsheet formula set up, you can use it again and again for other companies and other industries.

Real Estate Applications

The key to sound analysis is the cash flow. Real estate gets complicated by confusions between price and cash, between interest rates and cash, and among taxes and other elements. Forget price; interest rates are more important. Don't forget taxes. Cash is to real estate analysis as votes are to political analysis: After all the rhetoric, truth sits with the cash and votes.

Real Estate Loans, Amortization

Real estate is where the classroom analyst discovers what interest rates really mean. Buy a house and quickly learn that the interest rate and financing package make a lot more difference than the transaction price does. This is the real world.

Given financing packages and their principal variables, some people buy an expensive calculator to figure loan payments. It's simpler just to build a payment schedule into your spreadsheet. With the way interest rates and financing packages vary these days, you may be using this setup more often than you'd like.

The amortization formula is one of the classics of finance. This is what we use to find out monthly payments for a loan of a given number of years at a given interest rate. It also provides a good example of how to use standard variables on a spreadsheet. The formula is based on mortgage amount P, interest rate I, and mortgage period Y.

We use this formula on the following real estate model. Notice that the mortgage amount P is in cell D4; the interest rate I is in cell D5; and the mortgage period Y is in cell D10. We can use these cell references as simply as if they were variables A, B, and C.

In the first step, since the figuring gets complicated, you should take the interest rate I and convert it to a new variable called, in this case, B3, which is

$$(I/100)/12$$

In our spreadsheet version, it is located in cell B3 and is

$$(D6/100)/12$$

Now, go to the key number that is often called M in the financial textbooks. This number is the basis for getting the monthly payments and comes from a fancy formula:

$$I/((1+I)^2(Y*12)-1)+I$$

Put that in the spreadsheet as C3, with the formula

$$B3/((1+B3)^2(D10*12)-1)+B3$$

With that done, the monthly payment comes from multiplying the M value by P, the loan amount, in cell D3, the formula of which is

$$C3*D5$$

Then we pull that result back onto our list of variables in the real estate model. *Voila!* Change the interest, amortization period, or loan amount, and get instant monthly payments. All we have to do now is write the checks for the next 30 years.

Notice, by the way, that by breaking a formula down, we come up with a simple way to run through the variables using cells. For purists, the formula for monthly payments is

$$P*(((I/100)*12))/((1+((I/100)/12)^2(Y*12)-1))+(((I/100)/12))$$

Table 6-10: Real Estate Analysis

	B	C	D	E	F	G	H
1:		Real estate model:					
2:	I. Variables:						
3:	.01	.01	1592.93				
4:	Buy	Price:	190000.00		Rent	Monthly	950.00
5:		Financed:	144000.00			Misc.	10.00
6:		Int. rate	13.00			Increase	
7:		Monthly	1592.93			Straight	1.00
8:		Yearly	19115.13			Yearly	5.00
9:		Amort.	1.00				
10:		Length	30.00			Yearly	11520.00
11:		Closing:	1000.00				
12:		Apprec.:					
13:		Straight	1.00				
14:		Yearly	5.00				
15:		Prop. tax	2000.00				
16:		Insurance	475.00				
17:		Maint.	950.00				
18:		Increase %	5.00				
19:							

That's what we just did. It seems a lot simpler in the spreadsheet, doesn't it?

Of course, there is more than just monthly payments working in the real estate model. It also sets up the groundwork for some additional analysis and establishes other useful real estate variables.

Notice the use of switches. There is one in cell D9, another in D13, and a third in cell H7. Each adds convenience to the working model.

Let's take the one in D9 as an example. It works on cell D7, the monthly payments, and allows us to choose an interest-free loan in which there is no amortization. The actual formula for cell D7 is

IF(D9=1,D3,((D6/100)*D5)/12)

It says IF D9=1, then this cell is equal to D3, which is the monthly payment we figured using our special formula. If not, then we use the formula behind the second comma

((D6/100)*D5/12)

It takes our interest rate in cell D6, divides it by 100 to convert it to decimal form, and then multiplies it by the loan amount, which is in D5. Therefore, D9 is a "switch" cell used to turn a process on and off.

The other two switches relate to the model we build with these variables. They allow us to take appreciation or rent increases either as a straight-line increase of the same percent every year or as a variable increase with the percent per year added for each year. This is convenient for the buy-versus-rent model, Table 6-11.

Table 6-11: Real Cost of Buy vs. Rent

A	B	C	D	E	K	L
20:	Purchase	Year 1	Year 2	Year 3	Year 9	Year 10
21:Down	47000.00					
22:Mortgage		19115.13	19115.13	19115.13	19115.13	19115.13
23:Interest		18694.32	18639.61	18577.79	17996.43	17850.99
24:Amortization		420.81	475.52	537.33	1118.70	1264.13
25:Principal	144000.00	143604.87	143158.38	142653.84	137908.83	136721.85
26:Property tax		2000.00	2000.00	2000.00	2000.00	2000.00
27:Insurance		475.00	498.75	523.69	701.79	736.88
28:Maintenence		950.00	997.50	1047.38	1403.58	1473.76
29:Marginal tax		.45	.46	.47	.53	.54
30:Tax effect		9312.44	9494.22	9671.56	10598.11	10719.54
31:Cash flow	-47000.00	-13227.69	-13117.16	-13014.63	-12622.40	-12606.23
32:Appreciation						
33:Value	190000.00	199500.00	209475.00	219948.75	294752.36	309489.98
34:Equity	46000.00	55895.13	66316.62	77294.91	156843.53	172768.13
35:Equity plus		9895.13	10421.49	10978.29	15086.25	15924.60
36:Cash-equity plus		-3332.56	-2695.66	-2036.34	2463.86	3318.36
37:						
38:Rent						
39:Increase		5.00	5.00	5.00	5.00	5.00
40:Rent + Misc.		-11520.00	-12096.00	-12700.80	-17020.29	-17871.30
41:$41K plus		4600.00	4600.00	4600.00	4600.00	4600.00

The Real Cost of Buying

In real estate, the real cost of buying is complicated by the effects of tax deductions and equity appreciation. Using the variables established in the first real estate analysis, we sort through some of these complications in the buy-versus-rent model.

This model sits on the same spreadsheet as the real estate variables but in different cells. Hence, it refers to those variables in several places. Notice that we skip some columns (F through J are missing), but this is just to make the model fit on the page. Who needs years four to eight, anyway?

Row 22 is taken straight from the other model. Row 23 estimates how much of the mortgage payment is interest and how much is principal, which is important for figuring tax deductions. The formulas for that row are based on an IF function that estimates amortization if amortization is in effect and takes interest only for an interest-only loan. For cell C23 the formula is

```
F(D9=1,((D6/100)*B25)-((D6/100)*(6*(D7-(((D6/100)*B25)/12)))),
(D6/100)*B25)
```

The most important phrase of this formula is the one between the two commas, the one that is active if D9=1. (We explained this switch in the previous section.) This phrase takes the interest payment you'd have on an interest-only loan:

```
(D6/100*B25)
```

It subtracts from it the interest on the amortized portion of the principal (that's where you see D7, the payment, less ((D6/100)*B25)/12, which would be interest-only payments) for six of the twelve months. The amortization isn't exact, but it's very close.

To figure it exactly, you must take each payment and calculate its interest and amortization figures; this is not hard to do on the spreadsheet, but it would take up a lot of space and is hardly worth the effort. This formula, though, provides a good solid approximation.

Rows 26 through 28 estimate other cash-flow items. Property tax is estimated at 1 percent of the value of the house, plus $100; this is an approximation of California rates. Maintenance is estimated at .5 percent of the value of the house in a year, and insurance is estimated at .25 percent of the value of the house.

Then we deal with the tax implications. Row 29 is an input value for the marginal tax rate of the buyer—how much of each new dollar earned is collected by the income taxes. This is important because the tax deductions affect cash flow in relation to the marginal tax rate; if you only pay 10 cents on every new dollar to the tax collector, then you don't get a big tax break out of interest deductions. You save only 10 cents on each dollar. But if you're paying the government 90 cents on every dollar, then you should buy everything on credit; the government will pay 90 percent of your interest payments by deducting those from your taxable income.

Row 30 shows exactly how those deductions work with the marginal tax rate. Labeled "tax effect," it takes the deductible portions of the payments and multiplies them by the marginal tax rate. For example, the formula for cell C30 is

C29*(C26+C23)

C26 is property taxes (deductible) and C23 is interest (also deductible). Tax effect is a positive factor—it's money that you won't pay to the government because of your tax deductions—so it reduces the actual cost of buying.

Row 31, then, is the actual cash flow, the sum of cash payments plus the tax effect. Rows 32 through 36 then look at equity appreciation as a benefit of owning the house and add this back to the cash flow. Notice that the appreciation row in 32 is blank; we chose a straight-line appreciation estimate in establishing our main variables. Otherwise, we would have had percentage growth rates in those cells. Value in row 33 goes up by 5 percent per year; equity in row 34 is simply value less the outstanding loan; and equity increase in row 35 is a simple subtraction of last year's equity from this year's equity. Row 36 adds these together to produce an effective yearly cost of buying, after taxes and appreciation.

Finally, we can compare the cost of buying to the cost of renting a house, which we figured back when we did the original variables. We have an estimated 5-percent annual rent increase and a token expense for incidentals, the little items the renter doesn't get back from the landlord. (Some cynics or experienced renters may find this figure too small.)

The comparison favors buying over renting. We have some additional comments: First, the buyer had about $46,000 in down payment to make; second, the buyer might have to alter the cash flow to reflect the other things that the $46,000 might have done.

Even at 10-percent interest in a bank, the money would have yielded another $4,600 per year, which could have paid for some of the rent. Just to keep things even, we added that $4,600 in on the rental side, in row 41. This is called an opportunity cost and is useful in some analyses.

Investment Property

Investment goals and tax structure change for a real estate investment analysis. Much of the same real estate calculation applies and is taken from the real estate variables and real estate buy-versus-rent model for use in the Investment model, Table 6-12. Notice that only a piece of the model is shown. The rest comes straight from the earlier two; this one, in fact, was produced by simple modifications of the other real estate versions.

The format in the following model follows a business presentation style. Revenues come first, then expenses, and then capital expenditures, which are called investment.

Table 6-12: Investment Property Analysis

	A	B	C	D	E	K	L
20:		Purchase	Year 1	Year 2	Year 3	Year 9	Year 10
21:							
22:	Revenue		11520.00	12096.00	12700.80	17020.29	17871.30
23:	Less costs:						
24:	Interest		18694.32	18639.61	18577.79	17996.43	17850.99
25:	Property tax		2000.00	2000.00	2000.00	2000.00	2000.00
26:	Maintenence		950.00	997.50	1047.38	1403.58	1473.76
27:	Insurance		475.00	498.75	523.69	701.79	736.88
28:			--------	--------	--------	--------	--------
29:	Profit (loss)		-10599.32	-10039.86	-9448.06	-5081.51	-4190.34
30:	Tax benefit		4769.69	4618.34	4440.59	2693.20	2262.78
31:							
32:	Investment:						
33:	Down	47000.00					
34:	Amortization		420.81	475.52	537.33	1118.70	1264.13
35:			--------	--------	--------	--------	--------
36:	Investment (ca	-47000.00	-420.81	-475.52	-537.33	-1118.70	-1264.13
37:	I.T.C.	4700.00	42.08	47.55	53.73	111.87	126.41
38:		--------	--------	--------	--------	--------	--------
39:	Net cash flow	-42300.00	-6208.35	-5849.49	-5491.07	-3395.14	-3065.27
40:	Cumulative cash		-48508.35	-54357.84	-59848.91	-85391.39	-88456.66
41:	Equity	46000.00	55895.13	66316.62	77294.91	156843.53	172768.13
42:		--------	--------	--------	--------	--------	--------
43:	Profit		7386.77	11958.78	17446.00	71452.14	84311.47
44:	Transaction costs		-14962.50	-15710.63	-16496.16	-22106.43	-23211.75
45:	Capital gains		1515.15	750.37	-189.97	-9869.14	-12219.94
46:			--------	--------	--------	--------	--------
47:	Net profit		-6060.58	-3001.48	759.87	39476.57	48879.77
48:	NPV calc		.91	.83	.75	.42	.39
49:	PV Investment	-42300.00	-47943.96	-52778.25	-56903.77	-71148.62	-72330.41
50:	PV return		38588.88	42443.28	45536.28	52956.21	52949.14
51:			--------	--------	--------	--------	--------
52:	NPV		-9355.07	-10334.97	-11367.49	-18192.41	-19381.27
53:	Discount rate:	10.00					

Revenues are equal to assumed rent income. You might want to adjust it for vacancies (multiply rent by .8 or .9, for example), but this model assumes full rent for the duration of the analysis period.

Aside from the order of presentation, tax treatment changes. Now all expenses, including interest, property tax, maintenance, and insurance, are deductible. The going business of property rental produces a loss, which, in turn, produces a tax benefit that is related as before to the investor's assumed marginal tax rate.

Also, we want to look at the non-deductible investment part of the picture, which produces an investment tax credit as shown in rows 36 and 37. For the purposes of this analysis, the investment tax credit is assumed to be 10 percent of the investment. That's a simplification the accountants can worry about.

Then we cumulate the total cash expended on the deal. This is done by adding B39 to C39 to get C40, then by adding D39 to C40 for D40, and finally by replicating D40 onto E40 through L40. We do the cumulation routine in other parts of this book as well, so it's a good one to remember.

Now, we can look at some measures of profit. We take the equity value from earlier calculations—the ones for the real estate variables and the buy-versus-rent model—and put it into row 41. Then, the value of our equity (less what we've invested to own it) becomes profit, as in row 43. Subtract from that the real estate selling transaction cost (estimated at 7 percent of selling price) in row 44 and the capital gains tax (20 percent of profit) in row 45 to get the net profit, which is in row 47. Notice how that starts out negative, but, given our assumptions on equity appreciation and rent increases, turns positive with time and downright lucrative by the tenth year. It makes real estate look like an attractive investment, even at the basically absurd (though not unrealistic, at least for Northern California in 1983) price and interest levels assumed.

Yes, but we're forgetting one of our basic principles: the time value of money! That's when rows 48 through 52 come in. We want to discount those cash flows for time to produce a net present value of the investment.

This is done as we suggested earlier in this chapter. The NPV calculation in row 48 is the same calculation we used to make our present value multiplier. In this model, we are discounting at 10 percent per year, using cell B53 to hold our discount rate. We discount each of the negative cash flows by the NPV calc factor to produce the numbers in row 49. Then we discount our net return (equity less transaction cost less capital gains tax) by the same factor to get the number in row 50. The formulas are, beginning with cell C49

```
C40*C48
```

Then, for cell C50 (equity is not shown on the model, because it is in the earlier model and is identified as EQUITY rather than its cell symbol), the formula is

```
C48*(EQUITY+C44+C45)
```

Table 6-13: Property Investment at a Lower Discount Rate

: A	:: B	:: C	:: D	:: K	:: L :
47:Net profit		-6060.58	-3001.48	39476.57	48879.77
48:NPV		.97	.94	.77	.74
49:PV Investment	-42300.00	-48327.53	-53841.23	-80119.47	-82400.32
50:PV return		41211.43	48408.30	95700.90	102191.21
51:		--------	--------	--------	--------
52:NPV		-7116.10	-5432.93	15581.43	19790.89
53:Discount rate:	3.00				

Notice that we add transaction costs and taxes because those are in the model as negative numbers; we are in a cash-flow mode. Then, finally, we can subtract the present value of total investment from the present value of its return, producing the net present value of the investment, which is in row 52.

This is a good example of how important the present value calculations are. They just turned the tables on what looked like a good investment, making positive numbers negative. Is that realistic? We think so; after all, the investor spent a fair amount of money up front and spends more each year only to get a return 10 years later. If the banks were paying 10 percent on safe investments, profits would have been much higher just by leaving the money in a bank.

This also shows how much the NPV analysis pivots on discount rates. The investment looks quite good at a 3-percent discount rate, as shown in Table 6-13.

Bonds, T-Bills, Money Market Funds, etc.

Sometimes it seems that the secret to these money market investments is understanding the terminology. You must deal with coupon rate, sinking funds, call price, maturity, serial bonds, debentures, subordinated debentures, mortgage bonds, trust bonds, income bonds, convertible bonds, convertible debentures, certificates of deposit . . . an endless list. But this is not the place for a course in Wall Street jargon.

The key to this kind of analysis is to avoid getting blown away by the terminology. When you don't understand a word, ask; don't nod your head knowingly when analysts get into the details, and don't be embarrassed by what you don't know. Wall Street is always inventing new buzzwords; since no one can follow them most of the time, you'll look even more knowledgeable when you ask a question.

The spreadsheet is a good test of your own knowledge. If you can't sit down and model a bond yield in a spreadsheet, then you must ask more questions. Your model should follow the patterns we've already shown in this chapter, with the original purchase price in the first column as a negative, interest yield over the life of the bond as a positive, and the final selling price or redemption value as a positive. Then you can figure out an internal rate of return, or return on investment, or net present value. Then you can compare one bond or money market fund to another. If you don't have enough information to estimate a cash flow by now, you're in trouble.

The Standard Analysis

The standard analysis is the cash flow, as shown in Table 6-14, which was produced by modifying the real estate models in the previous section, thus saving time on column headings and labels.

Table 6-14: Simple Bond Analysis Model

	A	B	C	D	K	L
1:	Basic bonds model					
2:		Variables:				
3:						
4:			Price	130000.00		
5:			Par	150000.00		
6:			Int. rate	13.00		
7:			Monthly	1625.00		
8:			Yearly	19500.00		
9:						
10:						
11:			Commission	520.00		
12:			Rate	.004		
13:			Discount	10.00		
14:			Tax rate	.45		
15:						
16:		Purchase	Year 1	Year 2	Year 9	Year 10
17:						
18:	Purchase	-130000.00				
19:	Commission	-520.00				
20:	Yield		19500.00	19500.00	19500.00	19500.00
21:	Less taxes		-8775.00	-8775.00	-8775.00	-8775.00
22:	Redemption					150000.00
23:		----------	-----------	-----------	----------	-----------
24:	Net cash flow	-130520.00	10725.00	10725.00	10725.00	160725.00
25:	Cumulative cash		-119795.00	-109070.00	-33995.00	126730.00
26:	PV calc	1.00	.91	.83	.42	.39
27:	PV cash flow	-130520.00	9750.00	8863.64	4548.45	61966.45
28:	NPV	-6788.02				

Notice that one chronic confusion on bonds is the price and the par value. The par value is the original issue value of the bond, and this is the figure that determines the interest to be paid. But these things are traded, so as market rates go up and down, the prices of the bonds go up and down, above and below the par value. So you need to look at the price paid,whatever that is, and the par value. These important variables are in cells D4 (the price) and D5 (the par value) of the model.

Please note that we've edited the model again for display purposes. Columns E through J are not shown.

Cash flow on the bond is calculated much as other cash flows are. Interest yield is determined by the par value, and its formula is simple. The cells in row 20 are taken from cell D8, which is the sum of cell D5 multiplied by (D6/100). The commission is a transaction cost that is produced by the commission rate (in cell D12) times the price paid (cell D4). Tax effects are treated as they were treated for real estate analysis, with the effective tax rate (the marginal rate or the incremental tax on each incremental dollar) input as a constant variable in cell D14 and with this rate applied to the income from the bond to produce the tax effect row (21). Redemption comes at the end of the period, when the bond is redeemed for its par value; that's in row 22 (at the end of the tenth year, it's in cell 22L). Don't forget that the bond is redeemed at its full $150,000 par value, even though it was purchased for $130,000.

Now, look at the cash flow discounted for present value. Use the same formulas used in other calculations, with the discount rate in cell D13 and the discount factor loaded into row 26.

When this standard bond transaction is carried back to its present cash-flow value at 10 percent, it's a losing proposition. The net present value is negative, meaning the investment is not attractive in a 10-percent discount rate environment. Why not? It doesn't earn enough. Why doesn't it? The main reason is that you have to wait 10 years to get your money back.

Bond Valuation

The valuation model makes a very simple modification of the basic bond model to show how to calculate a bond valuation. Basically, it is as simple as leaving out the price to see where the bond valuation comes out. Then run the discounted present value calculations to determine that this bond is worth just a little bit less than $124,000. This is just the other side of the analysis we did for the basic model. In that case, we said it was overpriced at $130,000; the difference takes us exactly to where this theoretical valuation ends up.

Table 6-15: Bond Valuation Model

	A	B	C	D	K	L
1:	Basic bonds model					
2:		Variables:				
3:		.01	.01	1659.30		
4:			Price	.00		
5:			Par	150000.00		
6:			Int. rate	13.00		
7:			Monthly	1625.00		
8:			Yearly	19500.00		
9:						
10:						
11:			Commission	.00		
12:			Rate	.004		
13:			Discount	10.00		
14:			Tax rate	.45		
15:						
16:		Purchase	Year 1	Year 2	Year 9	Year 10
17:						
18:	Purchase	.00				
19:	Commission	.00				
20:	Yield		19500.00	19500.00	19500.00	19500.00
21:	Less taxes		-8775.00	-8775.00	-8775.00	-8775.00
22:	Redemption					150000.00
23:		--------	--------	--------	--------	--------
24:	Net cash flow	.00	10725.00	10725.00	10725.00	160725.00
25:	Cumulative cash		10725.00	21450.00	96525.00	257250.00
26:	PV calc	1.00	.91	.83	.42	.39
27:	PV cash flow	.00	9750.00	8863.64	4548.45	61966.45
28:	NPV	123731.98				

Generalized Bonds/Money Market Analysis

When the bond buzzwords start flying, use the cash flow to deflate a lot of the high-flying words and to bring them right back down into dollars and sense. Sometimes we get the impression that simple formulas scare the interest rates off the money market wizards. But remember—if you can't do a spreadsheet cash flow, it hasn't been explained very well, and you won't know what you're getting into.

Some of the different savings/investment instruments are distinguished by different risk structures. Debentures are normally considered bonds that are not backed by specific collateral. Subordinated debentures are last in line for what's left if the issuing company goes bankrupt. Concepts like these don't change your cash-flow analysis, but they might change the discount rate used to go back to present value. It would be better to increase the discount rate as the perceived risk increases.

Another set of instruments is distinguished by extra provisions, such as call prices or convertibility, that add special options. A bond with a call price can be called in by its issuer at specified times for specified amounts of money. The $150,000 bond might, for example, be callable at the fifth year for $160,000. A convertible bond can be turned into common stock at a specified formula price. With these options, it's better just to run the cash flow to see how things would look when and if the options are exercised. How does your investment look when it turns into equity, for example? Build the model to this end and take a good look.

Summarizing Investment Analysis

In this chapter, there are some common themes that we'll examine now in focus.

1. Analysis depends on guessing the future. Don't be fooled into thinking all those fancy numbers are objective, dependable facts. They aren't. They are the well-formatted output of someone's hunches. Question the assumptions.

2. Investment analysis pivots around discount rates. You can change almost anything in this field from "go" to "no-go" simply by changing to present value from the rate at which you are discounting. No other single element counts half as much. But often the discount rate is not determined by any cold, hard, justifiable method. Never forget how much uncertainty surrounds discounted numbers.

3. Cut through the fancy words straight to the cash flow. Cash flow is what rests at the bottom of all the rhetoric. It's where investment analysis really is.

SEVEN

Pro Formas and Business Planning

Care and Feeding of Pro Forma Statements

Pro forma accounting statements are plans written in accounting language. A pro forma statement is a representation of business plans as they'd look in accounting form, after the fact, if they were to come off exactly as planned. Write an income statement for next year, and you have a pro forma income. It's a model of what the numbers are supposed to look like, it's an income statement model for future income, it's a cash-flow plan, and it's a model of the balance sheet as it would look if the cash flow and future income statement worked out.

Using Pro Forma Statements

Standard pro forma statements are standard building blocks in business. They are an integral part of planning, budgeting, and finance. They are the most important single component of the business plans used by venture capitalists to judge potential businesses seeking venture financing.

Pro forma statements are very useful pieces of information. They are the bones of business plans, the structure that holds the text together to give the plans substance. You can't really define a business idea without defining its probable costs, revenues, financing requirements, and profits. This is what pro forma statements do for a plan.

Plans take many different forms, and pro formas will vary from one to another depending on the nature of the business. But there are some basic structures that are common to all pro forma accounting statements. In this chapter, we'll emphasize the business plan for the prospective new company looking for venture financing; pro forma statements are about the same for this case as for many others. Pro formas are also used widely in established businesses as part of the normal planning functions. They are very often an integral part of the budgeting process and are used to tie budgets together in a projected cash flow, income, and balance statement for a division, for a group, or for a company as a whole. The pro forma is also the key presentation document for obtaining bank financing, venture financing, or other long-term corporate credit. The people putting this money into a business want to see financial reports showing actual performance and pro formas showing projected performance. New companies can't provide actual financial statements because they don't have a history; but very few companies have ever been financed without some pro forma projections.

Preparing Pro Forma Statements

The details of a pro forma statement depend on individual styles and the nature of the business. Some people can scratch up a pro forma for a small business in a few minutes, using pencil and paper. Some businesses require long hours of computer time to consolidate huge, complex, multiple-division results. Industry sourcebooks provide estimates of standard and average percentages paid for different income statement items such as average percent of general and administrative expenses of the cement business, or average cost of goods sold for the auto manufacturers. These industry averages can help provide you with estimates. Build a pro forma statement on as much industry knowledge as you can. You can also benefit a great deal from proper use of the spreadsheet program.

With the spreadsheet program, you'll use most of the tools we've discussed in the previous chapters. Remember, spreadsheets were used first by accountants trying to figure out pro forma statements. The design is ideal for the task. Most of the work is on the level of fairly simple commands—for column labels, for row labels, for straightforward increases, and for sums—combined with careful considerations.

Some Words of Warning

Remember that each company is different and each situation is different. In the rest of this chapter we will prepare some standard pro forma statements based on a computer software start-up business. Much of the basics of the pro formas we'll use should be applied to any pro forma for any business anywhere. But there will be differences also. Please use these examples as samples rather than as rigid rules for format, form, or structure. The key market is the boss, the audience, or the person with the money. Make your own pro formas the way the market wants to see them. The spreadsheet is certainly flexible enough to do this in a number of different ways.

More Examples

In this chapter, we will build integrated pro forma cash-flow, income, and balance-sheet statements. Some additional examples are provided at the end of the following chapter, which presents them as illustrations of the link between the pro formas on the spreadsheet and the business plan.

The Pro Forma Cash Flow

We already did a pro forma cash flow in Chapter Five. At that time, it was called a cash budget; now it's called a pro forma. It's still basically the same thing. We must project revenue when the check arrives or when the cash register rings rather than when the sale is made. This usually means a lag on sales, as we discussed earlier. Also, we must project expenditures when money leaves in cash or when the checks are written. When this is done, suddenly the old "time value of money" takes on a new and very exciting meaning. Companies have gone broke while running good income statements: no cash flow. It's important.

To make a pro forma cash flow on the spreadsheet, start with some lines for revenues. Do you have more than one stream of revenues? Several products or product lines? Will you receive financing, loans, slush funds, or lunch money? If so, put them in the revenue section. Remember one of our basic principles, "divide and conquer," which argues that the more you break things down, the easier you'll be able to deal with them later on.

Your time line—your columns—depends on needs. Using the pro forma statement determines whether you want months, years, quarters, or days. Cash flow on a daily basis sounds like desperation but can be important when companies are in financial trouble or when large companies manage large amounts of cash. Interest on a daily balance of cash for a multibillion-dollar corporation can run to tens of thousands of dollars.

The examples here assume the planning of a start-up software company that is just beginning to receive some revenue. We show just a few months, a piece of a larger statement. After we finish the routine with months, we can translate into years.

Table 7-1 has the first pro forma cash flow. It looks familiar because it's much like Table 5-9 and the following. But each company is different, and so is this one.

Notice that we have some months in the middle of the year and none before or after these. Cumulative cash (row 47), for example, doesn't begin with the first month on the table. The reason is that this is a real planning document, and since the first five months have no revenue and very few salaries, they didn't serve the purposes of this exercise. This is a slice of a planning piece that included two years by months and three more years by year.

Table 7-1: Pro-Forma Cash Flow

Pro-Forma Cash Flow
Start-Up Software Company

		June	July	August	September
		-----6-----	-----7-----	-----8-----	-----9-----
1	Sales:				
2	units	10.00	15.00	23.00	35.00
3	unit price	55.00	55.00	55.00	55.00
4	Value	550.00	825.00	1,265.00	1,925.00
5	Revenue:				
6	Unit sales	-	-	550.00	825.00
7	OEM contracts	-	-	10,000.00	20,000.00
8	Other	500,000.00	-	-	-
9	Subtotal	500,000.00	-	10,550.00	20,825.00
10	Direct costs:				
11	Units	15.00	23.00	35.00	100.00
12	Direct materials per	10.00	10.00	10.00	10.00
13	Shipping, etc. per u	2.00	2.00	2.00	2.00
14	Materials costs	150.00	230.00	350.00	1,000.00
15	Materials expenditur	-	150.00	230.00	350.00
16	Documentation fees	500.00	500.00	500.00	500.00
17	Shipping, etc.	20.00	30.00	46.00	70.00
18	Total cost of good	520.00	680.00	776.00	920.00
19	Product Development				
20	Salary 1	2,500.00	2,500.00	2,500.00	2,500.00
21	Consultants	2,250.00	2,500.00	2,750.00	3,000.00
22	Hardware/software pu	500.00	500.00	500.00	500.00
23	Supplies, miscellane	500.00	600.00	700.00	800.00
24	Development subtot	5,750.00	6,100.00	6,450.00	6,800.00
25	Marketing/sales				
26	Salary 1	1,250.00	1,250.00	1,250.00	1,250.00
27	Salary 2	2,500.00	2,500.00	2,500.00	2,500.00
28	Salary 3	-	-	-	2,500.00
29	Commissions	11.00	16.50	1,025.30	2,038.50
30	Advertising etc.	-	-	-	25,000.00
31	Travel	1,000.00	1,200.00	1,400.00	1,600.00
32	Office expenses	300.00	350.00	400.00	450.00
33	Marketing subtotal	5,061.00	5,316.50	6,575.30	35,338.50
34	General & Administrative				
35	Salary 1	5,000.00	5,000.00	5,000.00	5,000.00
36	Salary 2	1,200.00	1,200.00	1,200.00	1,200.00
37	Utilities	125.00	126.25	127.51	128.79
38	Insurance	100.00	102.00	104.04	106.12
39	Rent	750.00	750.00	750.00	750.00
40	Miscellaneous	100.00	150.00	200.00	250.00
		-----------	-----------	-----------	-----------
41	G&A subtotal	7,275.00	7,328.25	7,381.55	7,434.91
42	Interest	-	-	-	-
43	Taxes	-	-	-	-
44	Capital expenditure	100.00	100.00	100.00	100.00
45	Total expenditure	18,706.00	19,524.75	21,282.85	50,593.41

The spreadsheet part is the easiest. First, let's take the revenue section, which starts with projected sales.

1	Sales:				
2	units	10.00	15.00	23.00	35.00
3	unit price	55.00	55.00	55.00	55.00
4	value	550.00	825.00	1,265.00	1,925.00

This is simple mathematics, but it is still important. There is a lot of very important information in this simple units-times-price calculation. We spent all of Chapter Four doing sales forecasting, just to come out with line 2, units. The unit forecast is quite probably the most far-reaching row of numbers in all pro formas, and it is certainly one row that is going to get a lot of attention as time goes on. This is where forecasting goes from theory to business reality.

Of course, sales aren't money. Ask the people who deal with accounts receivable—remember those ratios we did last chapter? We've got a sales forecast, but we need to turn sales into revenues. We did that in Chapter Five, and our software company has a similar revenue lag. Note the rows here:

5	Revenue:				
6	unit sales	—	—	550.00	825.00
7	OEM contracts	—	—	10,000.00	20,000.00
8	other	500,000.00	—	—	—
9	Subtotal	500,000.00	—	10,550.00	20,825.00

The sales revenue is a simple two-month lag on sales. Look at it again:

4	value	550.00	825.00	1,265.00	1,925.00
6	unit sales	—	—	550.00	825.00

We assume that we'll get our money two months after we make our sale. That's a 60-day collection period, which is hardly unusual. We discussed the revenue lags in Chapter Five.

The "other" row is our equity financing. The pro forma cash flow calls for half a million dollars in venture capital financing for this start-up company. That is or isn't realistic, depending on a number of things, including how convincing the pro forma cash flow is. Do you want to put money into this company? You'd certainly want to see more than just four months.

Now start with expenditures, beginning with the direct costs of production:

10	Direct costs:				
11	units	15	23	35	100
12	direct materials per	10.00	10.00	10.00	10.00
13	shipping, etc. per u	2.00	2.00	2.00	2.00
14	materials costs	150.00	230.00	350.00	1,000.00
15	materials expenditure	—	150.00	230.00	350.00
16	documentation fees	500.00	500.00	500.00	500.00
17	shipping, etc.	20.00	30.00	46.00	70.00
18	Total direct costs	520.00	680.00	776.00	920.00

The unit number on production is different from units in sales. Compare them:

2	units	10	15	23	35
11	units	15	23	35	100

The difference is that you have to produce items before you can sell them, so the unit production comes roughly a month before unit sales. It's expected that you won't really be able to forecast sales well enough to produce exactly as many items in one month as you'll sell in the next; but you have a rough estimate with which to get started. So on the cost side of cash flow, the number of units is generally greater than the number in the same column's sales.

Costs follow those production units. Material cost is figured on production units and is then lagged—notice lines 14 and 15:

14	materials costs	150.00	230.00	350.00	1.000.00
15	materials expenditure	—	150.00	230.00	350.00

Assuming we'll have 30 days to pay production bills, wait until they're due before we pay them.

Shipping costs of $2 per unit are spent on receiving raw materials and on shipping finished goods. Take them as a function of production units, and they're the product of line 12 times line 11. No time lag here, because small accounts must pay shipping at once—at least until they become big accounts.

Notice in these discussions of pro formas that whenever there's a judgment call on when to take costs, or on when to take revenues, these models fall on the conservative side. It is much easier to defend a conservative forecast than an aggressive one; therefore, it is better to underestimate rather than overestimate profits and sales: This tactic seems to make life more comfortable when the pro formas come back for comparison to actual performance. You could lag shipping costs or tie shipping to sales and underestimate, but it's better to overestimate expenses, when in doubt.

Beware of a tricky, potentially confusing situation: The cash-flow plan wants direct expenses entered according to the timing of the cash disbursement. The income statement, which follows, wants the same costs related as the cost of the goods each month. The income statement wants the $150 of material costs recorded the same month the 15 units are sold. The cash flow wants it the month that the check is written. Sometimes this is a significant difference.

The rest of the pro forma cash flow tracks actual costs as the company expects to incur them. Salaries, rent, purchases, and travel are paid as incurred; commissions hold for sales revenue. Each item is supposed to represent actual planned payments. This is less spreadsheet and more standard, hands-on planning. Question yourself, associates, textbooks, bankers, and anyone or anything else; use all your business experience. Take the line items, one by one, and guess (estimate) what is going to happen with them.

Realism is the goal. That's much more important than how a table looks, or how elegant a model is. The best possible pro forma is based on close and detailed projections from actual past results. There's no better starting point for next year than last year. Why are things going to change, and what is going to change them? How does the pro forma compare to the actual?

Comparison is a good guideline. The best possible way to judge your pro forma is to get some real numbers from your company. Second best is to get real numbers from a similar company with which you have contact. Third best is to inspect library information showing average numbers for companies in the same kind of business. If you can't find any of these guidelines, then think through each line very carefully. At this point in the process, spreadsheet finesse is worth much less than good guessing about what's going to happen with your company.

There are many different ways to arrange items. Most people prefer sales, then revenue, and then direct costs; this order fits conveniently with a standard income statement format, which goes from sales to cost of goods sold to gross margin. Accountants are used to that order. After ordering, you want to try to group your items to produce one subtotal line for general and administrative expenses (G&A), one subtotal for marketing and sales, and other subtotals that make sense with your business. The sample company here lists product development as an important item, because that's where it's going to account for all programming costs.

Include whatever expenditures you plan to make. We don't have much in taxes because we don't have profits here. But you might want to include taxes, in the months they are paid, with a formula to take taxes as a function of income. You may have interest expenses; if so, put them in the month that you'll write the checks. Include the company picnic, the Mercedes—whatever you're going to pay for in the month you're going to pay for it.

The mechanics of these expenditures is not difficult to fathom; getting the numbers straight is a lot harder. The models in Chapter Five offer some additional cash-flow examples, and more are wherever your library keeps financial statements.

The Pro Forma Income Statement

The *income* statement is the granddaddy of them all and the father of the expression "the bottom line"; the bottom line of the income statement is the net profit, the "after all is said and done" of business.

Not that there isn't plenty of opportunity for creative writing with income statements. A good accountant can play any number of legitimate options to speed up recording of profits, to manipulate the time when losses are taken, and otherwise to change or to influence that famous bottom line. Working the income statement can be taken as one of the world's great living chess games or as an intricate puzzle. Some respected stock market analysts base lucrative consulting practices on the ability to see through the accounting into the real value of earnings. Soft earnings are inflated, hard earnings are the product of conservative accounting.

While there may be too much creative accounting in the income statements of the real world, that is not the subject of this book. We'll explain how to do a basic pro forma income statement—we'll base it on fact and turn to the conservative side whenever a reporting choice comes up. If you want to play around with creative accounting, at least you've got a spreadsheet program that lets you experiment with numbers and return to the real world at appropriate intervals.

Income statements have a standard form. Sales and service incomes come first, at the top. Then comes cost of goods sold. Gross margin is calculated as sales less cost of goods sold. After that come sales and marketing, research and development (R&D), and general and administrative expenses (G&A), though not necessarily in this order. Take gross margin and subtract marketing/sales, R&D, and G&A to get earnings before interest and taxes (EBIT). Then subtract interest and taxes to arrive at the famous bottom line, the net profit or loss.

The best way to make a pro forma income statement is to modify a pro forma cash flow. Take a look at how this is done in Table 7-2. See where we modify back from cash to accepted accounting practices to preserve the relationship between income and cash flow.

Look first at sales, which are once again recorded in the month they're booked. Notice that the revenue lag is irrelevant in the income statement, and the direct costs are those associated with the actual goods sold that month. The cost of goods sold is the direct cost per unit times the units sold. If factory overhead and indirect costs were allocated to each unit, these would also be put into the cost of goods sold for the month as a function of sales booked during that month.

Accountants are sensitive about booking sales. The OEM contracts, which appeared on the cash flow, drop out of the income statement. That's because these contracts are not sales until the related products are actually shipped. The OEM contract is an agreement to buy, not a sale. It goes into the accounting books as advance payments on goods to be delivered at a later date; the actual sales are booked only when the goods are delivered.

The income statement follows the cash-flow numbers for product development, sales and marketing, and G&A expenses. These are considered expenses as they are paid out month by month, so they need little or no modification as they move from cash flow to income statement.

Neither capital expenditures nor expenses incurred building inventory for next month's sales appear on the statement. Both items are sensitive to creative accounting. There is always a temptation to capitalize payments that might be considered expenses, such as certain programming and related product development costs. Sometimes money paid for useless work and waste, such as programming on projects that don't produce a decent product, is recorded as if it were building inventory. Inventory will then accumulate an imaginary value that will have to be written off eventually as overvalued inventory.

Table 7-2: Pro-Forma Income Statement
Start-Up Software Company

		June	July	August	September
		-----6-----	-----7-----	-----8-----	-----9-----
1	Sales:				
2	units	10.00	15.00	23.00	35.00
3	unit price	55.00	55.00	55.00	55.00
4	OEM contracts	-	-	10,000.00	20,000.00
5	Total sales	550.00	825.00	1,265.00	1,925.00
6	Cost of goods sold				
7	Direct materials per	10.00	10.00	10.00	10.00
8	Shipping, etc. per u	2.00	2.00	2.00	2.00
9	Materials costs	100.00	150.00	230.00	350.00
10	Shipping, etc.	20.00	30.00	46.00	70.00
11	Total cost of good	120.00	180.00	276.00	420.00
12	Product Development				
13	Salary 1	2,500.00	2,500.00	2,500.00	2,500.00
14	Consultants	2,250.00	2,500.00	2,750.00	3,000.00
15	Hardware/software pu	500.00	500.00	500.00	500.00
16	Documentation fees	500.00	500.00	500.00	500.00
17	Supplies, miscellane	500.00	600.00	700.00	800.00
18	Development subtot	6,250.00	6,600.00	6,950.00	7,300.00
19	Marketing/sales				
20	Salary 1	1,250.00	1,250.00	1,250.00	1,250.00
21	Salary 2	2,500.00	2,500.00	2,500.00	2,500.00
22	Salary 3	-	-	-	2,500.00
23	Commissions	11.00	16.50	1,025.30	2,038.50
24	Advertising etc.	-	-	-	25,000.00
25	Travel	1,000.00	1,200.00	1,400.00	1,600.00
26	Office expenses	300.00	350.00	400.00	450.00
27	Marketing subtotal	5,061.00	5,316.50	6,575.30	35,338.50
28	General & Administrative				
29	Salary 1	5,000.00	5,000.00	5,000.00	5,000.00
30	Salary 2	1,200.00	1,200.00	1,200.00	1,200.00
31	Utilities	125.00	126.25	127.51	128.79
32	Insurance	100.00	102.00	104.04	106.12
33	Rent	750.00	750.00	750.00	750.00
34	Depreciation	135.00	136.66	138.33	140.00
35	Miscellaneous	100.00	150.00	200.00	250.00
36	G&A subtotal	7,410.00	7,464.91	7,519.88	7,574.91
37	Interest	-	-	-	-
38	Taxes	-	-	-	-
39	Net profit	(18,291.00)	(18,736.41)	(20,056.18)	(48,708.41)
40	Cumulative results	(65,099.33)	(83,835.74)	(103,891.92)	(152,600.33)

Capital expenditures should be on the internal spreadsheet matrix, though, even if they don't come into the income statement. They are required for figuring depreciation.

Depreciation is a function of capital expenditures. Tax laws and accepted accounting principles allow subtraction of depreciation from net income because equipment is being worn out. Many different rules and formulas are involved in figuring depreciation, but they are too elaborate to fit into the scope of this book. Nonetheless, depreciation is a serious accounting question.

Here, simply assume each piece of equipment is depreciated over a five-year period, with no value left over. This means we take one-sixtieth of its value as depreciation each month. In the spreadsheet, the depreciation formula is tedious to write because, for each month, one-sixtieth of the money spent in all previous months has to be taken. This must be done until the five-year assumed life of the good is over. This is so tedious that most people take depreciation just once per year, at the end of the year, to simplify calculations. We do it month by month because we need it for the balance sheet model, which is related to the income statement. Depreciation for July, under this simplified formula, would be the sum of one-sixtieth of each of the capital expenditure numbers for January through July.

This set of pro formas was written in MicroPlan because MicroPlan's accounting orientation, tables consolidation, and programming option are ideally suited for this use. Depreciation, however, is easier in one of the calc programs. Take last month's depreciation and add this month's capital expenditures (divided by 60) to produce this month's depreciation. If we assume for a moment that capital expenditures are in row 60, then depreciation for the first month (cell B34) would be

B60/60

To do the rest of depreciation, make C34 equal to

B34 + (C60/60)

and replicate across the rest of the row.

Some of the more advanced spreadsheets have facilities for handling depreciation formulas. Both MicroPlan and the VisiCalc Advanced Version provide some options on which depreciation formula to work with; neither of them is convenient to use. Both assume yearly rather than monthly depreciation. Lotus 1-2-3 and Multiplan are better. Even in the worst case, you can still resort to just writing in the whole formula.

Taxes are figured at 50 percent of taxable income, which is sales minus expenses. Net income is taxable income minus taxes.

There are many variations on income statements. We probably should include a line for gross margin because analysts look at gross margin as an indicator of the underlying profitability of the product and the market. This example doesn't add it only because of constraints imposed by the page size. We could also take rent and utilities and divide them among product development, sales, and administrative expenses. This is called allocation, which is used to provide better insight on real costs of each general expense heading. Product development actually costs a portion of rent and overhead, as well as the salaries and expenses that appear in Table 7-2.

As with the cash flow, the pro forma income statement is simple to manage with spreadsheets. Build the income statement off the cash flow by saving the cash flow on disk with a file name and then by modifying it to produce the income. With a spreadsheet like MicroPlan, which allows programming, turn on the program mode, and the software remembers the steps taken to turn cash flow into income statement. Thus, when you change an item or two in the cash flow, you can run the MicroPlan program memory to produce a new income statement. You don't have to repeat the whole procedure every time you change the cash plans.

Even if you don't have the programming option, you can save some time by reading parts of one file into the other. In VisiCalc, do this by saving the modified portion of the cash flow as a DIF file. From the command menu you get with a slash key, choose S for STORAGE, then S for SAVE, and then # to indicate you want the DIF file format. VisiCalc prompts you for the cells to be saved as DIF, and you answer with a range of cells. Then you go to the income statement, call in the DIF file with a slash, then S for STORAGE, L for LOAD, and # for the DIF facility. The computer asks you for the file name used with the DIF file and brings the file into your spreadsheet at the point where you left the cursor. Update the income statement and recalculate. SuperCalc and Multiplan have similar facilities for bringing rows and columns from one model into another.

You can also move simply from monthly to quarterly to yearly recording. Usually, detail in a monthly statement is necessary for the company's first couple of years, but after that the future is so uncertain that it makes little sense to produce many years of planning in month-by-month detail. Instead, put a column on the end of the 12 months to sum the total of the months and to produce a year summary. Then you can use that year to estimate results for the following years without going back into months. Most of the time you are only applying percentage growth rates to the items in the first-year summary. Remember, turn months into years by adding 12 together—any spreadsheet can do this for you—and turn them into quarters by adding three together. It's easy.

Expect your income statement to vary. The income statement has to fit the crime, and every company is different. The key is to get good information and make good estimates. A pro forma is supposed to be based on some kind of objective possibility.

The Pro Forma Balance Sheet

The balance sheet is like the income statement; it's an important document fundamental to business analysis. Whole textbooks have been written on financial statement analysis, and the business schools teach classes on it.

The balance sheet is a financial still life of the company—it lays out in glorious detail how the company stands on the day the balance is dated. The detail includes how much cash, inventory, plant, equipment, accounts receivable, accounts payable, debt, and owners' equity the company has. The balance is where experts often catch up with the creative accounting on the income statement. If, for example, a company has been calling production "waste" inventory, then eventually its balance will show a huge (and highly suspect) inventory buildup. Back when companies were capitalizing R&D expenses, balances began to accumulate R&D as if the spent money were some valuable asset. The balance sheet reports the end result of the business: what you have got.

Balance sheets are based on a fundamental equation: Total assets must always be equal to debt plus equity ownership:

$$\text{ASSETS} = \text{DEBT} + \text{EQUITY}$$

This is where the term "balance" comes from; if the sheet doesn't balance, it isn't finished. At least one unbreakable rule exists amid the creativity in accounting.

When things are working right, you can take last year's balance sheet and adjust it according to this year's income statement to produce this year's balance. Figures should balance: Earnings are added to owners' equity, assets are added to the asset side, new debts are added to the debt side, and the fundamental equation should still stand. When it doesn't, the accountants go back to work.

All this is a lot easier to do on a spreadsheet that deals with pro forma statements because you don't have reality getting in the way. There aren't any lost accounting entries, misfiled invoices, or slipups among buying materials, production, and eventual sales. The pro forma balance sheet represents a glimpse of a perfect world in which the systems work.

Table 7-3 produces a pro forma balance sheet for our start-up company after its first year. The model was built by bringing up the same cash-flow and income statements we had before and by modifying them to produce the balance. Although we work with 12 months on the computer, we only show you the four in the middle; so, let's look first at the cash-flow statement for January of that year to get a starting balance. The statement shows that we started with $50,000 in cash from equity financing and purchased $3,000 in capital equipment. Our balance at the end of the month will be capital equipment minus depreciation plus leftover cash on the asset side, and $50,000 in capital minus the expenses (which become loss, or negative earnings) on the debt and equity side.

Assets		Debt + Equity	
Cash	$34,850	Capital	$50,000
Equipment	3,000	Earnings	(12,200)
Depreciation	(50)	Total	37,800
Total	37,800		

Table 7-3 shows how the January cash flow is involved:

That should give you the idea. From there, go to the real thing, writing a model that will absorb the cash-flow and the income statement to produce a standard balance sheet. Table 7-4 shows the resulting balance sheet from the same months shown for Tables 7-1 and 7-2.

Table 7-4 is the last piece of a set of models that include Tables 7-1 and 7-2, which work together to produce the three key pro forma documents. They are interactive. If you change cash flow, you should also see some change in the income statement and balance.

In SuperCalc, VisiCalc, and most other calc programs, this is written in one model with all the information necessary for printing each of the three segments. In MicroPlan, there are three separate models, but—using MicroPlan's programming mode—they can be programmed to update one another on demand.

Table 7-3: Pro-Forma Cash Flow

Start-Up Software Company

		January ----1----
1	Sales:	
2	units	-
3	unit price	55.00
4	Value	-
5	Revenue:	
6	Unit sales	-
7	OEM contracts	-
8	Other	50,000.00
9	Subtotal	50,000.00
10	Direct costs:	
11	Units	-
12	Direct materials per	10.00
13	Shipping, etc. per u	2.00
14	Materials costs	-
15	Materials expenditur	-
16	Documentation fees	-
17	Shipping, etc.	-
18	Total cost of good	-
19	Product Development	
20	Salary 1	-
21	Consultants	2,000.00
22	Hardware/software pu	5,000.00
23	Supplies, miscellane	100.00
24	Development subtot	7,100.00
25	Marketing/sales	
26	Salary 1	-
27	Salary 2	-
28	Salary 3	-
29	Commissions	-
30	Advertising etc.	-
31	Travel	-
32	Office expenses	-
33	Marketing subtotal	-
34	General & Administrative	
35	Salary 1	5,000.00
36	Salary 2	-
37	Utilities	-
38	Insurance	-
39	Rent	-
40	Miscellaneous	50.00
41	G&A subtotal	5,050.00
42	Interest	-
43	Taxes	-
44	Capital expenditure	3,000.00
45	Total expenditure	15,150.00
46	Net cash results	34,850.00
47	Cumulative cash result	34,850.00

Balance sheets also obey traditions about item order. On the asset side, first put short-term assets and then long-term assets. Short-term assets come in order of decreasing liquidity, from cash to accounts receivable to inventory. When you get into a big complicated balance, you can refer to accounting textbooks or to additional examples. This convention will almost always be followed.

Table 7-4: Pro-Forma Balance Sheet
Start-Up Software Company

		June -----6-----	July -----7-----	August -----8-----	September -----9-----
1	Short-term assets:				
2	Cash	476,819.00	457,294.25	446,561.40	416,792.99
3	A/R calc #1	550.00	825.00	1,265.00	1,925.00
4	A/R calc #2	-	550.00	825.00	1,265.00
6	Accounts receivable	550.00	1,375.00	2,090.00	3,190.00
7	Inv. calc	-	50.00	130.00	250.00
8	Inv. calc #1	50.00	80.00	120.00	650.00
9	Inventory	50.00	130.00	250.00	900.00
10	Total short-term asset	477,419.00	458,799.25	448,901.40	420,882.99
11	Long-term assets:				
12	equipment	8,100.00	8,200.00	8,300.00	8,400.00
13	(depreciation)	135.00	136.66	138.33	140.00
14	(depreciation)	468.33	604.99	743.32	883.32
15	Total long-term assets	7,631.67	7,595.01	7,556.68	7,516.68
16	TOTAL ASSETS	485,050.67	466,394.26	456,458.08	428,399.67
17	Debt and equity				
20	Accounts payable	150.00	230.00	350.00	1,000.00
21	Advances from client	-	-	10,000.00	30,000.00
22	Paid-in capital	550,000.00	550,000.00	550,000.00	550,000.00
23	Retained earnings	(65,099.33)	(83,835.74)	(103,891.92)	(152,600.33)
24	DEBT & EQUITY	485,050.67	466,394.26	456,458.08	428,399.67

On the debt and equity side of the balance, short-term debt comes before long-term debt, and all debt almost always comes before equity ownership. Sometimes debt will appear below with equity capital because it is invested in a way that makes it work very much like equity capital.

Table 7-4 depends on the earlier models and draws most of its data straight from the other two. Let's look at it in detail.

1	Short-term assets:				
2	cash	476,819.00	457,294.25	446,561.40	416,792.99
3	A/R calc #1	550.00	825.00	1,265.00	1,925.00
4	A/R calc #2	—	550.00	825.00	1,265.00
6	accounts receivable	550.00	1,375.00	2,090.00	3,190.00
7	inv. calc	—	50.00	130.00	250.00
8	inv. calc #1	50.00	80.00	120.00	650.00
9	inventory	50.00	130.00	250.00	900.00
10	Total short-term asset	477,419.00	458,799.25	448,901.40	420,882.99

Short-term assets have several standard components. Cash is taken directly from the cumulative cash line of the cash-flow module. Accounts receivable is the sum of this month's sales plus last month's sales, which is in lines 3 and 4 above. That's a MicroPlan version using the LAG (72) function to lag sales. In SuperCalc or VisiCalc, you have an easier procedure: Just set up an accounts receivable row and make the formula equal to this month's sales plus last month's sales.

Inventory is a similar problem. Take last month's inventory and put it into row 7, which is row 9 lagged by one period. Then subtract the direct material cost of this month's sales and add the direct material cost of this month's production. That is in row 8. When these two are added together, which is done in row 9, the result is an estimate of inventory in each month.

1. CALC PRODUCTS

In SuperCalc or VisiCalc, you can once again do the operation faster by writing the formula identifying last month's inventory plus the adjustment for this month's.

2. MICROPLAN

MicroPlan requires a couple of lines with lags and so forth, as we did before with lags, because the program doesn't refer back by row and column at the same time, that is, it can't take (column-1) when it is working with rows.

Since this is a pro forma balance sheet, calculations assume perfect management of inventory and materials. These approximations are close enough for planning purposes.

Now, look at long-term assets:

11	Long-term assets:				
12	equipment	8,100.00	8,200.00	8,300.00	8,400.00
13	(depreciation)	135.00	136.66	138.33	140.00
14	(depreciation)	468.33	604.99	743.32	883.32
15	Total long-term assets	7,631.67	7,595.01	7,556.68	7,516.68
16	TOTAL ASSETS	485,050.67	466,394.26	456,458.08	428,399.67

These are taken straight from the cash-flow and income statements, which give us row 12 for the accumulated capital expenditure on equipment and row 13 for the depreciation in each month. Row 14 cumulates row 13 using MicroPlan's CUMULATE (49) command. Row 15 computes total long-term assets as the sum of row 12 minus row 14. Row 16 adds long- and short-term assets to produce a total-assets number.

Then we have the debt and equity side of the balance. Accounts payable is equal to last month's direct material cost because we take 30 days to pay that bill. We have some OEM-customer advances that haven't been booked as sales, so they better show up on the balance sheet somewhere. They offset cash assets, so they must be on the debt and equity side. Paid-in capital is the sum of the financing paid into revenue as "other" revenue. Then we can assume that all this must equal total assets, so we make earnings a "plug" figure:

Earnings = Total assets – debt – equity

That makes the balance balance. A plug figure is one that is left to the end of a calculation, when it is calculated in a way that makes it fit into a necessary equation.

17	Debt and equity				
20	accounts payable	150.00	230.00	350.00	1,000.00
21	advances from client	—	—	10,000.00	30,000.00
22	paid-in capital	550,000.00	550,000.00	550,000.00	550,000.00
23	retained earnings	(65,099.33)	(83,835.74)	(103,891.92)	(152,600.33)
24	DEBT & EQUITY	485,050.67	466,394.26	456,458.08	428,399.67

Now, go back and check. If the model works, the retained earnings will be equal to the cumulated earnings on the net income statement. In this case, it works.

These calculations are easy to foul up. Watch very closely for the accounts receivable, accounts payable, and inventory lines, in which lags and confusions can make errors.

Be especially careful of circular loops, which occur quite often in balance sheet models. Loops tend to appear as rows are lagged. In this model, for example, row 7 in one month is supposed to be the same as row 9 in the previous month. Then calculate row 8, row 9, and the sum of 7 and 8. Recalculate row 7, because parts of row 9 have changed. You can avoid this by changing the order of the rows, but the easiest way is just to calculate over and over again until the entries stop changing when you recalculate. Some newer spreadsheets have safeguards against these circular problems, but if yours doesn't, just recalculate repeatedly. This will make sense if you try it on your computer.

Balance sheets can be enormously complicated. The standard corporate balance takes up five or more pages of fine print, including a lot of notes. You can manage a complicated model by following through on each step; our balance is short, but it has all of the elements of the most complicated ones.

EIGHT

The Business Plan

The business plan is a magical document. It represents an idea in detail, the basic seed from which a company grows. It represents a thoroughly thought-out and researched business idea. It summarizes the product, the people, the strategy, the market, and the financing.

Business plans are used in many different facets of business. For small businesses, they are essential for the first financing that turns a business idea into a company. Also, small businesses will use them occasionally for negotiation of financing with bankers. For large businesses, the business plan is equivalent to the proposal that a manager uses to win approval for a new idea.

This chapter focuses on the business plan as a necessary part of the process of raising investment capital. This is the business plan that occurs most often in the computer software business. But, whatever your business plan, our model is good to follow.

Attracting investors is a lot more complicated than just forming a business plan. Generally, a start-up idea will not be financed unless the idea sellers have good, convincing presentations and good ''track records''; it can also fail because the market isn't attractive, because the financial community believes the product can't actually be produced, or because of any number of additional reasons. The financing process has a large assortment of ''necessary but not sufficient'' conditions—which means you can't get financing for sure without them, but you might not make it even with them. If you want a list of selling points, include people, markets, sales, something new and/or different about the product, technical innovation, and—another "necessary but not sufficient" one—the business plan.

Once in a great while you hear about a major start-up that secures venture financing without having a business plan. Compaq, the company that makes IBM-PC-compatible portable computers, was supposedly started by three computer executives who were known by the venture people and who were able to arrange financing before they wrote a plan. This happens very rarely.

Spreadsheet Blocks

Experience with these start-ups, in fact, led to writing this book. Chapter by chapter, we went through the same series of steps for individuals and explained to talented engineers and market wizards how to put all these ideas into the number games the financial community wants to see.

Sales and Market Forecasts

The sales forecast is essential. It drives the sales and revenues numbers in the pro formas and provides the foundations for the business plan. If you don't expect to sell a whole lot of products, you probably don't have an interesting new business idea. That's what the sales forecast is about: how many products you can sell.

The sales forecast often involves a whole-market forecast. This depends on the business. It's comfortable to know how your sales compare to the apparent or projected performance of an entire market. Prospective investors want to know what kind of market share you intend to capture: If the business looks attractive at less than a percent of the total market, for example, it's probably more interesting than one with great numbers predicated on capturing a 50-percent market share. Very few start-ups go from nowhere to 50 percent of the market.

Both sales and market forecasts are part of spreadsheet analysis, as we showed in Chapter Four. They're building blocks one and two of the business plan. (Although they're not the first chapters to appear, they may be the first ones to be written.)

At the end of this chapter, there's an example of the spreadsheet components of a real business plan. It includes several different but related market forecasts and some product-specific information, all of which back up the sales forecasts that are included in the pro forma financial section. There are many ways to make a business plan; this is one example.

Budgets

The next step is to do some budgeting, as in Chapter Five of this book. Consider how much equipment you need and when you'll need it. Call this the capital budget. Then figure out how much office space, how many people, how much travel, how much production space, how many workers, and what else you'll need to get the business going. All this is budgeting. It'll fit just fine on your spreadsheet.

You'll probably need the following:

— Capital expenditures budget

— Office budget

— Production budget

At this point, you're into an iterative process, which means you'll repeatedly modify those budgets until everyone is satisfied. If you're a production-oriented person, your sales and marketing person should be adding input about the needs of the marketing side of the business. Financial people may suggest you're too thin on this number and too thick on that one; your sales budget may change as you revise forecasts. Remember the rule to design those models in such a way as to make them easy to change when the time comes.

In the real-world example at the end of this chapter, the capital budget is presented separately. This company's business idea involved a fair number of up-front expenditures, so potential investors needed this information. The capital expenditures budget is linked into the pro forma financial statements. These pro formas also absorb an office budget and a production budget.

Pro Forma Financials

This is the part we finished in Chapter Seven. The heart of the business plan is the pro forma financial statements including cash flow, income statement, and balance. Most business plans contain three to five years of information, with the first year or two broken down into months or quarters.

Financials are subject to an awful lot of scrutiny. Make them solid, make them stand up to detailed study. You'll feel much better if your estimates are conservative—when doubting Thomases point to your sales forecast or projected profits, be able to assure them that "it's *at least* that." Be able to show them why it's probably much more than that.

In the example at the end of the chapter, the cash flow, income statement, and balance sheets are linked by the spreadsheet program. So is the market forecast, which is part of the financials. When the links are set up right, changes in the cash flow will automatically be reflected in the income statement and balance.

Investment Yield

When you finish the financials on your company, consider for a while the whole deal from the investors' point of view. What part of the ownership of the company are you offering in return for the financing you need? Would *you* make that investment? What is its yield, its net present value, its ROI? You don't have to put these things in the plan, but you ought to consider them. Negotiations are much simpler when you know what the other person is thinking.

A Business Plan Outline

There is no single outline that's best for a business plan. Each needs some basic answers to very standard, almost obvious questions. Order is not that important.

Don't overemphasize the business plan. Recently, a prominent investor told a crowded auditorium that one thing he doesn't want to see in a new business plan is "100 pages." Length is not a good substitute for thoroughness and detail, and apparently the venture capitalists have trouble justifying for themselves the time spent on a plan that long. Present a business document, not a novel. Usually, 20 pages is long enough if the plan contains all the right information. Style and grammar are not nearly as important as content.

A sample outline follows. Adjust it, as you like, to fit your own business plan needs, but you should include the key information: product, people, and business prospects.

I. EXECUTIVE SUMMARY

Nobody reads this anymore. Give potential investors a break with a single page that tells them what you've got. Some of them aren't at all interested in your kind of product, or your kind of business, or you; let them off the hook early.

The executive summary should be just one page that sums up what the product is, what its market looks like, and what kind of people are in on the deal. Don't summarize the financials because, if they weren't interesting, you wouldn't be writing the plan. Besides, most venture capitalists summarize the financials for themselves just by looking at the bottom line.

II. THE PRODUCT

What is it, what's new about it, and what's different about it? If you have advertising copy or product literature, keep text to a minimum; that will always be better than adding special text about the product. People believe what's typeset and printed in offset before they believe output from a word processor or a typewriter.

III. THE PEOPLE

Business records of the principals are probably the most important part of any venture capital financing decision. Investors want to see what you've done. There is no substitute for hard experience, especially experience in line management of a similar company, of another start-up, or of part of a larger company in a similar business.

Resumés will be checked. Don't stretch the truth. There is a story about a deal that went sour when the president of the would-be start-up insisted he had volume manufacturing experience. His resumé indicated he didn't, and the financial people checked the references on the resumé. Better to admit the gaps in the background and to offer to bring in the necessary people. Not everyone can do everything a business needs done: If you are a good technical type, don't pretend to know everything about marketing, and vice versa.

IV. THE MARKET

Here's where your market forecast and sales forecast come in. Back up numbers with lots of facts but use as little text as possible to do so. People are not interested in a detailed market survey that ought to be sold by the market research houses; they want to make sure that you have places to sell your products.

The sales forecast is part of this section. The same rules apply: Back numbers up with lots of objective facts and good analysis.

Both forecasts are basically spreadsheet output with some text thrown in.

In the equipment company example that follows, the market forecast is presented in detail; product orders of the equipment company are added in this section. Then the sales forecast is included with the pro forma financial summaries.

V. STRATEGY

This is where you talk about how you plan to position your product against the rest of the market, what you plan to do about distribution, and about other key variables. Strategy can be extremely important to some ventures and nothing more than cosmetics for others. A technology-driven new product, with no competition, needs less strategy than a market-driven product based on a market niche and on proper positioning.

VI. FINANCIALS

Throw in all your budgets, all your pro formas, and whatever information you have to document their reasonableness and realism.

In the equipment company example that follows, the plan includes summaries as well as detailed pro formas. A simple summary in front, providing a condensed income statement of cash flow for a few years, is probably a good idea.

VII. APPENDICES

Appendices should include more product literature, product literature from competitors, magazine articles, market research, detailed resumés, etc. Some people like to include a year-by-year summary of financial performance in the financials section of the text and a month-by-month summary of the first two years in the appendix.

Real-World Examples

The following material is taken from real business plans that were actually presented to venture capitalists in 1982 and 1983. All of it was prepared on a 64K CP/M microcomputer using SuperCalc and MicroPlan in conjunction with WordStar word processing.

The examples show how much spreadsheet material is included in the business plan. All texts and all names of people, companies, and products are left out.

Table 8-1: Product Order Information

Equipment Purchase Orders

October 1981 - April 1982

Purchaser	Product	P.O. Amount
Fairchild Bipolar	Automatic fluid dispenser	$ 43,700
	Tools & parts	5,213
	Manual dispenser	2,970
	Special bench	2,520
Fairchild Automotive	Wire welder	29,780
	Solder bump screener	39,500
	Passive trim station (2)	57,740
GTE Lenkurt	Reflow welder	3,870
Intel Magnetics	Manual work station	2,830
Northern Telecom	Fuse welder	6,003
Infomag	Welder stage	25,805
Astec Systems	Mag feeders	63,320
	" "	47,490
National Semiconductor	Dispense feeder	15,520
	" "	143,000
Total (through April 16, 1982)		490,361

Table 8-2: Whole Market Information

Semiconductor Assembly Equipment

(millions of 1980 dollars)

Product	Market Revenues
1. Dicing saws	14
2. Die Attach machines	13
3. Ultrasonic manual bonders	3
4. Thermocompression manual bonders	8
5. Automatic bonders	52
6. Gang bonders	2
7. Belt furnaces	6
8. Cap Welders	2
9. Molding presses	8
10. Molding dies	32
11. Finishing equipment	4
12. Marking machines	8
13. Other	27
	179

Source: Rose Associates

Table 8-3: Whole Market Information

Programmable Controllers

(millions of 1981 dollars)

	1982	1983	1984	1985	compound growth rate
automotive	35	45	59	76	29.3%
aerospace	7	9	12	15	30.3
miscellaneous nonelectrical	139	181	235	306	28.3
miscellaneous industrial	161	208	270	351	29.9
other	7	9	12	15	28.9
	-----	-----	-----	-----	-----
Total	349	452	588	763	29.9%

source: Creative Strategies International

Table 8-4: Whole Market Information

Light- and Medium-Duty Industrial Robots

(millions of 1981 dollars)

	1982	1983	1984	1985	compound growth rate	
machine shop products	30	51	86	147	86.0§	%
fabricated metals	9	15	25	42	85.6	
stamping and forming	30	51	86	147	86.0	
Other	17	29	49	84	85.7	
	-----	-----	-----	-----	-----	
Total	85	145	247	419	86.0%	

source: Creative Strategies International

Table 8-5: Capital Expenditures Budget

	Capital Expenditure	Leasable Amount
Leasehold improvements:		
Total leasehold improvements	25,000	
Equipment:		
Machine shop and grinding room		
Mill	10,000	10,000
Lathe	8,000	8,000
Bench EDM	10,000	10,000
Optical Comparator	5,000	5,000
Surface plate	-	-
Band saw	4,000	4,000
Sheet metal shear	3,000	3,000
Sheet metal break	3,000	3,000
Sheet metal punch	3,000	3,000
Drill presses	-	-
Abrasive cutoff saw	-	-
Surface grinder	5,000	5,000
Other smaller items (total)	34,000	-
Total machine shop and grinding room	85,000	51,000
Electronic Development Equipment:		
Development system	90,000	90,000
Logic analyzer	15,000	15,000
Oscilloscopes	9,000	9,000
Other items (total)	36,000	12,000
Total electronic development equip.	150,000	126,000
Engineering		
CAD (CAD/CAM) system	200,000	200,000
Drawing boards, etc.	10,000	-
Other items (total)	5,000	-
Total engineering equipment	215,000	200,000
Inspection Room		
Optical comparator	18,000	18,000
Microscope	7,500	-
Lightsources	-	-
Gauge blocks, height gauges, etc.	-	-
Surface plate	-	-
Other items (total)	49,500	-
Total	75,000	18,000
	-	-
Lower assembly (total)	10,000	-
Upper assembly (total)	20,000	-
	-	-
Miscellaneous plant equipment	-	-
Gas storage	-	-
Precision tools	-	-
Welding equipment	-	-
Stockroom	-	-
Parts inventory	-	-
Other items (total)	100,000	-
Total	100,000	-

Table 8-5 *(continued)*

	Capital Expenditure	Leasable Amount
Office/administration expenditures	-	-
Data processing	25,000	25,000
Office furniture	15,000	-
Miscellaneous other office equipmen	10,000	5,000
Other	5,000	-
Total office equipment	55,000	30,000
Totals:		
Total Product Development Equipment	414,500	326,000
Total Production Equipment	215,000	51,000
Total other equipment & capital exp.	80,000	30,000
Total capital expenditure (phase one)	709,500	407,000
Estimated monthly lease payments	-	10,175
Non-leasable capital expenditure	302,500	-

Table 8-6: Summary Pro-Forma Income Statement

	Year 1	Year 2	Year 3	Year 4	Year 5
Sales:					
Systems	840,000	3,960,000	6,930,000	12,127,500	21,223,125
Custom	1,500,000	2,300,000	3,450,000	5,175,000	7,762,500
Other	630,000	1,300,000	1,950,000	2,925,000	4,387,500
(Less returns)	(59,399)	(151,199)	(246,599)	(404,549)	(667,462
Total sales	2,910,600	7,408,800	12,083,400	19,822,950	32,705,663
Cost of goods sold					
Production	1,056,800	2,894,500	4,692,890	7,680,015	12,671,713
Engineering (80%)	395,440	602,360	798,476	1,077,642	1,479,279
Depreciation	60,000	60,000	75,000	100,000	125,000
Gross margin	1,398,360	3,851,940	6,517,034	10,965,293	18,429,670
Less:					
General & adminis	343,500	780,375	1,017,483	1,369,224	1,902,021
Cost of sales	370,400	1,178,000	1,905,580	3,119,033	5,150,952
Engineering (20%)	98,860	150,590	199,619	269,410	369,820
Interest	8,350	33,400	50,000	75,000	100,000
Taxes	230,900	683,830	1,337,741	2,453,050	4,362,751
Net Profit	383,853	1,078,278	2,006,612	3,679,576	6,544,126

Assumptions are presented in detail at the end of the plan, in an appendix.

Table 8-7: Summary Income Statement

(first eight quarters)

	Quarter 1	Quarter 2	Quarter 3	Quarter 4
Sales:				
Systems	-	60,000	240,000	540,000
Custom	300,000	350,000	400,000	450,000
Other	90,000	135,000	180,000	225,000
(returns)	(7,800)	(9,700)	(11,600)	(13,500)
Total sales	382,200	535,300	808,400	1,201,500
Cost of goods:				
Production	131,825	188,075	292,325	444,575
Engineering (80%)	85,660	94,460	103,260	112,060
Depreciation	15,000	15,000	15,000	15,000
Gross margin	149,715	237,765	397,815	629,865
Less:				
General&Administra	59,813	70,813	95,313	117,563
Cost of sales	30,800	53,400	112,400	173,800
Engineering (20%)	21,415	23,615	25,815	28,015
Interest	-	-	3,340	5,010
Taxes	15,075	35,975	64,379	122,191
Net profit	22,613	53,963	96,569	183,287

(first eight quarters)

	Quarter 5	Quarter 6	Quarter 7	Quarter 8
Sales:				
Systems	720,000	900,000	1,080,000	1,260,000
Custom	500,000	550,000	600,000	650,000
Other	250,000	300,000	350,000	400,000
(returns)	(15,000)	(17,000)	(19,000)	(21,000)
Total sales	1,455,000	1,733,000	2,011,000	2,289,000
Cost of goods:				
Production	565,000	670,750	776,500	882,250
Engineering (80%)	134,390	145,190	155,990	166,790
Depreciation	15,000	15,000	15,000	15,000
Gross margin	740,610	902,060	1,063,510	1,224,960
Less:				
General&Administra	159,844	183,344	206,844	230,344
Cost of sales	215,600	268,200	320,800	373,400
Engineering (20%)	33,598	36,298	38,998	41,698
Interest	8,350	8,350	8,350	8,350
Taxes	129,288	162,348	195,408	228,468
Net profit	193,931	243,521	293,111	342,701

Table 8-8: Pro-Forma Cash Flow

(first eight quarters)

	Quarter 1	Quarter 2	Quarter 3	Quarter 4
Revenue:				
Systems	-	-	60,000	240,000
Custom	-	300,000	350,000	400,000
Other	-	90,000	135,000	180,000
(returns)	-	(7,800)	(9,700)	(11,600)
Total revenue	-	382,200	535,300	808,400
Expenditures:				
Production	131,825	188,075	292,325	444,575
Engineering (80%)	85,660	94,460	103,260	112,060
General&Administra	59,813	70,813	95,313	117,563
Cost of sales	30,800	53,400	112,400	173,800
Engineering (20%)	21,415	23,615	25,815	28,015
Interest	-	-	3,340	5,010
Capital expenditur	302,500	15,000	16,500	18,150
Tax payments	-	14,000	35,000	64,000
Gross cash flow	(632,013)	(77,163)	(148,653)	(154,773)
Financing	-	-	200,000	100,000
Net cash flow	(632,013)	(77,163)	51,348	(54,773)
Cumulative cash flow	(632,013)	(709,175)	(657,828)	(712,600)

	Quarter 5	Quarter 6	Quarter 7	Quarter 8
Revenue:				
Systems	540,000	720,000	900,000	1,080,000
Custom	450,000	500,000	550,000	600,000
Other	225,000	250,000	300,000	350,000
(returns)	(13,500)	(15,000)	(17,000)	(19,000)
Total revenue	1,201,500	1,455,000	1,733,000	2,011,000
Expenditures:				
Production	565,000	670,750	776,500	882,250
Engineering (80%)	134,390	145,190	155,990	166,790
General&Administra	159,844	183,344	206,844	230,344
Cost of sales	215,600	268,200	320,800	373,400
Engineering (20%)	33,598	36,298	38,998	41,698
Interest	8,350	8,350	8,350	8,350
Capital expenditur	19,965	21,962	24,158	26,573
Tax payments	122,000	130,000	165,000	195,500
Gross cash flow	(57,246)	(9,093)	36,361	86,095
Financing	200,000	-	-	-
Net cash flow	142,754	(9,093)	36,361	86,095
Cumulative cash	(569,846)	(578,939)	(542,578)	(456,483)

Table 8-9: Pro-Forma Balance

	Quarter 1	Quarter 2	Quarter 3	Quarter 4
Assets:				
Cash	34,248	23,740	43,135	45,505
Inventory	136,990	94,960	172,538	182,020
Accounts receivab	382,200	535,300	808,400	1,201,500
Total short-term as	553,438	654,000	1,024,073	1,429,025
Equipment	302,500	317,500	334,000	352,150
Depreciation	15,000	30,000	45,000	60,000
Total plant and equ	287,500	287,500	289,000	292,150
Total assets	840,938	941,500	1,313,073	1,721,175
Capital and Liabilities				
Accounts payable	53,250	77,875	123,500	190,125
Accrued taxes	15,075	37,050	66,429	124,620
Short-term debt	-	-	200,000	300,000
Total short-term de	68,325	114,925	389,929	614,745
Long-term debt	-	-	-	-
Total liabilities	68,325	114,925	389,929	614,745
Paid-in equity	750,000	750,000	750,000	750,000
Retained earnings	22,613	76,575	173,144	356,430
Total Equity and Li	840,938	941,500	1,313,073	1,721,175

Table 8-9 *(continued)*

	Quarter 5	Quarter 6	Quarter 7	Quarter 8
Assets:				
Cash	82,481	89,962	106,534	133,053
Inventory	329,923	359,849	426,138	532,214
Accounts receivab	1,455,000	1,733,000	2,011,000	2,289,000
Total short-term as	1,867,403	2,182,811	2,543,672	2,954,267
Equipment	372,115	394,077	418,234	444,808
Depreciation	75,000	90,000	105,000	120,000
Total plant and equ	297,115	304,077	313,234	324,808
Total assets	2,164,519	2,486,888	2,856,906	3,279,075
Balance sheet items				
Accounts payable	232,250	278,750	325,250	371,750
Accrued taxes	131,908	164,255	194,663	227,630
Short-term debt	500,000	500,000	500,000	500,000
Total short-term de	864,158	943,005	1,019,913	1,099,380
Long-term debt	-	-	-	-
Total liabilities	864,158	943,005	1,019,913	1,099,380
Paid-in equity	750,000	750,000	750,000	750,000
Retained earnings	550,361	793,883	1,086,994	1,429,695
Total Equity and Li	2,164,519	2,486,888	2,856,906	3,279,075

INDEX

N

O

P

T

U

V

W